Feminist Comedy

EARLY MODERN FEMINISMS

Series Editor
Robin Runia, Xavier University of Louisiana

Editorial Advisory Board
Jennifer Airey, University of Tulsa
Paula Backscheider, Auburn University
Susan Carlile, California State University
Karen Gevirtz, Seton Hall University
Mona Narain, Texas Christian University
Carmen Nocentelli, University of New Mexico
Jodi Wyett, Xavier University

Showcasing distinctly feminist ideological commitments and/or methodological approaches, and tracing literary and cultural expressions of feminist thought, Early Modern Feminisms seeks to publish innovative readings of women's lives and work, as well as of gendered experience, from the years 1500–1800. In addition to highlighting examinations of women's literature and history, this series aims to provide scholars an opportunity to emphasize new approaches to the study of gender and sexuality with respect to material culture, science, and art, as well as politics and race. Thus, monographs and edited collections that are interdisciplinary and/or transnational in nature are particularly welcome.

Series Titles
A Genealogy of the Gentleman: Women Writers and Masculinity in the Eighteenth Century, by Mary Beth Harris
Objects of Liberty: British Women Writers and Revolutionary Souvenirs, by Pamela Buck
Fictions of Pleasure: The Putain Memoirs of Prerevolutionary France, by Alistaire Tallent
The Visionary Queen: Justice, Reform, and the Labyrinth in Marguerite de Navarre, by Theresa Brock
Eliza Fenwick: Early Modern Feminist, by Lissa Paul
The Circuit of Apollo: Eighteenth-Century Women's Tributes to Women, edited by Laura L. Runge and Jessica Cook

Feminist Comedy

WOMEN PLAYWRIGHTS OF LONDON

WILLOW WHITE

UNIVERSITY OF DELAWARE | UNIVERSITY OF DELAWARE PRESS

NEWARK

Library of Congress Cataloging-in-Publication Data

Names: White, Willow, author.
Title: Feminist comedy : the professionalization of women playwrights in London, 1750–1800 / Willow White.
Description: Newark, DE : University of Delaware Press, 2024. | Series: Early modern feminisms | Includes bibliographical references and index.
Identifiers: LCCN 2023044920 | ISBN 9781644533406 (paperback) | ISBN 9781644533413 (hardback) | ISBN 9781644533420 (epub) | ISBN 9781644533437 (pdf)
Subjects: LCSH: Women dramatists, English—18th century—Biography. | English drama—Women authors—History and criticism. | Feminist drama, English—History and criticism. | Women in the theater—England—London—History—18th century. | BISAC: LITERARY CRITICISM / Women Authors | HISTORY / Women
Classification: LCC PR719.W66 W45 2024 | DDC 822.6—dc23/eng/20240129
LC record available at https://lccn.loc.gov/2023044920

A British Cataloging-in-Publication record for this book is available from the British Library.

Copyright © 2024 by Willow White
All rights reserved

No part of this book may be reproduced or utilized in any form or by any means, electronic or mechanical, or by any information storage and retrieval system, without written permission from the publisher. Please contact University of Delaware Press, 200A Morris Library, 181 S. College Ave., Newark, DE 19717. The only exception to this prohibition is "fair use" as defined by U.S. copyright law.

References to internet websites (URLs) were accurate at the time of writing. Neither the author nor University of Delaware Press is responsible for URLs that may have expired or changed since the manuscript was prepared.

∞ The paper used in this publication meets the requirements of the American National Standard for Information Sciences—Permanence of Paper for Printed Library Materials, ANSI Z39.48-1992.

udpress.udel.edu

Distributed worldwide by Rutgers University Press

Contents

Figures vii
Tables ix
Acknowledgments xi

Introduction 1

1. Comic Resurgence: *Catherine Clive* 18

2. Musical Comedy: *Frances Brooke* 39

3. Laughter and Femininity: *Frances Burney* 65

4. The Satirical Seraglio: *Hannah Cowley* 89

5. Sentimental Comedy and Feminism: *Elizabeth Inchbald* 113

Conclusion: *Feminist Comedy 250 Years Later* 139

Appendix: Women's Plays Staged in London's Patent Theaters, 1750–1800 147
Notes 153
Bibliography 181
Index 195

Figures

I.1. Rachel Brosnahan as Midge Maisel in *The Marvelous Mrs. Maisel*, 2018. 2

I.2. Robert White after John Riley, *Mrs. Behn* (1718). 6

1.1. William John Alais, after John Faber Jr., after Peter van Bleeck, *Catherine Clive as Phillida in Colley Cibber's "Damon and Phillida"* (1734). 20

2.1. Mariano Bovi after Catherine Read, *Mrs. Brooke* (1790). 40

2.2. W. Grainger, "Rosina & Belville," *The New Lady's Magazine; Or, Polite, Entertaining, and Fashionable Companion for the Fair Sex* (London) 5 (1790): 553. 57

3.1. Charles Turner after Edward Francisco Burney, *Frances "Fanny" Burney* (1840). 68

4.1. James Heath after Richard Cosway, *Comedy Unveiling to Mrs. Cowley* (1783). 90

4.2. William Hogarth after Jean Baptiste Vanmour, *The Seraglio* (1724). 105

5.1. Wooding after John Russel, *Mrs. Inchbald* (1788). 115

5.2. James Heath after John Opie, *Mary Wollstonecraft Godwin* (c. 1797). 116

5.3. C. Sherwin after H. Ramberg, *Mrs. Inchbald in the Character of Lady Abbess* (1785). 118

5.4. Frontispiece of *Lovers' Vows*, in *The British Theatre*, vol. 23 (London: Longman, Hurst, Rees, and Orme, 1808). 135

C.1. Phoebe Waller-Bridge in *Fleabag*, 2019. 140

C.2. Issa Rae, Yvonne Orji, Amanda Seales, and Natasha Rothwell in *Insecure*, 2017. 141

C.3. Ilana Glazer and Abbi Jacobson in *Broad City*, 2016. 142

C.4. Ali Wong in *Hard Knock Wife*, 2018. 144

Tables

I.1. Plays by Women Staged in London, 1660–1800 8

1.1. New Plays by Women Staged during Clive's Playwriting Tenure, 1750–65 35

A.1. Women's Plays Staged in London's Patent Theaters, 1750–1800 147

Acknowledgments

The seeds of this project first took root in an undergraduate course on eighteenth-century drama taught by Alex Feldman at MacEwan University. Since that time, the fierce, funny, and feminist women playwrights of eighteenth-century London have captivated me. Over the years, I received generous support from many people as the project evolved from dissertation to monograph. In particular, at McGill University, I was fortunate to be mentored by Fiona Ritchie and Peter Sabor, who believed in the project at its nascent stages and provided expert advice and endless encouragement. I am further indebted to the stimulating and guiding conversations I have had with a community of scholars and theatre makers, including, though by no means limited to, Misty Anderson, Katherine Binhammer, Betsy Bolton, Tanya Caldwell, Alison Conway, Angelina Del Balzo, Gillian Dow, Isobel Grundy, Erin Keating, Heather S. Nathans, Alisa Palmer, Tiffany Potter, Diana Solomon, David Taylor, and Sue Williams. I also thank the American Theatre and Drama Society, the American Society for Eighteenth-Century Studies, the Canadian Society for Eighteenth-Century Studies, and the National Theatre School of Canada for providing venues to share, discuss, and improve my work year after year. Furthermore, several libraries, archives, and research centers gave me access to their materials that greatly enriched this project: the Beinecke Rare Book & Manuscript Library, the Bodleian Library, the British Library, the Burney Centre, the Chawton House Library, the Folger Shakespeare Library, the Houghton Library, the Huntington Library, McGill Rare Books and Special Collections, and the National Art Library.

For believing in my book even before I did, I heartfully thank my editor Julia Oestreich, as well as series editor Robin Runia. I also offer thanks to the anonymous readers who reviewed the manuscript and whose feedback strengthened the work. For generous financial support, I thank the Social Sciences and Humanities Research Council of Canada, the University of Alberta's Augustana Faculty, McGill University's Department of English, and the Literary Encyclopedia. I also thank the following journals for allowing me to reprint revised articles as the third and fifth chapters of this monograph: *Women's Writing*, 2021, copyright Taylor & Francis, available online: http://www.tandfonline.com/10.1080/09699082.2020.1847823; and *Eighteenth-Century Studies* 55, no. 3 (Spring 2022): 299–315. Published by

ACKNOWLEDGMENTS

Johns Hopkins University Press. Copyright © 2022 American Society for Eighteenth-Century Studies.

Many thanks are due to my steadfast partner of over a decade, Andrew Hochhalter, who has patiently learned more about eighteenth-century women writers than he ever imagined. I also thank my parents and family for their love and support, especially my two grandmothers, Carolyn Nemetchek (née Story) and Ruth White (née Ralston), who instilled in me a love of women's history. Lastly, I must thank my brilliant friend, confidant, and copy editor, Hannah Korell, alongside whom I survived the pandemic and the PhD.

I wrote this book in Montreal, Quebec, on the traditional, ancestral, and unceded lands of the Kanien'kehà:ka, and in Camrose, Alberta, Treaty 6 territory, home and traveling route of the Maskwacis Nêhiyawak, Niitsitapi, Nakoda, Tsuut'ina, and Métis Nations. I thank these friends and family for sharing their land and for their rich intellectual, spiritual, and emotional support.

Introduction

> A female culprit at your bar appears,
> Not destitute of hope, nor free from fears.
> Her utmost crime she's ready to confess,
> A simple trespass—neither more nor less;
> For, truant-like, she rambled out of bounds,
> And dar'd to venture on poetic grounds.
> —Prologue to Frances Sheridan's *The Discovery* (1763)

In the hit Amazon comedy series *The Marvelous Mrs. Maisel* (2017–23), Miriam "Midge" Maisel (Rachel Brosnahan), a young Jewish American wife and mother, struggles to make a career as a stand-up comedian in 1960s New York following her separation from an unfaithful husband. The series follows Midge as she navigates problems that arise in her personal and professional life as a result of her unconventional career in the male-dominated comedy industry. In episode 2 of season 2, "Mid-way to Mid-town," Midge endures a miserable night. She is at her first paid gig, but her set keeps getting pushed later and later, and fellow male comics openly harass her as she stands by. One implies that she slept with a major male comedian to get the job: "What he did for you was pretty big—you must have done something pretty big for him first!"[1] Another comedian, Stan, makes lewd comments about her from the stage: "We've got a girl comic coming up in a little bit, that oughta be entertaining. Madge or Marjorie, something like that. Don't get too excited fellas—she keeps her clothes on."[2] Moments before her set, Midge spills mustard across the front of her black dress and goes on stage with a yellow stain across her chest for a now sparse and boozed-up audience. Adding insult to injury, the emcee introduces Midge as an "adorable little lady, who, if she can't make you laugh, can at least make you dinner."[3] Once on stage, as depicted in figure I.1, Midge lets her fury fly, roasting the male comedians and ranting against their accusations that women cannot do stand-up: "[Men] run around telling everyone that women aren't funny. Only men are funny. Now think about this: comedy is fueled by oppression, by the lack of power, by sadness and disappointment, by abandonment and humiliation. Now, who the hell does that describe more than women? Judging by those standards, *only* women

Figure I.1. Rachel Brosnahan as Midge Maisel in *The Marvelous Mrs. Maisel*, screen grab, Amazon Prime Video, 2018.

should be funny—and Stan."[4] The audience roars with laughter as Midge demonstrates that comedy, though widely considered a masculine pastime, offers a powerful mechanism for women to call out the injustices they face as second-class citizens in a patriarchal society.

Written, directed, and produced by Amy Sherman-Palladino, *The Marvelous Mrs. Maisel* is inspired by the women of the mid-twentieth century U.S. comedy circuit, including Jackie "Moms" Mabley, Phyllis Diller, Lucille Ball, Carol Burnett, and many more. Like the fictional Midge Maisel, these women developed a specific throughline of comedy in response to the social conditions they encountered, including rampant sexism, racism, and antisemitism. Each used her comedy to spotlight inequities and elevate women's experiences. Though trailblazers in their own era, these women were part of a centuries-long genealogy of women comedians using humor to resist patriarchal oppression. This book looks further into the past, to mid-eighteenth-century London, when another cohort of women writers and performers flocked to the comic stage to earn a living, critique patriarchal authority, and celebrate women's lives. Like Mrs. Maisel, one of these women once quipped in 1707: "Why this Wrath against the Women's Works? Perhaps you'll answer, because they meddle with things out of their Sphere: But I say, no; for since the Poet is born, why not a Woman as well as a Man?"[5]

In the eighteenth century, stage comedy was the most in-demand genre in London's massive theatrical mediascape. During the annual 180-day theater season, the number of comedies performed outnumbered tragedies roughly five to one, according to *The London Stage*, entertaining thousands of patrons each night. Those who could not afford to attend the theater regularly could read summaries of plays and critical reviews in one of London's many print periodicals.[6] While most of those writing for and about the theater were men, approximately one hundred women wrote and produced hundreds of plays throughout the century, the vast majority of which were five-act comedies, lighthearted musicals, and comic afterpieces. Altogether, women playwrights made up only a small percentage of dramatists of the period, about 7 percent, but their plays contain valuable commentary on gender and professional identity.[7]

Feminist Comedy recovers a renaissance of women playwrights producing comic plays in London between 1750 and 1800. During this fifty-year period, approximately thirty-seven women staged seventy-five comic entertainments at the patent theaters.[8] In this study, I concentrate on the histories and creative works of five of these women—Catherine Clive, Frances Burney, Frances Brooke, Hannah Cowley, and Elizabeth Inchbald—to investigate the intersection of feminism and stage comedy during this period. These women playwrights seized the rare opportunity afforded them by the comic stage and denied to them in other male-dominated spheres, such as coffeehouses, newspapers, and Parliament, to further their own careers, challenge power structures, and further the status of women. I argue not only that stage comedy was crucial to women's success within the professional theatrical establishment, but also that their professional negotiations, including circumventing sexist gatekeeping in the industry, imbued their comedies with feminist impulses that are central to understanding how those plays engaged with eighteenth-century audiences. Ultimately, *Feminist Comedy* identifies the comic stage as an essential site of liberal feminist discourse and practice in the eighteenth century.

While feminist scholarship of the late twentieth century—including David D. Mann and Susan Garland Mann's crucial survey of women's plays between 1660 and 1823 and Nancy Cotton's comprehensive study of early women dramatists—did much to counter the historical disregard of eighteenth-century women playwrights, such studies were invested mainly in recovering what have been considered women's "serious" contributions, referring to full-length dramas and tragedies.[9] A scholarly inclination for studying novels over drama has further clouded women's contributions to stage comedy. However, recent studies by Emily H. Anderson, Paula Byrne, Nora Nachumi, and Francesca Saggini have highlighted the centrality of comedy in women's novels of the period.[10] Lisa Freeman and Gillian Russell have drawn much-needed attention to the connections between gender identity and genre on the eighteenth-century stage, and Betsy Bolton,

Anne K. Mellor, and Daniel O'Quinn have identified the radical, political, and social commentary within many women's comedies of the period.[11] I build on all of these projects with a particular debt owed to two texts on which I expand: Ellen Donkin's *Getting into the Act: Women Playwrights in London, 1776–1829* (1995), one of the first studies to focus on the professional barriers eighteenth-century women playwrights faced in the latter half of the century, and Misty Anderson's *Female Playwrights and Eighteenth-Century Comedy: Negotiating Marriage on the London Stage* (2002), which traces women playwrights' treatment of marriage in comedy. I engage Donkin's and Anderson's studies through my identification of a feminist voice in women's comedies of the eighteenth century and through my focus on women playwrights' interconnectedness with one another as a network of women working in a male-dominated field.

While previous studies have been hesitant to apply the label of "feminist" or prefer to use the term "proto-feminist" for women authors writing prior to Mary Wollstonecraft—author of the foundational liberal feminist text *A Vindication of the Rights of Woman* (1792)—I argue that foregrounding the feminist vein that runs through women's comedy of the eighteenth century is vital to understanding their work. I therefore take up Sarah Apetrei's call to expand the boundaries of feminism to include the work of historical women whose writing shares certain traits: "a call for women's equal moral, intellectual and spiritual status to be acknowledged; the critique of strategies employed by men to dominate women and keep them in subjection; and the claim that the sexual inequalities that existed in society were constructed by custom and convention and bore no relationship to a state of nature."[12] Recognizing the irony of placing boundaries around a set of ideas and practices rooted in women's emancipation, I embrace an expansive definition of historical feminism, which, in turn, allows me to consider a wider range of eighteenth-century women writers, mainly working women, under the banner of feminist discourse than has been previously acknowledged.

I argue that considering a broader tradition of women's practical and creative resistance to patriarchal oppression does not water down the history of feminism; instead, it reveals the complex and extensive strategies women from different social and political backgrounds have employed for centuries to claim liberation. For example, Burney's *The Witlings* (1779) could be understood as anti-woman for its mockery of certain characters—it was certainly interpreted so by her father.[13] Yet, Burney's play portrays women from an unprecedented range of socioeconomic positions, including women operating a milliner's shop, offering audiences a glimpse of the lives of women rarely centered in the drama of the period. Burney further portrays the women-only space of the shop as a productive site of economic exchange and working women as powerful gatherers and sharers of information. In analyzing a vibrant period of women's comic output in the second half of the eighteenth century, I reveal such patterns of unexpected and rebellious feminist themes and techniques that appear in women's comedies, sometimes masked by, or presented in conjunction with, popular comic tropes. Throughout this book, I explore the comic stage as a rich source of feminist innovation and circulation in the eighteenth century and beyond.

Prologue to Change

When Charles II decreed in 1662 that women could perform on stage for the first time in England's history, he inadvertently transformed the theater into a vibrant space of professional opportunity for women. Not only did women then work as actresses, playwrights, and managers, but they were also drawn to ancillary professions around the theater, including costuming and set creation, food and beverage service, and sex work. Katherine Philips's 1663 translation of Pierre Corneille's *La Mort de Pompeé* (1643) was the first play written by a woman to be staged in London.[14] It was followed by Frances Boothby's *Marcelia; or, The Treacherous Friend* in 1669. After these early experimental efforts, the prolific career of Aphra Behn (figure I.2) truly marked women's sustained entrance into the world of commercial playwriting. Behn bluntly declared her desire for wealth, writing that she "was forced to write for bread and not ashamed to owne it [sic]."[15] She learned quickly that stage comedies made the most money. Between 1670 and 1689, Behn generated eighteen new plays, nearly all of which were comedies. Behn's plays teem with gendered commentary and criticism, and they set the tone for women's comedy for centuries. In her preface to *The Lucky Chance* (1687), Behn begs for equal treatment for women from audiences, critics, and other playwrights:

> All I ask, is the Privilege for my Masculine Part the Poet in me, (if any such you will allow me) to tread in those successful Paths my Predecessors have so long thriv'd in. If I must not, because of my Sex, have this Freedom, but that you will usurp all to your selves I lay down my Quill, and you shall hear no more of me, no not so much as to make Comparisons, because I will be kinder to my brothers of the Pen, than they have been to a defenceless Woman. . . . I value Fame as much as if I had been born a Hero; and if you rob me of that, I can retire from the ungrateful World, and scorn its fickle Favours.[16]

Figure I.2. Robert White after John Riley, *Mrs. Behn* (1718), © National Portrait Gallery, London.

As the first woman to have a sustained career as a professional playwright, Behn established a unique voice, what Susan Carlson identifies as a "countertradition," by distinguishing herself from male playwrights through her focus on her own gender identity and that of her women characters.[17] Over the following century, the women playwrights who followed Behn would continue to draw and expand on her feminist legacy.

Following Behn's death in 1689, a rising group of women playwrights, known as the Female Wits (Delarivier Manley, Mary Pix, and Catherine Trotter), mimicked her demands for fair financial remuneration and gender equity in the business.[18] The success of the Female Wits was surpassed with the appearance of Susanna Centlivre, who wrote nineteen plays, mostly women-centric comedies, over the first two decades of the eighteenth century, including *The Basset Table* (1705), *The Busie Body* (1709), and *A Bold Stroke for a Wife* (1718). Many of these plays became part of the standard eighteenth-century repertoire and secured women's comedy as a standard offering at the theaters. Centlivre earned the status of top woman dramatist of the century in terms of the number of plays she produced and the number of years in which they were performed.[19] Though Behn, Centlivre, and other women playwrights experienced remarkable success writing for the comic stage, the meteoric rise of the professional woman playwright was not without setbacks.

The 1737 Stage Licensing Act resulted in a decline in the number of women's plays produced in the decades following the act's passing. The act gave the office of the Lord Chamberlain sole responsibility to vet all new plays and ban any deemed too politically sensitive, while strictly limiting performances to only a few venues.[20] Those "sensitive" topics included many issues of concern for women, such as domestic violence, divorce, and women's sexual pleasure. Ambitious playwrights were limited to Drury Lane, Covent Garden, and, as of the 1760s, the Haymarket during the summer season—though an illegitimate performance culture continued to exist on the margins.[21] For women, the Act only increased the sexist gatekeeping of the patent theaters. The managers who ran these houses, all men, were often playwrights themselves who tended to reserve spots for their plays and were not inclined to take a risk on a new woman playwright.[22] Additionally, the women who had found a welcoming venue at Henry Fielding's Haymarket in the 1730s—Eliza Haywood, Charlotte Charke, Elizabeth Cooper, and others—found themselves without a home and welcoming venue for their works. Table I.1 shows the number of plays staged by women in the 1730s at ten, which dropped to six in the 1740s, and reached a dismal two by the 1750s.

My study begins during this mid-century lull, when many women writers had abandoned playwriting despite the encouraging precedent set by Behn, Centlivre, and others. In 1750, thirteen years after the passing of the Licensing Act, at a time when no other women were staging plays, the comic actress Catherine Clive staged her first comedy, a short but fierce feminist rebuttal to men's dominance over the theatrical market. Though it was largely ignored by modern scholars, I argue that Clive's *The Rehearsal; or, Bayes in Petticoats* (1750) played a key role in the resurgence of women staging comedy for the remainder of the century. Not only did Clive reintroduce audiences to the idea of a woman playwright, but she also directly supported the women comedians who followed her, Frances Sheridan and

TABLE I.1. PLAYS BY WOMEN STAGED IN LONDON, 1660–1800

Decade	Number of Plays
1660	3
1670	12
1680	10
1690	14
1700	22
1710	9
1720	7
1730	10
1740	6
1750	2
1760	13
1770	19
1780	33
1790	29

Source: Judith Stanton, "'This New Found Path Attempting': Women Dramatists in England, 1660–1800," in *Curtain Calls: British and American Women and the Theater, 1660–1820*, ed. Mary Anne Schofield and Cecilia Macheski (Athens: Ohio University Press, 1991), 327.

Elizabeth Griffith, who in turn were followed by Jane Pope, Dorothy Celesia, Charlotte Lennox, Hannah More, Frances Burney, Sarah Cheyney Gardner, Elizabeth Craven, Ursula Booth, and Elizabeth Richardson in the 1770s. In the final decades of the century, Hannah Cowley and Elizabeth Inchbald dominated the comic stage in London, each producing more than a dozen plays that appeared alongside the works of many other less well-known women playwrights, including Mariana Starke, Catherine Metcalfe, Charlotte Smith, and dozens of others.[23] At the end of the century, approximately one hundred women had written and staged comic entertainments in London's patent theaters.

While there was little racial diversity among this group of women, they did represent surprisingly diverse backgrounds in terms of their class, faith, and sexual orientation.[24] Many, if not most, women playwrights came from working-class or ambiguous backgrounds and pursued the comic stage to make a living. These include some of the most famous playwrights of the century: Behn, Centlivre, and Haywood. Others, like Brooke and Burney, came from middle-class families and saw the possibility of creative and financial gain in writing for the stage. At least one Jewish woman, Jael-Henrietta Pye, staged a comic afterpiece at London's Drury Lane in 1771, and the most famous of all eighteenth-century women comedians, Inchbald, was Roman Catholic. Although same-sex relationships between women were not strictly illegal in the eighteenth century, they were certainly taboo; yet, in her private life, Clive maintained sexual and romantic relationships with women.[25] Despite differences in their identities, women playwrights shared a consistent interest in comedy as a means to engage with the social, political, financial, and cultural aspects of their gendered lives.[26] *Feminist Comedy* is the first sustained study to explore this flourishing period of comic output by women playwrights between 1750 and 1800 and situate their plays as an index of feminism in the eighteenth century.

Feminist Techniques in Women's Comedy

The concept of feminist comedy provides the theoretical basis for each of the five chapters in this book. Comedy is a mechanism to dissect, challenge, and laugh at the social systems and dynamics that shape everyday human life. For women and gender-diverse people living in patriarchal societies, comedy offers a distinct opportunity not only to direct an audience to bear witness to their marginalized position in society, but also to scrutinize and laugh at the absurdity of this discrimination. Such comedy not only works to raise awareness regarding issues of gender oppression, but also creates an "insider" humor among women by drawing on their shared experiences and binding them together as a group within a specific cultural, social, and historical moment. This is not to say that there is an essential biological quality to comedy by women, but rather that feminist comedy is grounded in gendered experiences and, I argue, in resisting patriarchal oppression—whether explicitly or implicitly in content—through the very practice of making comedy. Regina Barecca writes, "Anytime a woman breaks through a barrier set by society, she's making a feminist gesture of a sort, and every time a woman laughs, she's breaking through a barrier."[27] Barecca's sentiment promises that the history of women's comedy offers a rich archive of feminist practice, empowerment, and solidarity.

While the term "feminism" was not coined until the nineteenth century, principles of modern liberal feminism—particularly advocacy for gender equality in the public sphere—consistently appear in the works of women writers of the eighteenth century.[28] Audrey Bilger explains that women writers of this period deployed a distinctly feminist humor to "subject prejudices against women to rational scrutiny in order to expose the absurdity and encourage readers to laugh at the folly of sexist views."[29] The comedies of eighteenth-century women playwrights consistently center and celebrate women's experiences, agency, and desires in the face of sexist barriers and prejudices. Numerous feminist studies of women playwrights of the eighteenth century reveal that companionate marriage, sexual attraction, access to education, and the subversion of patriarchal authority recur as significant themes in those women's comedies.[30] According to Jaqueline Pearson's analysis of women's comedies during the Restoration and the early part of the eighteenth century, the comedic genre "gives its female characters a more emphatic visibility, usually having a higher proportion of female characters to male, and allowing women to appear in more scenes, especially in more women-only scenes, to speak a higher proportion of the lines, and to open plays more often, thus presenting the play world through their eyes."[31] The same holds true for women's comedies in the latter half of the century. For example, in Cowley's *A Day in Turkey; or, The Russian Slaves* (1791), women, not men, orchestrate the play's sexual and political plots as they work to free themselves from imprisonment; Burney's *The Witlings* opens, unusually, on a scene of working women; and Clive's *Bayes in Petticoats* disrupts audience expectations by portraying a woman (rather than a man) directing a rehearsal.

Notably, throughout the century, women's comedies continued to be marketed to the public as *women's* comedies. Behn set a precedent for women to identify themselves as the authors of their plays, and theater managers capitalized on the apparent peculiarity of women playwrights by marketing their gender in advertisements and playbills. As Anderson writes, "The bodies, or at least the gendered identities, of the first female playwrights became a part of their comedies."[32] The melding of a woman playwright's gendered identity and her creative product invited the audience to interpret her plays through a woman's point of view and offered the playwright a chance to comment on women's social roles in a fictional setting with real-world implications. For example, Cowley's comedies, like Behn's, frequently feature women who insist on their own choice for a marital and sexual partner while subverting the will of a father figure.

In Judith Stanton's statistical account of women playwrights of the Restoration and eighteenth century, she estimates that 42 percent of plays written by women were comedies, while only 24 percent were tragedies.[33] The remaining 34 percent she categorizes as "miscellaneous" modes such as pastorals, afterpieces, interludes, farces, and opera.[34] These numbers align with Gwenn Davis and Beverly A. Joyce's estimate that comedy comprised 40 to 45 percent of plays written by women in the century.[35] However, I analyze these numbers from an alternative perspective, arguing that most so-called miscellaneous works can still be broadly defined as comic entertainment. Indeed, women's overwhelming preference for writing comedy has been masked by theater historians' tendency to define stage comedy as a five-act mainpiece. Yet, much of the energy of eighteenth-century playwriting went toward writing shorter, comic entertainments. In the century, an evening at the theater generally involved a performance of the mainpiece, usually a five-act comedy or tragedy, followed by one or two afterpieces, usually comic in nature. Performance records show that afterpieces drew audiences and made good profits for the house and the playwright.[36] Lighthearted dances and musical interludes were also regularly interwoven throughout the evening, and humorous prologues and epilogues were not mere addenda, but central components of the evening's entertainment.[37] Thus, to appreciate women's playwriting of the eighteenth century fully, I move beyond the conventional definition of stage comedy as a five-act spoken play ending in marriage and embrace a more expansive definition that includes the plethora of funny modes in which women regularly wrote. This inclusion of all comic theatrical entertainment that sought to provoke humor, amusement, and laughter in its audience reveals that comedy far eclipsed all other genres in terms of women's theatrical output (see table A.1).

While a handful of women playwrights wrote and staged tragedies in the second part of the century, these works often failed to achieve the same commercial success as the playwrights' comedies. Performance records show that women's tragedies often floundered while their comedies prospered. For example, Brooke spent decades attempting to produce a tragedy, only to achieve success as a playwright when she switched to comedy. Similarly, Cowley's two tragedies received tepid reviews, while her comedies made her famous. The only play Burney ever staged was a tragedy. Still, her contemporaries believed that comedy was her true forte, and the debut of her tragedy proved so disastrous that it was canceled after a single performance. Similarly, Inchbald pulled her tragedy *The Massacre* (1792) from publication on the advice of her friend and confidant William Godwin that the play would not be well received. These examples suggest that while tragedy appealed to women playwrights creatively, it was not a lucrative or rewarding genre for them professionally. Certainly, tragedy also represented a less popular genre among men, but they enjoyed more consistent success at tragedy than women. As I explore in chapter 2, literary men of the eighteenth century, including theatrical managers and critics, strongly associated tragedy with its classical roots and their formal education, and they therefore deemed women inappropriate authors of the genre. This attitude persisted well into the nineteenth century and helps explains why women's tragedies were so often poorly received.[38] Though women also experienced professional gatekeeping when it came to comedy, as I will discuss in the following chapters, powerful theatrical men—playwrights, managers, and critics—often viewed comedy as a lesser genre and therefore less threatening when written by women. Thus, stage comedy provided a useful means of making feminist content palatable to the Lord Chamberlain, management, and audiences.

Barriers to Funny Women

Despite her potential to earn an independent living as a comic playwright, a woman still faced discrimination when "going public" in such a highly visible venture. The popular belief that comic playwriting was unfeminine posed a constant threat to women playwrights of the latter half of the century and required a careful tread. As Burney's father told her when she wanted to produce her first stage comedy in 1779, "In the Novel way, there is no danger," implying that playwriting would foreground her identity as an author and make her more vulnerable to critique than novel writing.[39] Consequently, women's comedy after 1750 tended to be more cautious in terms of feminist delivery than the plays of Behn and Centlivre. Behn, who had set a critical precedent for women playwrights both in terms of her preference for comedy and her outspoken defense of women's ability to write brilliant plays, was increasingly viewed as morally degenerate as the century progressed. While the Female Wits and Centlivre had openly acknowledged their debt to Behn, it became hazardous for other women to do so as decades passed. For example, when a reviewer criticized Cowley's *The World as It Goes* in 1781, he used Behn's legacy to attack Cowley, writing, "It exceeds in gross ribaldry, the productions of the notorious Mrs. Behn."[40] This attack did not stop Cowley from continuing to draw on Behn's comedies for inspiration. Still, when she adapted Behn's *The Lucky Chance* as her own *The School for Greybeards* in 1786, she avoided naming Behn in her preface and instead referred to her cryptically as "a poet of the drama, once highly celebrated."[41]

While my study of women playwrights foregrounds their agency, it is also alert to the entrenched gendered hierarchy of the eighteenth-century theatrical institution, where men held the highest positions of power, and women went to extraordinary lengths to stage their work. Women faced formidable, gendered barriers within the theatrical establishment, particularly from prominent male playwrights and managers of the period. Between 1750 and 1800, Drury Lane was managed by David Garrick and Richard Brinsley Sheridan, Covent Garden by John Rich, John Beard, and Thomas Harris, and the Haymarket, which became London's third patent theater in 1767, by Samuel Foote, George Colman the Elder, and his son George Colman the Younger. This small group of men held total control over whose plays were produced and when, and they did not always operate in good faith. The correspondence, prefaces, and newspaper essays of women playwrights of the century are littered with complaints against these managers. For example, in 1779, Cowley accused Harris and Sheridan of teaming up to block the production of her play *Albina*, and in 1805, Inchbald had to publicly defend herself against Colman the Younger, who wrote a scathing and sexist attack about her theatrical criticism.[42]

Of the elite group of patent theater managers, Garrick alone had a reputation for supporting and producing women playwrights. During his tenure as manager of Drury Lane from 1747 to 1776, Garrick staged nearly three hundred plays written by women, while his rival theater, Covent Garden, staged just over one hundred.[43] Garrick also produced many first-time woman playwrights, including Clive, Frances Sheridan, Griffith, Pope, Celesia, Lennox, and Cowley. Additionally, he helped usher Hannah More's first play, *Percy* (1777), to production at Covent Garden the year after his retirement. But Garrick also acted as a powerful gatekeeper, supporting women when it suited him financially and professionally and sabotaging those who challenged his authority. As I describe in the second and fourth chapters of this book, Garrick actively sought to destroy Brooke's theatrical career, and Cowley suspected him of stealing ideas from her play manuscripts to augment the plays of her rivals. Yet, women continued to produce marketable new plays after Garrick's retirement in 1776, suggesting that his paternal benevolence toward some women was not the primary source of their success. His successor, Richard Brinsley Sheridan, hardly proved a champion of women: he barred his own wife, Elizabeth Ann Linley, who had established a successful singing career, from performing after they married.[44] However, women continued to stage plays under Sheridan's tenure. Consequently, *Feminist Comedy* argues that the success of late eighteenth-century English women playwrights is illuminated by their consistent preference for writing comedy, their fierce self-advocacy in the profession, and their support of one another, rather than their reliance on major male figures.

Structure and Chapter Summaries

In the following chapters, I study five women writers—Clive, Burney, Brooke, Cowley, and Inchbald—all of whom wrote innovative feminist comedies that raised critique of patriarchal systems while still netting financial, critical, and popular success. I have chosen these women because their experiences represent women working in the theatrical marketplace; they all faced significant sexist hurdles in their careers as playwrights and each used stage comedy to circumvent those barriers. Additionally, I have chosen women who experimented widely in comic form and style. Each chapter focuses on a different kind of comic entertainment: the afterpiece, musical comedy, satire, and five-act laughing and sentimental comedies. In my analysis of these plays, I consider the lived experiences that shaped each playwright's life as a working woman in a male-dominated industry, and I look for gendered reverberations in her works. My methodology in each chapter therefore includes both careful analysis of women's play texts as well as the study of their personal and professional lives through the examination of journals, correspondence, theatrical anecdotes and ephemera, and newspapers. Such analysis offers insight into women's motivations for writing comic plays and into the gendered experiences of women in the theatrical marketplace of the eighteenth century.

Clive opens the book as one of the mid-century's most popular and influential comic artists. While her remarkable performance career is well documented in historical biography and has been illuminated by modern feminist theater scholars, little has been written about her identity as a playwright. Yet, in the later half of her career, between 1750 and 1769, Clive wrote four comic afterpieces for her benefit performances, making her the most prolific woman dramatist of the mid-eighteenth century. Clive's first play, *Bayes in Petticoats*, is particularly remarkable for its explicit critique of the misogynistic erasure of women playwrights from the theatrical establishment. It was well received by audiences, revived numerous times, and published in 1753. The significance of Clive's innovative comic playwriting has been overshadowed by her astonishing acting career, as well as the theatrical dominance of her manager, colleague, and sometimes rival, Garrick. Chapter 1 recovers Clive as an essential woman playwright, as I argue that she was also a crucial link between women playwrights of the first and second halves of the eighteenth century. Clive's formidable efforts to reclaim women's status as playwrights, and her own successful strategy of drawing on the comic legacy of women like Behn and Centlivre to gain legitimacy, paved the way for other women to do the same and resulted in a resurgence of women playwrights of comedy that exceeded the success of such playwrights of earlier years.

The second chapter turns to the theatrical career of Brooke, who, like Clive, is rarely remembered as a comic playwright. Better known as a novelist, Brooke long fostered a dream of becoming a dramatist but struggled throughout her life to achieve this goal. Garrick rejected her first play, a tragedy titled *Virginia*, for production at Drury Lane. Instead, she published the play in 1756 and, in the same year, wrote a critical review of Garrick. Consequently, Garrick held a grudge against her for the rest of his life, and it was only after he died in 1779 that she was finally able to stage a play at a patent theater. Harnessing her knowledge as a managing partner of the London Opera House, Brooke wrote two commercially successful comic operas late in her career, *Rosina* (1782) and *Marian* (1784). Though musical comedy was seen as a lower form of entertainment than full-length tragedy, Brooke followed the precedent set by other women playwrights by identifying comedy as the best tool to propel her own professional success. Like many of her sister playwrights, she used her comic plays to refute patriarchal violence and celebrate women's relationships.

Turning to the well-researched censorship of Burney's first comedy *The Witlings* in 1779, chapter 3 investigates the struggle women writers of comedy faced when their work was deemed unfeminine. Following the publication of her first novel, *Evelina* (1778), Burney's comic talent was undeniable, and managers were eager to see her works produced at their theaters. This chapter draws attention to the development of Burney's comic voice and technique as she wrote her first play, with particular attention paid to the influence of the popular comic playwright Arthur Murphy. A little-known manuscript by Burney of adapted scenes from Murphy's play *All in the Wrong* (1761) provides evidence of Burney's interest in Murphy's playwriting and the development of her own comic voice in the style of laughing comedy. In comparing Burney's *The Witlings* and Murphy's *All in the Wrong*, I argue that Burney clearly wrote her play in the style of her mentor. However, I also propose that she deviated from his focus on sexual exploits and instead centered her play on women's experiences and relationships, resulting in a distinctly feminist intervention in the style of laughing comedy. Unfortunately, Burney's father Charles and Samuel Crisp, a family friend, believed laughing comedy to be fundamentally unfeminine and forbade her from staging the play. This chapter, therefore, is distinct from the others as it explores a never-produced comedy. Nonetheless, Burney's experience helpfully demonstrates the gendered barriers that women playwrights faced in accessing the theater. Despite her theatrical failure, she became one of the most important and widely known women writers of comedy in the late eighteenth century in the novel form.

While Burney was barred from comic playwriting due to the reputational concerns of her family, the fourth chapter offers an analysis of sexism experienced within the theater business. Cowley's penultimate and satirical comedy *A Day in Turkey* is undergirded by decades of her frustration with the patent theater system and dealings with sexist male managers and critics. After the promising reception of her first play, *The Runaway*, in 1776, Cowley struggled to have her plays produced by Sheridan at Drury Lane or Harris at Covent Garden. *A Day in Turkey* launches a complex satirical critique of the theatrical institution that created this struggle by drawing on stereotypes of the East as the background to an analysis of gender, power, and the stage. In the play, Cowley depicts women characters as powerful theatrical agents who use the seraglio (harem) as a platform from which to manipulate the voyeuristic gaze of the male characters and audiences. Not long after the play's production, Cowley retired from the theater, having generated one of the most prolific and successful careers of any woman playwright.

In the final decades of the century, comic trends shifted toward a strong embrace of feeling and sensibility, a precursor to nineteenth-century melodrama.[45] This late-century sentimental shift, which emphasized subservient daughters and benevolent patriarchs, is at work in Inchbald's 1798 play *Lovers' Vows*, an adaptation of the German playwright August von Kotzebue's *Das Kind der Liebe* (1790). Like Burney in her feminist repurposing of laughing comedy, Inchbald embraced shifting comic trends by writing in a popular style as a means to benefit her own career while continuing to subvert standard gendered tropes; Inchbald's women characters in *Lovers' Vows* are sexually experienced, clever, and sympathetic. However, in reviews of Inchbald's plays and novels, the feminist writer Mary Wollstonecraft identified her sentimental women characters as a betrayal of women. While Inchbald never wrote a public rebuttal to Wollstonecraft's criticism, I argue that *Lovers' Vows*, written the year following Wollstonecraft's death, can be read as a defense against Wollstonecraft's critique and an articulation of Inchbald's own feminist theatrical technique in which she harnessed sentimental comedy to shift public perception of women who break sexual norms.

The conclusion of *Feminist Comedy* looks to the current landscape of comedy in the English-speaking world, primarily in the United States, where the cities of Los Angeles and New York have eclipsed London as the epicenters of mass-market entertainment. Today, women and gender-diverse writers like Phoebe Waller-Bridge, Ali Wong, Hannah Gadsby,

Issa Rae, Abbi Jacobson, Ilana Glazer, Tig Notaro, and many more continue to write feminist comedy for the stage, film, and television to be performed by themselves and others. By considering some of the parallels between the women of this study and contemporary comedians, I reflect on the important ways in which feminist comedy has changed and the equally significant ways it continues to resist gender and sexual oppression.

Together, the chapters of this book explore the comic strategies that women playwrights adopted to achieve professional success and launch sustained critiques of the patriarchy. I demonstrate that the second half of the eighteenth century was a period of productive effervescence in the history of women's comedy that has had long-lasting influence. Furthermore, by focusing on the intersection of women writers and stage comedy, *Feminist Comedy* centers the theater as a nexus for the development of feminist thought, community, and activism.

1

Comic Resurgence
Catherine Clive

On December 15, 1774, the retired London actress Catherine "Kitty" Clive (née Raftor; 1711–85) offered encouraging advice in a letter to her protégée Jane Pope. The young actress had recently been cast in the minor role of Lucy in Richard Cumberland's comedy *The Choleric Man*, which was to debut on December 19, 1774, at Drury Lane. Pope was frustrated by the casting, but Clive soothed her anxieties, writing: "I am sorry to hear you have an indifferent part in the new Comedy, but I don't at all wonder when you tell me the author. He is a wretch of wretches, however I charge you to make a good part of it. Let it be never so bad, I have often done so myself therefore I know it is to be done[:] turn it & wind it & play it in a different manner to his intention and as hundred to one but you succeed."[1] In this remarkable letter, Clive proposes a model of women's theatrical agency that subverts the male-dominated theatrical establishment. Acknowledging that Pope has been given a meager part by a boorish male playwright—many theater professionals disliked Cumberland—Clive explains that Pope has the power to manipulate the part in a manner that will win audiences and improve her career, as Clive herself had "often done."[2] Indeed, an overview of Clive's career in the theater reveals her unrelenting efforts to influence and circumvent fickle playwright-managers, sexist critics, and demanding audiences for her own professional gain.

This chapter considers Clive's playwriting as an important extension of her efforts to claim professional success as a woman in mid-eighteenth-century London's male-dominated theatrical industry. During the final two decades of her acting career, from 1750 to 1770, Clive wrote four comic afterpieces, short plays that followed full-length mainpieces: *The Rehearsal; or, Bayes in Petticoats* (1750), *Every Woman in Her Humour* (1760), *The Sketch of a Fine Lady's Return from a Rout* (1763), and *The Faithful Irish Woman* (1765).[3] Unfortunately, Clive's afterpieces, or farces, have been neglected, and sometimes even disparaged, by modern theater scholars. One modern biography refers to Clive's plays as "clever, but clearly not work[s] of comic art," and another writes damningly that "for all [Clive's] sensitivity in interpreting other people's humour, and for all her own possession of much impromptu wit, she could not write farces."[4] In reality, Clive's plays were well liked by audiences. Furthermore, they helped advance both her own career and that of other woman playwrights in London following the implementation of the 1737 Stage Licensing Act, which had a devastating impact on the number of new women playwrights able to access the London stage. In fact, Clive's four afterpieces make her the most prolific woman playwright of the mid-eighteenth century.[5]

By recovering her playwriting career in comedy, this chapter argues that Clive played a crucial role in bridging the gap between the first and second waves of women writing for the London stage in the eighteenth century, by cementing the identity of the woman playwright as savvy negotiator, women's advocate, and jokester. Prior to writing plays, Clive sought to legitimize her identity as a theatrical woman through two major clashes with management, known as the Polly Row and the Drury Lane Rebellion. Therefore, I read her foray into playwriting in the mid-century as an extension of her effort to further circumvent sexist barriers in the industry and sustain her own professional career. Clive's first play, *The Rehearsal; or, Bayes in Petticoats*, features a feisty woman playwright named Mrs. Hazard who tries, and fails, to produce her work in the face of much sexist antagonism. In this short feminist play, Clive confronts the barriers facing women playwrights as she purposefully reappropriates the familiar misogynist comedy used against women playwrights since the Restoration. Unlike Clive's other plays, which received only one or two performances and were never published, *Bayes in Petticoats* was well received and had a continual influence; it was performed at least thirteen times between 1750 and 1762 at Drury Lane and was published in London and Dublin in 1753.[6] I argue that Clive's foray into playwriting, particularly her feminist theatrical commentary in *Bayes in Petticoats*, reminded audiences that women could write funny plays while also exposing the absurdity of a misogynist culture that kept women away from the stage in the first place. Though Drury Lane manager David Garrick is often given credit for reintroducing women playwrights to London in the second half of the century, I end my chapter by reorienting attention to Clive's role in this shift. I argue that Clive became a crucial model for the next generation of women playwrights, beginning with Frances Sheridan and Elizabeth Griffith in the early 1760s, resulting in a renaissance of women's comedy.

The Polly Row and the Drury Lane Rebellion

Throughout her career, Clive (figure 1.1) worked to transform her identity as a theatrical woman into that of a respected and skilled professional, setting an important precedent for the women, both actresses and playwrights, who followed her.[7] In the following section, I focus on two incidents, the Polly Row and the Drury Lane Rebellion, that best exemplify these efforts. Clive began performing in London in 1728 at the age of seventeen in minor roles and singing parts at Drury Lane.[8] William Chetwood, the prompter at the time of Clive's debut, recalled that the young actress "had a facetious Turn of Humour, and infinite Spirits, with a Voice and Manner in singing Songs of Pleasantry peculiar to herself."[9] She gained increasingly significant roles, and by 1732, Henry Fielding began to write parts specifically for

Figure 1.1. William John Alais, after John Faber Jr., after Peter van Bleeck, *Catherine Clive as Phillida in Colley Cibber's "Damon and Phillida"* (1734), © National Portrait Gallery, London.

her, including Isabel in *The Old Debauchees*, Kissinda in *The Covent Garden Tragedy*, and Lappet in *The Miser*.[10] But it was the role of Polly in John Gay's *The Beggar's Opera* (1728) that would become the most important of Clive's early career. When Gay's new ballad opera debuted in 1728 at Covent Garden, it "shattered theatrical conventions and box-office records" and became part of the repertoire for the remainder of the century.[11] The part of Polly, a young ingenue, was initially performed by seventeen-year-old Lavinia Fenton, who stirred much public sensation due to her "unschooled singing" and her offstage relationships.[12] As Berta Joncus summarizes, "Factions formed over whether Fenton was a notorious slut or a beguiling innocent [and] debates unfurled across an unprecedented volume and variety of media: prints, ballads, broadsides, and an avalanche of commentary."[13] Fenton left the stage suddenly when she began a relationship with the Duke of Bolton (the two later married following the death of Bolton's first wife), leaving the role open to other actresses. Clive's successful debut as Polly at Drury Lane on August 1, 1732, fortified her identity as one of London's top singers and actresses.

Various aspects of Clive's portrayal of Polly illuminate her early professionalization efforts. First, Clive managed to navigate the infamous role—sexualized both because of Polly's plot line and the sensation surrounding Fenton's initial portrayal—without garnering the same notoriety that had dogged Fenton, by resisting any association with sexual impropriety. This was no easy task, as Felicity Nussbaum points out, since the actress appeared on stage for the public's entertainment but had to appear "sufficiently distant from [the] commercial transactions" on which her very livelihood relied.[14] Unlike Fenton, however, Clive was married while playing the role of Polly.[15] Though her union with George Clive was not a love match—the couple were estranged shortly after their marriage—the arrangement allowed Clive to claim the respectability of a married woman. At the same time, her absent husband did not interfere in her business matters. Joncus argues that the union was likely a marriage of convenience for both parties, obscuring both Catherine's and George's homosexuality. Later in her life, rumors circulated about Clive's Sapphic tastes, but early in her career, she made a great effort to portray herself as an unimpeachable young wife.[16] Henry Fielding's dedicatory epistle to Clive in *The Intriguing Chambermaid* (1734) demonstrates her efforts:

> As great a Favourite as you at present are with the Audience, you would be much more so, were they acquainted with your private Character; cou'd they see you laying out great Part of the Profits which arise to you from entertaining them so well, in the Support of an aged Father; did they see

> you, who can charm them on the Stage with personating the foolish and vicious Characters of your Sex, acting in real Life the Part of the best Wife, the best Daughter, the best Sister, and the best Friend.[17]

Clive's public presentation of feminine virtuosity appears to have been an effective strategy. Her unusually long career as an actress, forty-one years, was notably free of sexual scandals.

While avoiding accusations that she might be another Fenton, Clive soon faced a different professional crisis in playing Polly. It was the convention of the eighteenth-century stage for performers to "own" parts—that is, to play a role until they retired or agreed to pass it on to someone else.[18] Thus, after Fenton left the stage, Clive was free to assume the part of Polly. However, in 1736, Theophilus Cibber, then the manager of Drury Lane, attempted to give his wife, the actress Susannah Cibber, the role of Polly and downgrade Clive to the more minor role of Lucy. Seeing this move as a clear threat to her livelihood and professional prospects, Clive turned to the public, publishing a complaint in the *Daily Post* on November 19, 1736: "Not only the Part of Polly, but likewise other Parts (as could be made appear) have been demanded of me for Mrs. Cibber, which made me conclude, (and, I think with Reason) that there was a Design form'd against me, to deprive by degrees of every Part in which I have had the Happiness to appear with any Reputation; and, at length, by this Method, to make me so little useful to the Stage, as not to deserve the Sallary I now have, which is much inferior to that of several other Performers."[19] Not only does Clive stake her claim to the role of Polly, but she also states her own professional rights and well-deserved financial remuneration. Drawing attention to her finances was an unusual and potentially risky move for the actress to make, but Clive carefully paired her complaint with a heartfelt appeal to her fans.

Though Clive's grievance was primarily with the conduct of Theophilus Cibber, her petition incited the press to suppose a sensationalized rivalry between herself and Susannah Cibber. Henry Woodward's pantomimic farce *The Beggar's Pantomime; or, The Contending Columbines* (1736) capitalized on the dispute and portrayed both Clive and Cibber as prima donnas profiting from, and enjoying, the public attention the row received.[20] In a dramatic ultimatum, Clive was allowed to perform Polly again on December 31, 1736, and the audience was permitted to make a final decision on who should play the part. According to a review in the *London Evening Post*, Clive won the audience over with a masterful speech:

> Mrs. Clive, who play'd the part of Polly, when she came forward, address'd herself to the House, saying Gentlemen, I am very sorry it should be thought I have in any Manner been the Occasion of the least Disturbance;

and then cry'd in so moving a Manner, that even Butchers wept. Then she told them, She was almost ready with her Part of Lucy, and at all Times shou'd be willing to play such Parts as the Town should direct, and desir'd to know if they were willing she should go on with the part of Polly; she behaving in so humble a Manner, the House approv'd of her Behaviour by a general Clap.[21]

Clive countered the press' depiction of her as demanding and mercantile, with a performance of feminine subservience and self-effacement. Her skillful maneuvering of the audience, both on stage and in the papers, proved effective. She, not Cibber, kept the part. Though the matter of two actresses quarrelling over a part may seem inconsequential, Joncus explains that the results of the Polly Row were "a benchmark in the history of actresses, and of the industry of eighteenth-century theatrical celebrity."[22] The incident not only drew attention to the precarity of actors' rights and compensation at that time, it also exposed the immense power that a canny performer like Clive could have over theatrical politics. For a woman, whose professional and financial gain always bordered on the indecorous, this was a powerful revelation. Stuart Sherman deems Clive a "sly feminist" for her innovative and strategic manipulation of print and playhouse that would come to define her career.[23]

Clive faced another highly publicized conflict with theatrical management in 1743, when the manager Charles Fleetwood refused to compensate the Drury Lane actors fully. As Judith Milhous and Robert Hume have shown, Fleetwood claimed that the theater was losing money because of the high salary of star performers like Clive, while the actors claimed that Fleetwood was stealing from the company.[24] The actors were, in fact, correct. According to Milhous and Hume, in order to pay his exorbitant gambling debts, "Fleetwood and his creditors were milking the theatre of every penny of cash they could squeeze out of it."[25] A group of actors including Clive, Garrick (who had joined the company in 1742 after his debut season at Goodman's Fields Theatre), Charles Macklin, and Hannah Pritchard joined forces to stop performing until they received proper compensation. They simultaneously petitioned the Lord Chamberlain to intercede and allow them a license to perform their own plays.

At the beginning of the dispute, known as the Drury Lane Rebellion, Clive's position was strong. Since the Polly Row, she had managed to maintain her virtuous reputation and celebrity authority. This new dispute, however, proved to be more complicated. As she had in 1736, Clive once again turned directly to her fan base, explaining why she was refusing to perform in a letter published in the *Daily Gazetteer* on September 23, 1743:

> I think it incumbent on me to let the Publick know (to whom I am alone obliged for all the Advantages I have receiv'd in my Profession) the true Reason for my not performing as usual.
>
> It is said, that I have quitted the stage, intending to Act no more; it is also reported, that my Demands on the Manager are so exorbitant, that it is impossible for him to comply with them.
>
> In answer to these Insinuations, or Assertions, (which I suppose are intended to injure me) they being false; I am obliged to say, that I have not a Fortune that can support me independent of the Stage; and so far from making extravagant Demands, that I have not made any. My Reason for not performing, is, That I have a very great Sum due to me from the Manager, for which I have often apply'd to him to no Purpose; therefore I hope, I shall be justified in not entering into fresh Agreements with one, who has broke through his Bonds and Promises of paying me, what is justly my Due.[26]

Here, Clive makes a reasonable argument, stating that she will not work for free. Fleetwood, in response, fought back by publishing an account of the actors' salaries in the papers in which he exaggerated Clive's income.[27] Only Garrick's earnings topped Clive's £525 wage per annum.[28] Both audiences and the Lord Chamberlain were disturbed by these large numbers, and in a major blow to the revolting actors, the Lord Chamberlain sided with management and refused to allow the actors to perform elsewhere. Without the ability to perform, the actors were forced to scramble for positions at the other patent theaters. Some, like Garrick, returned to Drury Lane, while Clive went to Covent Garden.

With the matter of the actors' pay left largely unresolved, Clive managed to survive the remainder of the 1743–44 season at Covent Garden until manager John Rich dismissed her. Clive addressed this indignity with her fans in the form of a short pamphlet titled *The Case of Mrs. Clive, Submitted to the Publick* (1744). She once again accused Fleetwood of stealing from her and other actors, defended the salary she had been paid, and chastised Rich for firing her without notice. She presents herself directly, clearly, and humbly to her readers, writing: "I am sorry I am reduced to say any thing in favour of myself; but, as I think I merit as much as another Performer, and the Managers are so desirous to convince me of the contrary, I hope I shall be excused; especially when I declare, that at this time, I am not the least vain of my Profession."[29] Clive's pamphlet was effective. Powerful fans, specifically the Prince and Princess of Wales, attended an impromptu benefit concert that resulted in Rich rehiring her for the 1744–45 season at Covent Garden.[30] She returned to Drury Lane for the 1745–46 season, by which point Fleetwood had sold his shares and left.

As Joncus emphasizes the historical significance of the Polly Row, so Nussbaum draws attention to the importance of Clive's role in the Drury Lane Rebellion: "Clive's polemical pamphlet marked a historical moment when an actress first made an extended public plea to be treated as a respected professional, and to be granted appropriate commercial reward."[31] However, Clive did not escape entirely unscathed from the rebellion. Her second highly publicized battle with management had cemented her reputation as a temperamental diva. Years later, Tate Wilkinson would summarize Clive's personality in his memoirs as "passionate, cross, [and] vulgar."[32] Exacerbating matters was the fact that Clive was getting older. By the mid-century, Clive was nearly forty and still playing the parts of young ingenues like Polly in *The Beggar's Opera* and Ophelia in Shakespeare's *Hamlet* (c. 1599–1601). Other actresses might have retired and passed on their roles to younger counterparts, but Clive was not one to bow to yet another sexist barrier of the theatrical institution—Garrick, after all, played Hamlet until he was fifty-nine. Instead, Clive cunningly shifted the trajectory of her career and began writing plays that displayed her enduring and multifaceted comic talent to her fans.

An Actress Turned Playwright

Over a fifteen-year period between 1750 and 1765, Clive wrote and staged four comic afterpieces at Drury Lane. All four plays were written and produced for her benefit performances, a convention of the eighteenth-century theatrical contract in which an actor was allocated the proceeds from one evening's performances after house expenses. Matthew J. Kinservik has demonstrated that benefit performances made up a sizable percentage of Clive's annual earnings, sometimes as much as half.[33] It is unsurprising, then, that Clive identified a financial and professional opportunity in writing her own afterpieces, which she could tailor to promote her renowned comic acting, singing, and, for the first time in dramatic form, writing.

As I explained in the introduction, the mid-century was a particularly difficult period for women playwrights following the vacuum left by the death of the prolific playwright Susanna Centlivre in 1723 and the implementation of the Stage Licensing Act in 1737. The Act gave the office of the lord chamberlain the power to prohibit any play deemed too political or disruptive and strictly limited performances to London's patent venues, though plenty of nonpatent, illegal, theatrical activity continued to occur.[34] Exacerbating matters, the men who managed the patent houses were often playwrights themselves and reserved spots for their own work.[35] Thus, the Act drastically limited access to the stage for aspiring playwrights, men and women alike; Kinservik shows that following the implementation of the act, premieres of new main pieces dropped by a staggering two-thirds.[36] For women playwrights, the gatekeeping of the theatrical market was only further entrenched by the Act. While a handful of women continued to write plays, the number of productions dwindled. Standouts include Charlotte Charke, daughter of Colley Cibber, who managed to stage a number of original productions in illegitimate venues, and Mrs. Hoper, of whom almost nothing is known except that she staged three short productions at the Haymarket in the 1740s: *The Battle of Poinctiers; or, The English Prince* (1747), *The Cyclopedia* (1748), and *Queen Tragedy Restor'd* (1749).[37] The poet Letitia Pilkington also managed to stage a comedy, *The Turkish Court, or The London 'Prentice*, in Dublin in 1748. When Clive's first afterpiece, *Bayes in Petticoats*, debuted on March 15, 1750, it became the first of only two women's new plays to be staged during the 1750s. The other was Susannah Cibber's afterpiece *The Oracle*, an adaptation of Germain François Poullain de Saint-Foix's *L'oracle* (1740), which debuted at Covent Garden on March 17, 1752. Like Clive's *Bayes in Petticoats*, *The Oracle* was a comic afterpiece written and performed for Cibber's benefit, suggesting that Cibber was inspired by Clive's success with the experiment.

Clive's *Bayes in Petticoats* is a timely and topical interrogation of the identity of a woman playwright, Mrs. Hazard, directing her first play. According to the Drury Lane prompter Richard Cross, the debut performance on March 15, 1750, "went off well," earning Clive £240 for her benefit that year, £34 more than the previous year.[38] Clive revived the piece more than a dozen times after its debut through 1762, both for her own benefit and for other minor actors.[39] Audiences of the 1750s, therefore, would have been familiar with *Bayes in Petticoats*, which was revived year after year, and as of 1753, they could purchase a copy of the text, published in London and Dublin. Capitalizing on the financial and popular success of *Bayes in Petticoats*, in 1760 Clive wrote another afterpiece, *Every Woman in Her Humour* (the title is a gendered inversion of Ben Jonson's 1598 play *Every Man in His Humour*). Though *Every Woman* was only performed once, on March 20, 1760, Nussbaum deems it "the best of [her] small corpus," and Frushell agrees, writing that it is "the play upon which [Clive's] reputation as a minor playwright primarily should rest."[40] *Every Woman* features a more complex plot and a larger cast of characters than *Bayes in Petticoats*, as a group of partygoers gather at the country home of Lord and Lady Byfield. Mrs. Croston, played by Clive, is a cantankerous widower who badgers her brother-in-law Sir John Byfield about his new wife's spending and parties:

> MRS. CROSTON. Dear, Dear Brother, let's have no more on't, you really make me sick to Death to hear you talk so. What cou'd you expect when you married such a woman?
> SIR JOHN. Such a Woman!
> MRS. CROSTON. Look ye there! ay I say such a Woman, you are always complaining and teazing me with her usage of you, and then if I speak, or attempt to advise you how to prevent your ruin (for that she must bring about if she goes on at this rate) then I am snapped and interrupted.[41]

At the end of the play, Mrs. Croston is banished from Sir John's house. A group of pseudointellectual women—Miss Gibberish, Lady Di Clatter, and Mrs. Goodfellow—add further entertainment to the play by debating the merits of science and philosophy.

Clive's next play, *The Sketch of a Fine Lady's Return from a Rout* (first performed on March 21, 1763), is more self-referential than *Every Woman*. Clive played Lady Jenkings, a would-be fine lady who loves to gamble at fancy parties; Clive herself was well known for loving cards. Lady Jenkings's husband, Sir Jeremy, finds her frittering of funds infuriating, and she in turn finds him obtuse and uninteresting:

> SIR JEREMY. So Deary what are you up and dress'd already?
> LADY JENKINGS. Up, why I am but just come in.
> SIR JEREMY. Ha, ha, ha, ain't you, ain't you; well, that's a very good joke I protest; but just come in. You must know Deary, I was so fatigue'd with business yesterday that I went to bed early, I was fast asleep by ten o'clock upon my credit Deary. I never miss'd you; 'tis a very good Joke tho, that you shou'd be out all night & I never miss you, ha, ha, ha, a very good joke indeed.
> LADY JENKINGS. Ha, ha, ha! a prodigious fine Joke to be sure; why, Sir Jeremy, you might be out of the House for ten years and I shou'd never miss you, ha, ha, ha![42]

After Lady Jenkings cleverly wins back her losses, she and her husband make amends. Clive later adapted this play into two acts and retitled it *The Faithful Irish Woman*, which debuted for her benefit on March 18, 1765. The adaptation has a similar plot and characters, but with Clive performing a new role, Mrs. O'Conner, who loves the Englishman Captain Truman. In the play, Clive parodies her own Irish heritage by adopting a heavy accent and incorporating new dialogue defending Irish culture. However, the play is not a cheap mockery of the Irish. Rather, Clive rejects English prejudice as Mrs. O'Conner presents herself as a proud dual citizen of "Irish English" identity.[43] Nussbaum observes that in the play Clive "personifies Ireland as a wealthy, propertied woman who generously assumes the debts of her lover, a suddenly destitute Englishman"—a refreshing alternative to the anti-Irish stereotypes that pervaded the English stage in this era.[44]

Together, all four of Clive's afterpieces are explicitly woman-centric and self-referential: *Bayes in Petticoats* highlights Clive's identity as an ambitious theater professional; *Every Woman in Her Humour* and *A Fine Lady's Return from a Rout* display her in the persona she had cultivated offstage, that of a witty and learned gentlewoman; and *The Faithful Irish Woman* rests on references to Clive's Irish heritage.[45] Clive invites her adoring audience to laugh with her at the antics of her characters, Mrs. Hazard, Mrs. Croston, Lady Jenkings, and Mrs. O'Connor, but underneath their absurdity, all of Clive's metatheatrical characters celebrate witty, gritty, ambitious women who pursue their own desires and operate events for their own gain.

Bayes in Petticoats *and the Rehearsal Tradition*

While each of Clive's afterpieces is worthy of further scholarly attention, *Bayes in Petticoats* is particularly relevant to this study for its dramatization of a woman playwright and its interrogation of sexism within the theatrical establishment. *Bayes in Petticoats* is a parody of a famous rehearsal play—a comic play about a group of actors preparing for a performance—by the Duke of Buckingham, George Villiers.[46] First performed in 1671 and published in 1672, Buckingham's *The Rehearsal* features an inept playwright named Bayes who imitates the work of others to create a pastiche of heroic dramas. He openly brags about his imitation of the classics, not realizing that such a technique is passé: "Why, Sir, when I have any thing to invent, I never trouble my head about it, as other men do; but presently turn o'er this Book, and there I have, at one view, all that *Perseus, Montaigne, Seneca's Tragedies, Horace, Juvenal, Claudian, Pliny, Plutarch's lives*, and the rest, have ever thought, upon this subject: and so, in a trice, by leaving out a few words, or putting in others of my own, the business is done."[47] Buckingham wrote the character of Bayes to lampoon the poet laureate John Dryden and his heroic dramas, especially *The Conquest of Granada* (first performed in 1670), and he drew on an ancient Greek play for inspiration; Aristophanes's *The Frogs* features the playwrights Euripides and Aeschylus debating the merits of their tragic poetry. The so-called rehearsal play was also popular during the English Renaissance. Shakespeare's *A Midsummer Night's Dream* (c. 1595–96) features actors preparing for a performance of the story of

Pyramus and Thisbe; Ben Jonson's *Poetaster* (1601) mocks incompetent playwrights; and Francis Beaumont's *The Knight of the Burning Pestle* (1610) depicts actors passing as audience members—a grocer, his wife, and his apprentice—who interrupt the performance in order to perform a heroic drama of their own. Though Buckingham's *The Rehearsal* offered a highly specific parody of Dryden, its formula was timeless, and the piece remained popular long after both Buckingham's and Dryden's deaths. The broader themes of the rehearsal play—authorship, theatrical politics, and dramatic genre—proved to have enduring interest for audiences. *The Rehearsal* was performed more than 300 times throughout the century and its popularity helped usher in a series of new rehearsal plays by major eighteenth-century playwrights, including Colley Cibber's *The Rival Queens with the Humors of Alexander the Great* (1699), Thomas Durfey's *The Two Queens of Brentford; or, Bayes no Poetaster* (1721), Henry Fielding's *The Author's Farce* (1730) and *The Covent-Garden Tragedy* (1732), John Gay's *The Rehearsal at Gotham* (1730), Henry Carey and John Lampe's *The Dragon of Wantley* (1737), Garrick's *A Peep behind the Curtain; or, The New Rehearsal* (1767), and, late in the century, Richard Brinsley Sheridan's *The Critic; or, A Tragedy Rehearsed* (1779).[48]

When the theater historian Richard Frushell observes that Clive's rehearsal play marked her entrance into "a grand English theatrical tradition," he misses the most crucial element of Clive's contribution. In writing her own rehearsal play, Clive disrupted a grand, *male* English theatrical tradition.[49] Women had generally avoided writing in the rehearsal genre (Charlotte Charke's *The Art of Management* [1735] is a rare exception), as the genre was distinctly anti-woman and had been infamously used to attack women playwrights in the past.[50] In 1696, *The Female Wits; or, The Triumvirate of Poets at Rehearsal* (published anonymously in 1704) framed three women playwrights as incompetent frauds and sexually debased. The three-act play is modeled after Buckingham's *Rehearsal*, but with the satiric attack aimed at Delarivier Manley, Mary Pix, and Catherine Trotter. Likely written by a group of male actor-playwrights at Drury Lane, the play was a fretful misogynist response to the unprecedented increase in works staged by these women in the 1695–96 season.[51] That year, Manley, Pix, and Trotter staged five plays between them. The perceived professional threat posed by these women—that is, their potential to eclipse the commercial and critical success of their male counterparts—is apparent in the anxious and vicious attack against them in *The Female Wits*. In the play, Marsilia parodies Manley and is described as "[a] Poetess, that admires her own Works, and a great Lover of Flattery."[52] In reference to her weight, Pix is parodied as Mrs. Wellfed, "one that represents a fat Female Author."[53] Finally, Trotter is portrayed as Calista, "[a] Lady that pretends to the learned Languages."[54] The sexist agenda of the play is made clear in the prologue: "Thanks to the Strumpets that would mask'd appear, / We now in their True Colours see 'em here."[55] Thus, *The Female Wits* promises to unmask women playwrights as sexual deviants.

Claudine van Hensbergen has recently attempted to recover *The Female Wits* as a broader satire on theatrical conventions, rather than an anti-woman attack, writing, "We should be careful not to read a satire like *The Female Wits* solely through the lens of gender politics," as the play "speaks to [women playwrights'] commercial popularity" and suggests that male playwrights were "equally . . . condemned by contemporary satires."[56] However, this reading is not attuned to the power imbalance that existed between men and women playwrights during the Restoration, nor the fact that women were writing popular plays while simultaneously experiencing gender discrimination. As Laurie Fink writes, "The play does not merely satirize women playwrights: it seeks to deny them the authority to write."[57] Laura J. Rosenthal agrees, pointing out that the play "had real effects on the careers of these women."[58] Following its production in 1696, Manley, who bore the brunt of the satire, did not produce another play for a decade, and Pix and Trotter were forced to take their plays to different theaters. It is impossible to truly measure the detrimental impact of *The Female Wits* on women who might have tried writing drama at the time, but who abandoned their efforts following such highly publicized sexual harassment.

Clive, an experienced actress and theatrical insider, would have been familiar with the legacy of *The Female Wits* and, as Nussbaum writes, the "history of the rehearsal genre when it was earlier exploited to satirize women playwrights."[59] Indeed, at first glance, Clive's *Bayes in Petticoats* seems to be reviving much of the same anti-feminist satire at work in *The Female Wits* through Clive's portrayal of Mrs. Hazard as an incompetent woman playwright. However, in Clive's play, the satirical attack has the opposite effect. The humor of *Bayes in Petticoats* is rooted not in laughing at women who think they can write but rather in laughing at the men who think they cannot. By titling her play *Bayes in Petticoats*, and casting herself as Bayes, Clive presents her play as a gendered inversion of Buckingham's *The Rehearsal* and of the rehearsal tradition more broadly, resulting in a biting "feminist parody."[60]

A Woman's Rehearsal

In *Bayes in Petticoats*, Clive plays Mrs. Hazard; like the original Bayes, she imitates the work of others. Her servant, Gatty, reveals Mrs. Hazard's connection to Bayes as a plagiarist at the outset of the play: "Why, do you know 'tis none of her own? A Gentleman only lent it to her to read; he has been ill a great while at *Bath*; so she has taken the Advantage of that, made some little Alterations, had it set to Music, and has introduced it to the Stage as a Performance of her own."[61] Mrs. Hazard's borrowing might be read as a joke about women's ineptitude in playwriting if it were not for the obvious parody of Bayes. However, apart from their shared characteristics of being arrogant and unskilled, Mrs. Hazard is quite different from Buckingham's Bayes. Mrs. Hazard parodies Clive herself and her reputation for being temperamental, self-important, and ambitious. Even at the slightest of annoyances, Mrs. Hazard falls into an abusive rage:

> MRS. HAZARD. Why, what is the Meaning I must ring for an Hour, and none of ye will come near me, ye Animals?—
> GATTY. I was coming as fast as I could.
> MRS. HAZARD. As fast as you could! Why, you move like a Snail that has been trod upon, you creeping Creature.—Let me die, but she has provoked me into a fine Simile. Come, get the Things to dress me instantaneously. [Tom *with Tea and Coffee. She repeats Recitative*, Oh Corydon, &c.] You, *Tom*, I'm at home to no human Being this Morning but Mr. *Witling*. I've promised to carry him to the *Rehearsal* with me. [*Repeats Recitative*, Gatty *waiting with her Cap.*]
> GATTY. Madam, will you have your Cap on?
> MRS. HAZARD. No! You Ideot [*sic*]; how durst you interrupt me, when you saw me so engaged? As I am a Critic, this Creature will distract me!—Give me my Bottle of Salts.—She has ruined one of the finest Conclusions.[62]

In parodying her celebrity persona, Clive reclaims the nasty publicized assessments of her personality for her own advantage. Her comic technique is not self-derogatory, however. Rather, she mocks the ridiculous antics of Mrs. Hazard and invites the audience to laugh with her.

Making self-parody even more central to the plot, Mrs. Hazard casts Mrs. Clive in the lead role of her upcoming musical entertainment. In a dizzying display of meta-theater, Mr. Witling, a false friend, and Mrs. Hazard discuss Clive's upcoming role in the play:

> WITLING. Pray how many Characters have you in this thing?
> MRS. HAZARD. Why I have but three; for as I was observing, there's so few of them that can sing: nay I have but two indeed that are rational, for I have made one of them mad.
> WITLING. And who is to act that, pray?
> MRS. HAZARD. Why Mrs. *Clive* to be sure; tho' I wish she don't spoil it; for she's so conceited, and insolent, that she won't let me teach it

her. You must know when I told her I had a Part for her in a Performance of mine, in the prettiest manner I was able, (for one must be civil to these sort of People when one wants them) says she, Indeed, Madam, I must see the whole Piece for I shall take no part in a new thing, without causing that which I think I can act best. I have been a great Sufferer already, by the Manager's not doing justice to my Genius; but I hope I shall next Year convince the Town, what fine judgement they have: for I intend to play a capital Tragedy Part for my own Benefit.[63]

In this passage, Clive's self-parody becomes comically explicit as Mrs. Hazard claims that there are few performers who can sing, highlighting that she herself is one of the few. Of course, the character Mrs. Clive can never appear on stage since the real Clive is already performing as Mrs. Hazard. This absence becomes part of the larger joke:

MR. CROSS. Madam, Mrs. *Clive* has sent word, that she can't possibly wait on you this Morning, as she's obliged to go to some Ladies about her Benefit. But you may depend on her being very perfect, and ready to perform it whenever you please.

MRS. HAZARD. Mr. *Cross*, what did you say? I can't believe what I have heard! Mrs. *Clive* sent me word she can't come to my *Rehearsal*, and is gone to Ladies about her Benefit! Sir, she shall have no benefit. Mr. *Witling*, did you ever hear of a Parallel to this Insolence?[64]

In response to Mrs. Clive's tardiness, Mrs. Hazard decides to rehearse Mrs. Clive's part herself, that of the shepherdess Marcella in William Boyce's English pastoral *Corydon and Miranda* (1740). Emphasizing the irony of Mrs. Hazard taking Mrs. Clive's part, Mr. Cross, the prompter, jokes that Mrs. Clive's costume will fit Mrs. Hazard well since Clive is "much of her Size."[65]

In the musical interlude that follows, Clive neither remains in character as Mrs. Hazard nor slips fully into character as the lovestruck Marcella; instead, she shifts fluidly between both.[66] On the one hand, the musical interlude serves the important purpose of displaying Clive's singing abilities, but it also heightens the self-parodic effect. For example, at one point during the performance, Mrs. Hazard interrupts the singing to correct the actress rehearsing Miranda: "That's pretty well, Madam, but I think you sing it too much; you should consider *Recitative* should be spoken as plain as possible; or else you'll lose the Expression."[67] Joncus argues that the song offers a clever extension of Clive's burlesque, as the character of Marcella is "wealthy, vain, tyrannical, jealous, [and] volatile," the same features Clive lampoons in Mrs. Hazard.[68] Thus, in her performance of Mrs. Hazard performing Marcella, Clive engages in a clever layered parody of herself, which was no doubt delightful to audiences.

While the original staging of *Bayes in Petticoats* in 1750 ended with the musical rendition of *Corydon and Miranda*, an additional scene was later approved by the Lord Chamberlain for March 12, 1751.[69] The added scene introduces a new series of characters—Mrs. Giggle, Sir Albany Odelove, Mrs. Sidell, and Miss Daudle—and cements Clive's feminist intervention. The group interrupts the performance and mocks Mrs. Hazard, egged on by Mr. Witling, who seeks to ruin Mrs. Hazard's play: "If you'll join with me, we shall have the finest Scene in the World.—She has made me sick to death with her Stuff, and I will be revenged."[70] Initially, Mr. Witling asks the group to laugh loudly at Mrs. Hazard, but Miss Giggle has the better idea of encouraging the odious Sir Albany to offer Mrs. Hazard criticism: "Oh, I'll tell you what; let's set *Odelove* upon her to enquire into the Plot of her Play.—He'll plague her to death, for he's immensely foolish."[71] In turn, Sir Albany, who embodies the conventional misogynist belief that playwriting is unsuitable for women, torments Mrs. Hazard:

> I say, Madam, will you give me leave, as you're going to entertain the Town, (that is, I mean, to endeavour, or to attempt to entertain them) for let me tell you, fair Lady, 'tis not an easy thing to bring about. If Men, who are properly graduated in Learning, who have swallowed the Tincture of a polite Education, who, as I may say, are hand and glove with the Classics, if such Geniuses as I'm describing, fail of Success in Dramatical Occurrences, or Performances, ('tis the same Sense in the Latin) what must a poor Lady to expect, who is ignorant as the Dirt.[72]

Sir Albany disregards women writers on the grounds that they lack formal education, and he goes on to suggest that Mrs. Hazard get advice from her "Male Acquaintance," perhaps intended to reference Garrick, who can coach her on the classical unities.[73] Of course, Clive's physical presence on stage serves as a constant reminder that a woman authored this play, inviting audiences to laugh not at women playwrights, but at Sir Albany and the attitudes he represents.

Ultimately, in *Bayes in Petticoats*, Clive harnesses Buckingham's stock rehearsal play to promote herself through a complex exploration of her own identity as a professional theatrical woman, complete with her exposure of powerful men who disparage her contributions. Clive displays her multifaceted talent as an actress, comic playwright, and singer as she mocks the notion that theatrical women are in any way inferior to their male colleagues.

Clive and the Resurgence of Women Playwrights

By the time Clive staged *The Faithful Irish Woman* in 1765, two other women playwrights had established themselves in London: Frances Sheridan and Elizabeth Griffith. As I described in the introduction, the resurgence of women playwrights in London following the lean years of the mid-century has often been attributed to Garrick, who was fond of supporting aspiring women writers, as Ellen Donkin describes: "Garrick took pride in his reputation for helping new playwrights, but he took particular pride in having helped new women playwrights. He took pleasure in their public demonstrations of gratitude, usually in prefaces, and occasionally indulged himself by reflecting on the women he had helped in letters to friends."[74] There is no doubt that Garrick played a major role in the reintroduction of women playwrights in the mid-century by accepting their plays for production. Of the eight new plays by women staged during Clive's playwriting tenure, 1750 to 1765, Garrick produced seven of them at Drury Lane. Not only did he produce all four of Clive's plays, but in 1763 he also produced Sheridan's *The Discovery* and *The Dupe*, and a few years later, in 1765, he produced Griffith's debut play *The Platonic Wife*. He also later staged Griffith's *The School for Rakes* in 1769, by which time other women had entered the market. These mid-century plays by Clive, Sheridan, and Griffith mark a major shift in women's access to the London stage, as evidenced by table 1.1.

Garrick's motivation for staging women's comedies, however, was rooted not in altruism, but in profit—he was a businessman. The success of Clive's *Bayes in Petticoats* proved that there was still a market for plays by women, specifically women's comedies. In fact, we can see evidence of Garrick's realization that a woman's gender could be harnessed as a selling point in the epilogue he wrote for *Bayes in Petticoats*, added to the revival of the play on March 19, 1751, and delivered by Clive:[75]

> A woman write! Hey-day! Cry one and all!
> No wonder truly, Bedlam, is too small,
> Should this whim circulate & grow a fashion,
> Each House would be a Mad one thro' the Nation—
> But pray, Sirs, why must we not write, nor think?
> Have we not Heads and hands, and Pen and Ink?
> Can you boast more, that are so wondrous wise?
> Have Women then no weapons but their Eyes?
> Were we, like you, to let our Genius loose
> We'd top your wit, and Match you for abuse.[76]

TABLE 1.1. NEW PLAYS BY WOMEN STAGED DURING CLIVE'S PLAYWRITING TENURE, 1750–65

Debut	Play	Playwright	Venue	Manager	Genre/Form
March 15, 1750	The Rehearsal; or, Bayes in Petticoats	Catherine Clive	Drury Lane	David Garrick	Comic afterpiece
March 17, 1752	The Oracle	Susannah Cibber	Covent Garden	John Rich	Comic afterpiece
March 20, 1760	Every Woman in Her Humour	Catherine Clive	Drury Lane	David Garrick	Comic afterpiece
February 3, 1763	The Discovery	Frances Sheridan	Drury Lane	David Garrick	Comic mainpiece
March 21, 1763	The Sketch of a Fine Lady's Return from a Rout	Catherine Clive	Drury Lane	David Garrick	Comic mainpiece
December 10, 1763	The Dupe	Frances Sheridan	Drury Lane	David Garrick	Comic mainpiece
January 24, 1765	The Platonic Wife	Elizabeth Griffith	Drury Lane	David Garrick	Comic mainpiece
March 18, 1765	The Faithful Irish Woman	Catherine Clive	Drury Lane	David Garrick	Comic afterpiece

Source: Matthew J. Kinservik, "Garrick's Unpublished Epilogue for Catherine Clive's The Rehearsal: or, Bays in Petticoats (1750)," Études Anglaises 49, no. 3 (1996): 326.

Garrick's epilogue reflects a common marketing strategy for eighteenth-century women's comedy: framing the play as having a woman-friendly message, while also capitalizing on a sort of misogynist surprise that a woman has written a play at all.[77] The misogyny, in this case, is undercut by Clive's delivery of the prologue and the foregrounding of her own authorship. Similar epilogues were used to market women's plays for the remainder of the century, long past the point that it was unusual to see a new play written by a woman.

While Garrick supported many women in his role as manager, he also was a powerful gatekeeper, as I will discuss further in the following chapter. He regularly undervalued the women he worked with, as evidenced in his financial negotiations with Clive herself. In 1768, for example, Garrick attempted to reschedule Clive's benefit performance, a major source of her annual income, to follow that of other actresses. Clive felt this was a slight to her standing in the company that would have a negative effect on the financial gains of her own benefit, which she explained to Garrick bluntly in a letter:

> Any one who sees your letter wou'd suppose I was kept at your Theatre out of Charitey [sic]; if you still look over the number of Times I have play'd this season—you must think I have desarvd [sic] the monney [sic] you give me. You say you give me the best day in the week; I am sorry to say I cannot be of your opinion. . . . You say that you have fixt the day and have drawn a line under it that I may be sure that I can have no other: therefore, I must take it—But I must think it (and so will every impartial person) very hard that Mrs Dancer should have her Benefit before Mrs Clive.[78]

Clive's unwavering defense of her own professional rights—as evidenced by this letter and her numerous other negotiations with theatrical management—may have encouraged Garrick to take other women playwrights more seriously. Though some scholars have framed Clive's career as benefiting from Garrick's "friend[ship]," the truth is that she had a strong sway over him.[79] As Nussbaum points out, in 1767 Garrick wrote his own Buckingham-style rehearsal play, *A Peep Behind the Curtain; or, The New Rehearsal*, suggesting "Clive's influence on Garrick rather than the reverse."[80]

While Garrick was pivotal to the reintroduction of women playwrights both during the lean years of the mid-century and in the decades that followed, I want to reorient attention to Clive's role in this shift. Clive's plays set a precedent for Sheridan and Griffith, both actresses, to claim playwriting once again as a legitimate profession for women. When Sheridan staged her comedy *The Dupe* in 1763, Clive not only performed in the play as Mrs. Friendly—a part that Sheridan wrote especially for her—but she also delivered the epilogue. Yet, Clive's role in supporting *The Dupe* has been almost entirely overlooked and even misrepresented. A claim made by Sheridan's granddaughter, Alicia Le Fanu, in her 1824 biography of her grandmother—and repeated in the current entry on Sheridan in *The Oxford Dictionary of National Biography*—places blame for the play's supposed failure (it was performed only three times) on Clive, who, Le Fanu argues, "vowed immortal hatred" on Thomas Sheridan and ruined his wife's play to take revenge.[81] The play's anonymous epilogue, clearly written by or in collaboration with Clive, contradicts Le Fanu's account. The epilogue offers a feminist interrogation of the theatrical establishment as Clive addresses the women in the audience, explaining that no man was willing to write an epilogue for Sheridan's play, so she did:

> Not Mrs. Friendly now, I'm Mrs. Clive;
> No character from fiction will I borrow,
> But if you please, I'll talk again to-morrow.
> Then you conclude, from custom long in vogue,
> That I come here to speak an Epilogue;
> With satyr, humour, spirit, quite refin'd,
> Double-entendre too, with wit combin'd;
> Not for the ladies—but to please the men;
> All this you guess—and now you're out again:
> For to be brief, our author bid me say
> She tried, but cou'dn't get one to her play.
> No Epilogue! why, Ma'am, you'll spoil your treat,
> An Epilogue's the cordial after meat;
>
> . . .
>
> She took the hint—Will *you*, good Sir? or *you*, Sir?
> A sister scribbler! sure you can't refuse her!
>
> . . .
>
> What's to be done, she cry'd? can't *you* endeavour
> To say some pretty thing?—I know you're clever.[82]

Though Clive ends her epilogue with a note that she was "unable to succeed" in helping Sheridan, she explains that she has "finely dup'd" the audience into listening to her recount the interaction.[83]

Clive similarly supported the work of Griffith by delivering an epilogue advocating for the woman playwright for *The Platonic Wife*. Griffith wrote a role for Clive in her first comedy, which debuted on January 24, 1765, at Drury Lane. As she had done for *The Dupe*, Clive performed the epilogue for *The Platonic Wife* (also by an anonymous writer that could have been Clive, or at the very least, someone with whom Clive collaborated) in which she gives a similar defense of the playwright. This elaborate epilogue involves Clive marching on stage with a piece of paper in hand. In the satirical style of the bombastic Mrs. Hazard, Clive is displeased with the male-authored epilogue and says that she will "write an air, myself, to't—then you'll roar / Bravo! bravissimo! divine! encore!"[84] In mock airheadedness, Clive gets flustered, saying: "Dear me! What is't that I was going to say? / Lord, I'm so flounder'd! so confused!"[85] While the humor in this epilogue appears to lie in the sexist notion that women cannot write, the joke is inverted by Griffith's authorship of the play and Clive's delivery of the epilogue itself.

Indeed, Clive employs the same comic feminist technique that she used in *Bayes in Petticoats*. As she bungles her lines and becomes increasingly hysterical, the joke is not aimed at women writers, but the tired stereotypes about them. In a reciprocal display of solidarity, Griffith addressed Clive in her preface to her 1769 play *The School for Rakes*, in which Clive played Mrs. Winifred and delivered another epilogue. Griffith thanks Clive for her "study of a new part," the last new role of Clive's career, and for her "kindness to the author."[86]

Clive's epilogues for Sheridan and Griffith set a precedent for women playwrights to find professional legitimacy in their connections to one another, and to see their gender not as a detriment but a marketable strength. In 1767, Clive's friend and romantic partner Jane Pope followed in her mentor's footsteps and wrote her own benefit afterpiece, *The Young Couple*, based on Sheridan's first play *The Discovery* (1763). No doubt inspired by Clive, Pope did not wait for a man to write her a good part, but created her own.

Following her retirement from the stage in 1769, Clive moved to the countryside. In a 1771 study of Twickenham country homes, Jael-Henrietta Pye describes Clive's house as "a little cottage of plain appearance" with gardens "laid out in excellent taste," culminating in a "charming Retirement."[87] Clive wrote to Pope describing her contented life in retirement: "I have ten times more business now than I had when I playd the Fool as you do, I have engagements every day of my life. Routs either at home or abroad every night all the nonsense of having my hair not done time enough for my parties as I used to do for my parts with the difference that I am losing money instead of getting some but I dont mind that for I am in such good health, and such fine spirits that it is impossible for any one to be happyer."[88] Clive passed away at seventy-four years of age on December 6, 1785. Her will was executed by her good friend and neighbor, the writer Horace Walpole.

While Clive's influence as a playwright has been long overlooked, she played a key role in the resurgence of women writing for the London stage. Her fierce defense of her professional rights, her quick-witted feminist comedies, and her advocacy for other women in the theater provided a model that other women playwrights could, and did, repeat. Though Clive wrote her last play in 1765, the traits she exemplified as a playwright can be identified in the careers of many women who succeeded her in the latter half of the century. In the following chapter, I turn to one such woman, Frances Brooke, who, despite Garrick's decades-long efforts to sabotage her career, managed to become one of the first woman managers of a patent theater in London and staged two immensely successful comic operas.

2

Musical Comedy

Frances Brooke

While Frances Brooke (née Moore; 1724–89) is remembered primarily as a novelist, she long harbored a dream of becoming a professional playwright, and over a span of more than three decades, she wrote at least six plays, four of which were published, and three of which were produced on the London stage. Brooke may have experienced even more success as a playwright had it not been for her longtime feud with playwright-actor-manager David Garrick. After rejecting her first play, *Virginia*, in 1754, Garrick blocked Brooke's access to the London stage during his lifetime. Unlike many other women in the latter half of the eighteenth century who strategically ingratiated themselves with Garrick to stage their works, Brooke refused to grovel to him, and he resented her for it. After realizing that she had been blacklisted, Brooke decided to challenge the all-male theatrical administration head-on.

In 1773, Brooke, seen in figure 2.1, became the part owner and manager of the King's Theatre, London's opera house, which she ran successfully until 1778. After Garrick died in 1779, Brooke harnessed her newfound knowledge as a manager to stage one of her own plays, *The Siege of Sinope*, which debuted at Covent Garden in 1781, more than a quarter of a century after she had written *Virginia*. *Sinope* was a moderately successful tragedy; it ran for ten performances but was not revived in later seasons. The following year, Brooke wrote a massive commercial success, a two-act comic opera, or burletta, titled *Rosina* (1782). *Rosina* became the second-most performed afterpiece of the late eighteenth century, staged more than 200 times by 1800, and was followed by another successful comic opera, *Marian*, in 1788.[1] Although not a record-breaking hit like *Rosina*, *Marian* was performed an impressive forty times between 1788 and 1800. Thus, Brooke's long and storied theatrical career ended on a high note; she died shortly after *Marian* debuted on January 23, 1789.

This chapter explores Brooke's commercially successful but critically overlooked plays, *Rosina* and *Marian*. Despite the immense popularity of

Figure 2.1. Mariano Bovi after Catherine Read, *Mrs. Brooke* (1790), © The Trustees of the British Museum.

these two comic operas, they have generally been treated as less important than Brooke's other works, deemed to lack the seriousness and complexity of her novels, poetry, translations, periodical essays, and tragedies. In 1986, the prominent musicologist Roger Fiske assessed both of Brooke's librettos as "insipid."[2] Even feminist theater historians have fallen prey to the same diminishing narrative. Ellen Donkin misrepresents the final stages of Brooke's career as "stalemated," when in fact, *Rosina* and *Marian* marked an enormous critical and financial boon for Brooke, and Jodi L. Wyett, who applies a feminist lens to Brooke's *Sinope*, refers to *Rosina* and *Marian* as mere "puff pieces."[3] However, a small body of recent scholarship has sought to counter the dismissive assessments of Brooke's comic operas. Leslie Ritchie has contextualized *Rosina* and *Marian* within a larger body of late eighteenth-century pastorals—comic musical afterpieces depicting rural life—pointing out that *Rosina* became the "pastoral to which all others were compared."[4] Betty Schellenberg reads *Rosina* and *Marian* as an extension of Brooke's participation in "the political public realm."[5] Finally, a recent article by Paula R. Backscheider demonstrates how Brooke harnessed her expertise as a manager to create her plays, although her study focuses primarily on *Sinope*.[6]

Building on the efforts to redeem *Rosina* and *Marian*, this chapter also seeks to analyze the two musicals as part of Brooke's professional strategy while also situating Brooke within the index of women playwrights of comedy in the eighteenth century. I trace Brooke's professional development from the 1750s, when she arrived in London hoping to stage her first play, through her ensuing battles with Garrick—the most powerful figure in London's theater industry—to her eventual success as a manager and playwright. At first glance, *Rosina* and *Marian* appear to be conventional pastoral afterpieces, shoring up nationalistic and patriarchal values: the eponymous heroines of both plays are young, virtuous women who fall in love against the background of rural beauty where farmers labor happily under the benevolent gaze of aristocratic overlords. However, in my reading of *Rosina* and *Marian*, I argue that Brooke makes daring critiques of gender, class, and power, and deviating from previous studies that have highlighted Brooke's contributions to opera and pastoral, I place her work within the tradition of feminist comedy.

This chapter relies on the only surviving correspondence between Brooke and her friend, the poet Richard Gifford, held by the Houghton Library at Harvard University.[7] Brooke and Gifford shared an interest in music and theater and discussed the creation of Brooke's plays, including *Rosina*. Her unpublished letters to Gifford offer critical insight into Brooke's determination to become a professional playwright and her remarkable resourcefulness in pursuing this goal despite the entrenched sexism of London's theater industry.

The Feud of Frances Brooke and David Garrick

Like most women writers of the eighteenth century, Brooke received her education at home. Her father, the Reverend Thomas Moore, was the rector at Claypole, Lincolnshire, but died in 1727, leaving his three young daughters, Frances, Catherine (who died in childhood), and Sarah, to be raised and educated by their mother, Mary.[8] The small family initially lived with Mary's widowed mother, but both mother and grandmother died by the time Frances was a teenager. The Moore sisters then moved in with their aunt, Sarah Steevens, and her husband, the Reverend Roger Steevens, the rector of Tydd St. Mary, Lincolnshire. Lorraine McMullen observes that Brooke's education was likely augmented by her upbringing in these various rectories where she was influenced by highly educated men, and unusually well-educated women, with consistent access to a home library. She developed a strong knowledge of French and Italian, and she was well read in both English literature and English translations of classical Greek and Roman literature.[9] Her classical education—the norm for English schoolboys but unusual for a young woman—had an important influence on her later dramatic works; her two tragedies were based on Roman history, and her comedies were written in the pastoral tradition that can be traced back to ancient Greece. Additionally, all her plays are marked by an adherence to the classical unities of action, time, and place.

As a young adult, Brooke was in the unusual position of being a single woman with financial independence. She received £500 from her father's will when she and her surviving sister Sarah reached the age of majority, and possibly had more funds left to her by her mother. Combining her creative talent, professional ambition, and financial freedom, Brooke moved to London in the late 1740s to pursue a career as a playwright. During this period, she married Reverend John Brooke, made friends in London's literary and theatrical circles, and pursued the production of her first play, a full-length tragedy titled *Virginia*. It was bad luck that the story on which Brooke based her play, Livy's tale of Appius Claudius's abduction of Virginia, had also been dramatized by two other playwrights at the same time. All three dramatists—Brooke, Samuel Crisp, and John Moncrief—were possibly inspired by the same edition of Livy's *Ab urbe condita* prepared by the French author Jean-Baptiste Louis Crevier in the late 1740s.[10] Though Brooke submitted her play to Garrick at Drury Lane before the two men had submitted theirs, her play was rejected. Crisp's *Virginia* beat out Brooke's for the spot at Drury Lane in 1754, and John Moncrief's version, titled *Appius*, was staged at Covent Garden in 1755 under the auspices of manager John Rich. It was not the first time that the Roman tale had been dramatized: John Webster wrote *Appius and Virginia* in the early seventeenth century and it was published in 1654. With such an esteemed male lineage, from ancient Rome through the early modern stage, it is highly possible that the classical subject matter, "overwhelmingly associated with masculine freedom and authority," was deemed inappropriate for a woman's pen by the managers.[11]

With both playhouses staging a version of the tragedy by her male rivals, Brooke realized that her play would never be staged. Instead, she published *Virginia* in 1756, alongside a selection of original and translated poetry, and appended a preface defending her play:

> The Author of these poetical Attempts, begs Leave to say, that she should not have printed them, but that she is precluded from all Hopes of ever seeing the Tragedy brought upon the Stage, by there having been two so lately on the same Subject. If her's should be found to have any greater Resemblance to the two represented, than the Sameness of the Story made unavoidable, of which she is not conscious, it must have been accidental on her side, as there are as many Persons, of very distinguished rank, and unquestionable Veracity, who saw her's in Manuscript before the others appeared, and will witness for her, that she has taken no advantage of having seen them.[12]

By drawing attention to the timeline of her manuscript submission to Garrick, Brooke refutes any possibility that she plagiarized Crisp's or Moncrief's plays. She also draws attention to her gender as a possible reason for her play's rejection and alludes to the possibility that Garrick *could* have read her manuscript while working on her rival's play. The small number of women playwrights producing work in the 1750s also adds important context to Garrick's rejection of *Virginia*. As I argue in the first chapter, the mid-century was a difficult decade for women playwrights. Only the actresses Catherine Clive and Susannah Cibber were able to stage plays during the 1750s, and both plays were comic afterpieces. While Garrick later became known for producing work by women, at the time that Brooke submitted *Virginia* he had only ever produced the work of one woman, Clive. It was not until the 1760s that he seems to have fully realized the marketability of women's comedies.[13]

Frustrated by her fruitless efforts to stage *Virginia*, in 1755 Brooke took on an entirely new project, a periodical titled *The Old Maid*. The satirical journal was published under Brooke's pseudonym, Mary Singleton, and promised, tongue in cheek, "a little court of female criticism, consisting of myself and six virgins of my own age, to take into consideration all stage offences against sense and scenery."[14] Not all of Brooke's theatrical criticism was accepted as satiric, however. In an essay on Shakespeare's *King Lear* (c. 1606), Brooke criticized Garrick's choice to stage Nahum Tate's adaptation rather than the original, writing on March 13, 1756: "Mr. *Garrick*, who professes himself so warm an idolater of this inimitable poet, and who is determined, if I may use his own words, in the prologue to the *Winter's Tale*, 'To lose no drop of this immortal man,' should yet prefer the vile adulterated cup of Tate."[15] Making matters even more personal, Brooke went on to praise Spranger Barry, Garrick's rival, as the better Lear. Garrick, who prided himself on his affinity to Shakespeare and was famous for playing Lear, was deeply offended by Brooke's criticism, jest or no. Less than a year later, in October 1756, he produced a new version of Tate's *Lear* that included more of Shakespeare's original text, though he mainly restored Lear's lines to showcase himself in the role.[16]

There is concrete evidence that Garrick spoke negatively about Brooke among the literary and theatrical community following her article in *The Old Maid*, and that he sought to sabotage her career. In January 1757, six months after the final publication of *The Old Maid*, Brooke began writing a new play. Perhaps realizing that the masculine perception of Latin literature had contributed to her play being passed over in favor of adaptations by two men, Brooke changed tactics with her next project and wrote a comic pastoral afterpiece titled *The Shepherd's Wedding*. In a letter to her friend Gifford, she explains that the piece will be produced by Rich at Covent Garden: "You must know, I am about a pastoral piece of two Acts, I think Rich will play it; we are gracious; he came to see me Sunday last sennight: it, the piece, is to be call'd *The Shepherd's Wedding*: send the Songs in a few days, & I'll love you for ever: I shou'd like a Duet between the two Lovers, who are parted, because the Shepherdess is found out to be of superior Rank."[17] Though Brooke's letter indicates that Rich expressed sincere interest in the play, for unknown reasons *The Shepherd's Wedding* was not staged (although it shares similarities with *Rosina* and *Marian*, produced decades later). In 1761, Brooke wrote and tried to produce another, unnamed, farce. But Garrick declined to read it: "He refus'd to take it [the manuscript], saying he had one on the same plan in his hands of Frances's [Sheridan]."[18] Garrick would later hold up his support of other women playwrights like Sheridan as proof that he did not reject Brooke's plays due to sexism.

Further evidence of Garrick's efforts to derail Brooke's career can be found in his correspondence with Marie Jeanne Riccoboni in 1765, ten years after the publication of *The Old Maid*. Riccoboni asked Garrick's opinion of Brooke and whether she should agree to let Brooke translate one of her novels. Brooke had already translated a novel by Riccoboni into English, *Lettres de milady Juliette Catesby à milady Henriette Campley, son amie* (1759). Her translation, first published in 1760 under the title *Letters from Juliet, Lady Catesby, to Her Friend, Lady Henrietta Campley*, was in its fourth edition by 1765, and Brooke wanted to repeat the success. Riccoboni sought Garrick's advice, and he responded unequivocally:

> I am not acquainted with Mrs. Brooke: she once wrote a play, which I did not like, & would not act, for which heinous offence she vented her female Spite upon Me, in a paper she publish'd call'd *The Old Maid*, but I forgive her as thoroughly as her Work is forgotten—I am told she has merit & is very capable of a good translation, tho not of an Original—*five hundred* of her will not make half a Riccoboni. You will be civil to her & no more, all this is Entre nous [between us].[19]

Riccoboni trusted Garrick and gave the translation to his friend Thomas Becket, even though Becket had done a poor job translating another of her novels as *The History of Miss Jenny Salisbury* (1764).[20] Becket continued to translate Riccoboni's novels at Garrick's behest, but none were as successful as Brooke's *Letters from Juliet*. Donkin argues that Garrick's advice to Riccoboni cost both Riccoboni and Brooke financial and professional gain.[21] Garrick's disingenuous guidance reveals that he continued to hold a grudge against Brooke even a decade after the publication of *The Old Maid*.

Brooke's theatrical endeavors were put on pause when, between 1763 and 1768, she moved from London to the British colony of Quebec, where her husband had been appointed garrison chaplain.[22] While in Quebec, Brooke focused primarily on novel writing, but on her return to London in 1768, she once again set her gaze on the theater. She reconnected with the literary and theatrical community, no longer as a new member of London's literati, but as a respected author of two successful novels, *The History of Lady Julia Mandeville* (1763) and *The History of Emily Montague* (1769). Frances Burney, who was not yet a published author herself, praised Brooke in her journal around this time, writing that Brooke was "very well bred, and expresses herself with much modesty upon all subjects; which in an *authoress*, a woman of *known* understanding, is extremely pleasing."[23] Yet, despite the high regard that London's literary community held for Brooke, she continued to struggle with the theatrical establishment.

In the early 1770s, Brooke wrote the first draft of a play she titled *Rosina*, a comic opera like *The Shepherd's Wedding*. She collaborated closely on the project with Gifford, who according to their letters, wrote some of the songs and provided her with unceasing encouragement. But Brooke's letters to Gifford also reveal her ongoing difficulty getting her work accepted by the managers at any of the patent theaters. She first approached George Colman the Elder, the new manager at Covent Garden, about staging *Rosina*, but he was not accommodating. She feared that Garrick had poisoned Colman against her, writing to Gifford: "Colman has not yet sent an answer. I have a very bad opinion of all of these gentry [the managers], & my greatest hope is that as neither of the installations [the patent theaters] seem to please violently, one of them will have a vacancy & take it for their own sakes. I know neither will for mine. . . . There is nothing so astonishing to me as that Colman should be another Garrick, which I am told he is."[24] Brooke was determined that her play would be staged one way or another, and she explained to Gifford her plan if Colman remained unsupportive:

> My design is, if he refuses, to apply to G. [Garrick] & if he refuses[,] to apply to the Ld Chamberlain, for leave to act it at my own hazard, for twenty nights at Foote's, which if *thot* about, will probably pave the way for a third theatre, which is in agitation. I know the Lord Ch. is very angry at some instances of theatrical tyranny, & I think I can refer my story back up & back it with friends that will carry my point, & the best female singer we have, Miss Catley, is in town, & not engaged at either house, & as ready to take such a revenge as I can be; but if I hint my design, they will engage her, and prevent it.[25]

This letter reveals Brooke's resolve to circumvent the managerial boys' club by lobbying the Lord Chamberlain for a third patent for spoken drama to be performed in London. She even enlisted the support of another woman, the singer Ann Catley, in her scheme. According to *The London Stage*, Catley had not performed at Covent Garden between March 1771 and September 1772, for unknown reasons. Though the *Biographical Dictionary* suggests this absence was Catley's choice, Brooke's letter reveals that Catley was, in fact, being blocked from employment by the managers.[26] Considering Garrick's dislike for Brooke and the close relationship he had with Colman (the two co-authored a popular comedy, *The Clandestine Marriage*, in 1768), it is unsurprising that *Rosina* was not accepted by either theater. Brooke, facing the seemingly impossible barrier of convincing any of the London managers to stage her work, did not move forward with her plan to produce the play at the Haymarket, perhaps because, as performance records show, Catley was rehired by Colman at Covent Garden. Instead, she made the audacious decision to become the manager of a London theater herself.

Managing the Opera House

After *Rosina* was refused in 1773, Brooke and a small group of partners purchased the King's Theatre, colloquially known (and hereafter referred to) as the Opera House. Brooke, her husband, and her brother-in-law, along with the acting couple Richard and Mary Ann Yates, took over management of the Opera House in late 1773.[27] Like Brooke, Mary Ann Yates had reason to resent London's theatrical management. She had performed at Drury Lane from her debut in the 1750s through 1767, becoming one of the most highly celebrated actresses of her day, especially in tragedy. Following the deaths of two other great actresses, Susannah Cibber in 1766 and Hannah Pritchard 1768, and the retirement of Catherine Clive in 1769, Yates demanded to be paid a sum appropriate for her standing as London's top actress. Like Clive, Yates used the press to stake her claim for adequate remuneration in letters to the public.[28] Garrick was unmoved, however, and chose not to reengage her, so she and her husband moved to Covent Garden. But in the 1772–73 season, Yates left Covent Garden after quarrelling with Colman over the same issue; the manager consistently refused to pay her requested salary.[29] Yates was limited in her ability to negotiate because of the duopoly of London's patent system. By joining ranks to run the London Opera House, Brooke and Yates hoped that they could provide competition to Covent Garden and Drury Lane, and they planned to appeal to the Lord Chamberlain for a license to perform spoken drama and English opera alongside Italian opera.[30] If their patent was granted, Brooke could write plays, and Yates could perform in them.

Brooke's and Yates's status as women theater managers was not entirely unprecedented by the late eighteenth century, but it was extremely unusual.[31] A handful of women had ventured into the business of theater before them, including Ann Bracegirdle and Elizabeth Barry, who in 1695 became the first women managers of a London theater company following their petition for a license to form the United Company along with six male collaborators.[32] Other women worked in theater administration beyond the patent stages. For example, in the 1730s and '40s, Charlotte Charke successfully acquired a license to perform her own puppet shows and other theatricals at a variety of venues.[33] Teresa Cornelys established Carlisle House, a fashionable gathering place where patrons could purchase annual subscriptions for access to entertainments including masquerades, and, in the late eighteenth century, Elizabeth Craven organized private theatricals at her mansion, Brandenburgh House.[34] Still other women managed theaters outside the metropolis, such as Sarah Baker, who operated a traveling performance troupe and later opened four theaters in the provinces.[35]

Practically speaking, however, women's access to theatrical management in London was especially limited due to both the highly regulated nature of the industry and women's unequal legal standing. In 1745, actress Susannah Cibber harbored dreams of becoming a manager and tried to convince then-actor Garrick to go into business with her and purchase the patent at Drury Lane. Garrick was interested, but because Cibber was a woman, he questioned her ability to run the business effectively and independently. In December 1745, he explained his concerns to a friend, writing, "How can she be a joint patentee? Her husband will interfere, or somebody must act for her, which would be equally disagreeable."[36] Cibber's husband, Theophilus, was a notorious scoundrel who, as Fiona Ritchie observes, "would take any opportunity of exploiting his wife's success."[37] Garrick, pragmatically, did not want to deal with such complications, so he did not partner with Cibber. The issue of coverture also applied to Frances Brooke and Mary Ann Yates, whose management roles were possible only because their husbands were amenable co-conspirators. John Brooke and Richard Yates supported their wives' desire to purchase the theater and were willing to take a less prominent role in the business.

Shortly after their takeover in 1773, Brooke and Yates made their first application for a license to perform spoken drama at the Opera House on four nights of the week, but they were refused.[38] Consequently, the two women, who had no expertise in either management or Italian opera, were now in charge of curating London's opera season. According to Ian Woodfield, Yates played "the part of glamorous society hostess, holding court like a queen," while the "all-important responsibility of artistic policy... was assumed by Brooke."[39] Richard Yates served as front-of-house manager, while Brooke's husband and her brother-in-law were silent partners. A journal entry by Frances Burney from 1774 gives some indication of how this unusual managerial arrangement functioned:

> The first Opera [of the season] was performed last Tuesday. The morning before, Mrs Brooke, who lives in Market Lane, Called here, & very civilly invited my mother, Susy & me to go with her to the Opera the next Day.... Accordingly we went. Her House in Market Lane, by means of divers turnings & windings, has a passage to the Opera House. We intended to have sat in her Box, & have seen only her, but when we went, we found she was up stairs with Mrs Yates, & when she came down, she immediately asked us to go up stairs with her. This we declined, but she would not be refused, & we were obliged to follow her.... We were led up a noble stair case, that brought us to a most magnificent Apartment.... Here we saw Mrs Yates, seated like a stage Queen surrounded with gay Courtiers, & dressed with the utmost elegance & brilliancy.... With an *over done* civility, as soon as our Names were spoken, she rose from her seat hastily, & rather *rushed* towards us, than meerly advanced to meet us. But I doubt not it was meant as the very *pink of politeness*. As to poor *Mr* Yates, he presumed not to take the liberty, in his own House, to act any other part than that of Waiter, in which capacity he arranged the Chairs.[40]

Though Burney, and the public, may have raised their brows at women managing a theater while their husbands acted in subservience to them, by all accounts this managerial arrangement was a great success.

Woodfield observes that during her tenure at the helm of the Opera House, Brooke "demonstrated so sound a grasp of artistic planning and financial control that the King's Theatre began to prosper to a hitherto unprecedented degree."[41] Backscheider confirms this, writing that Brooke "learned from failures, experiments and innovative talent acquisition to make King's profitable, and, once again, a centre of London cultural life."[42] Though their application to perform spoken drama was denied (they once again applied, and were rejected, in 1775), Brookes and Yates made the best of the situation. Yates began performing once again at Drury Lane in 1774, splitting her time between her two professions as actor and manager, and leaving Brooke with foremost responsibility of managing the Opera House.

Notably, one of Brooke's main contributions in revitalizing the Opera House was to expand the comic opera program. In the year before her takeover, the season of 1772–73, the Opera House had staged only three comic operas, compared to fifty-nine serious or tragic operas.[43] This disparity was unusual: according to performance records from 1766 to 1772, comic opera had dominated the repertoire at the Opera House under the reign of the celebrated singer Giovanni Lovattini, who was known for his comic roles, but when Lovattini left the Opera House in 1772, there was no one to replace him, resulting in a critical imbalance in the repertoire.[44] Under Brooke's tenure, her main concern became restoring comic opera in London. On September 8, 1775, she wrote to her friend Ozias Humphrey, "At present the balance is terribly against us."[45] Humphrey, a London painter who happened to be in Italy, offered his services to the Opera House, and Brooke was quick to tell him what she needed:

> I had the pleasure of your letter from Florence a few days ago, & we are all extremely oblig'd to you for your polite remembrance of us, & your very kind offer of doing anything for us in Italy.
>
> We cannot show a sense of your kindness so strongly as by accepting it, & therefore I make no scruple to say that if there is any very good comic opera play'd this autumn at Florence set by a capital master, you will greatly oblige us by sending us the whole score & the book; I shou'd particularly wish it [Niccolò] Piccinni's or [Giovanni] Paesiello's, & if we cou'd have it directly I mean *instantly* it wou'd be of great service to us. If you can do this for us, & will be so obliging to draw on Mr Yates or my brother for the amount, you will lay us under a great Obligation. I am not sure there is a comic opera at Florence but I write on that supposition.[46]

Brooke's dogged efforts to import more comic opera resulted in a more diverse repertoire at the Opera House and significant commercial growth under her tenure.[47]

That said, Brooke's interest in comic opera was not purely commercial. In 1756, Brooke had praised Catherine Clive's opera singing in *Lethe*:

> I was particularly diverted by her *Italian Song* in which this truly humorous actress parodies the air of the Opera, and takes off the action of the present favourite female at the Haymarket [Regina Mingotti], with such exquisite ridicule, that the most zealous partisans of both, I think, must have applauded the comic genius of *Mrs. Clive*. . . . I am a lover of music, and no enemy to the Opera, have seen and heard this performer with pleasure, but have still been a good deal surprized, to hear persons not deficient in understanding, so lavish, as I have sometimes found them, in their praises of this Foreigner's action, of which by the way, not understanding the language, they can be but indifferent judges, when we have more than one actress on our own stage, so infinitely superior to her.[48]

In this passage, Brooke identifies a love for comic opera, and a belief that London has the talent and resources necessary to develop its own English-language opera that could compete with the Italian. Her praise of Clive also indicates her interest in highlighting women performers and singers, decades before she became manager of the Opera House.

As a manager, Brooke displayed a natural inclination for theater administration, demonstrated by her curation of a balanced program, her ability to charm subscribers, and her financial savvy. However, not all were impressed by the Brooke-Yates management team, especially the women's efforts to acquire a license to perform spoken drama. The managers of Drury Lane and Covent Garden had much to lose if another theater could break up their duopoly. As manager of one of these patent theaters, Garrick had more reason than ever to clash with Brooke. Their relationship further deteriorated after Yates chose to split her responsibilities as actress and manager. A letter from Garrick to Richard Yates regarding his wife's availability illuminates Garrick's frustration with the arrangement and his desire to bypass the two women altogether:

> I shall beg leave to discuss our Theatrical Matters with You, in order to prevent their being discuss'd any where else. . . . You left word with Mr. Hopkins *that we are to think no more of Mrs. Yates,'till She will let us know her pleasure*, or words to that Effect. Do You & Mrs Yates imagine that the Proprietors will submit to this manner of going on, or that they will pay such a large Sum of Money for having their Busines[s] so destroy'd,

as it was in great part of the last Season and has been wholly this, by waiting for Mrs. Yates's pleasure to perform?—She play'd but Thirty times last Season, and as She goes on, in the proportion of four times in Six weeks, she will play Twenty times in this Season.[49]

This particular dispute was resolved when Mary Ann Yates agreed to accommodate Garrick's demands to perform, but as McMullen points out, Yates mailed her acquiescence from the manager's apartment at the Opera House, perhaps as a reminder to Garrick, who had consistently undervalued and underpaid her, that she was his equal not his inferior.[50]

Other letters reveal that Garrick's already bitter relationship with Brooke further deteriorated during these years. In April 1776, Brooke asked Garrick to return a book lent to her that she had, in turn, lent to Garrick "at his request."[51] Garrick's response to Brooke's innocuous request is striking:

> From the great hurry and Multiplicity of Business in which I am engag'd, the misplacing or Mistaking a book belonging to no set, and there not of the greatest Value, may be a fault, but surely not of that Magnitude to merit so harsh a Letter.—Mr. Highmore whom I have not the honour to know, has been so obliging to give me my own time to find the lost Sheep, and to assure You that he is perfectly satisfy'd. This great & kind Civility has reliev'd my Mind from a most disagreeable concern, as it at once excuses you from the unpleasing task of writing Angry Letters, & me from the mortification of receiving them.[52]

Garrick's angry response to Brooke is peppered with gendered stereotypes: he accuses Brooke of overreacting and showing inappropriate anger. Though Garrick is obviously at fault for failing to return the book, his defensive response clearly displays his ongoing dislike of Brooke.

Brooke and Garrick's feud reached new heights in 1777 following the publication of Brooke's next novel, *The Excursion* (1777). Wyett describes the novel as revealing "the reality of brutal and often gendered politics of the theatre world," and Katherine Charles similarly summarizes the novel as "interested in critiquing corrupt theatrical politics."[53] The semi-autobiographical narrative features a young protagonist named Maria Villiers, who travels to London with a small inheritance and dreams of becoming a playwright, as Brooke did in the 1750s. Like Brooke, Maria submits a tragedy to be staged at Drury Lane theater, but Garrick—who is named in the novel and portrayed as an arrogant and mercenary figure—dismisses it: "These authors—and after all, what do they do? They bring the meat indeed, but who instructs them how to cook it? . . . 'Tis amazing the pains I am forced to take with these people, in order to give relish to their insipid productions."[54] The scene appears to reference the rejection of Brooke's *Virginia* by Garrick in the 1750s.

If Garrick still felt lingering bitterness over Brooke's article about him in *The Old Maid*, he was now enraged over her treatment of him in *The Excursion*. He had retired in 1776 and considered the lampoon a low blow. He had also recently assisted Brooke and Yates's most recent application for a theater patent, this time in Birmingham, by lobbying his friend, the MP Edmund Burke, to support the patent.[55] Garrick felt personally betrayed by Brooke's satire of him in the novel and believed she had delayed publication until the matter of the patent was decided. Of course, while Garrick claimed that his support of the Birmingham patent was altruistic, it also would have benefited him by conveniently removing two women competitors whom he disliked and who had challenged his authority. He vented his frustration in a letter to Frances Cadogan on July 17, 1777:

> You have seen how much I am abus'd in yr Friend Mre Brook's new Novel?—she is pleas'd to insinuate that [I am] an Excellent Actor, a so author, an Execrable Manager & a Worse Man.... She has invented a Tale about a Tragedy, which is all a Lie, from beginning to ye End—she Even says, that I should reject a Play, if it should be a Woman's—there's brutal Malignity for You—have not ye Ladies—Mesdames, *Griffith*, *Cowley* & *Cilesia* spoke of me before their Plays with an Over-Enthusiastick Encomium?—what says divine Hannah More?... What a Couple of wretches are ye *Yateses Brookes's* partners—I work'd with Zeal for their Patent—wrote a 100 Letters, & they were Stimulating Crumpling all ye while to Mischief, & they deferr'd ye publication till this time, that I might not cool in their Cause—there are Devils for You."[56]

As Misty Anderson observes, Garrick hated being called out as sexist and his "emotionally complex outburst echoes Lear's need for daughterly approval."[57] He prided himself on being seen as a champion of women, but his letter to Cadogan also reveals "his demand for absolute gratitude."[58]

Garrick did not limit himself to disparaging Brooke among his literary and theatrical network; he also published a deeply misogynist, anonymous five-page review of the novel in which he staunchly defended his own greatness and condemned Brooke: "Nothing can be more ungenerous than to attack a man, after he has quitted the field, and has retired, not only crowned with the laurel of genius, as Mrs. Brooke herself allows, but with the palm of virtue also, and ... with the good wishes and warm esteem of an admiring public."[59] Backscheider points out that he made a "mean-spirited" attack on Brooke's appearance in his anonymous review; Brooke was not an attractive woman, and Garrick used this against her to refute the biographical allusions in her book in which the heroine is described as a "great *beauty*."[60]

Brooke's tenure as a manager of the Opera House ended shortly after the publication of *The Excursion*, though not because Garrick had succeeded in bullying her away from the theater. Rather, Brooke and her partners sold the building and the patent for a significant profit of £14,600 on June 24, 1788.[61] It was purchased by the new manager of Covent Garden, Thomas Harris, and the manager of Drury Lane, Richard Brinsley Sheridan, who had succeeded Garrick following his retirement in 1776. The purchase of the Opera House by the other London managers suggests that under the Brooke-Yates partnership, it had begun to contend with spoken drama, even drawing customers who might otherwise have attended Drury Lane or Covent Garden. Perhaps Harris and Sheridan also feared that Brooke's applications for a license might eventually be approved, destroying their own duopoly over London's drama. As Backscheider points out, the two men took on significant debt to purchase the Opera House.[62] In a testament to the success of the Brooke-Yates tenure, Garrick himself purchased shares in the Opera House directly after Sheridan and Harris took over, noting that the investment was "a mine of gold."[63]

The Stage at Last

No longer a manager, Brooke was free once again to pursue the staging of her own plays. She began writing a new tragedy shortly after her retirement as manager, but other projects and ongoing illness slowed her progress. She wrote to her publisher, Thomas Cadell, about these matters on January 5, 1779: "My health has been so bad since the beginning of July, that I have not been able to do anything to any purpose, not even finish my tragedy. . . . I had every reason to believe it wou'd have come out this year if I had."[64] Despite these setbacks, Brooke finally staged her first play, *The Siege of Sinope*, at Covent Garden on January 31, 1781. It cannot be overlooked that Brooke's first produced play appeared only after Garrick's death in 1779, supporting the theory that Garrick had been blocking Brooke's work from the patent theaters for decades. Harris, the manager at Covent Garden, did not share Garrick's disdain for Brooke and was willing to take a risk on a new play, especially one by a playwright whose name was well known.

Like her first unperformed play, *Virginia*, Brooke's *Sinope* was also a Roman tragedy, based on Giuseppe Sarti's opera *Mitridate a Sinope* (1779), which, in turn, is based on Appian's *Roman History* and the story of Pharnaces, king of Pontus. Years before the action of the play begins, Thamyris, daughter of Athridates, had been promised in marriage to Pharnaces.

However, when Athridates rescinded this promise, Pharnaces kidnapped Thamyris and married her anyway. The play opens with Pharnaces and Athridates appearing to make peace after years of war over the matter, but Athridates betrays the accord and attacks the city. He eventually loses the battle and commits suicide, and Pharnaces and Thamyris are reunited with their young son. Though the play appears to focus on masculine subject matter—featuring two male characters who battle over territory, women, and power—much of *Sinope* is devoted to Thamyris and her negotiation of duty, love, and motherhood. Thamyris is torn between competing patriarchal loyalties to her husband, her father, and her son, and her suffering becomes the emotional center of the play. However, unlike other iconic tragic heroines of the century, such as Elwina in Hannah More's *Percy* (1779)—the most popular tragedy written by a woman in the eighteenth century—and Belvidira in Thomas Otway's perennially popular *Venice Preserv'd* (1682), Thamyris does not descend into madness and die. Instead, she is reunited with her family.

Brooke's experience managing the opera house, and her insider knowledge of theatrical production, factored greatly into her creation of *Sinope*. Unlike *Virginia*, which Brooke had written when she had no theatrical experience, *Sinope* was written with performance and production in mind. Not only did Brooke capitalize on Yates's celebrity status by writing the part of Thamyris for her, but she also took advantage of other marketing factors. As Backscheider explains, when *Sinope* debuted, the Opera House was staging a related work, Antonio Sacchini's *Mithridates*, the plot of which focuses on Pharnaces' father.[65] Audiences of both houses could experience a double-feature effect as they "follow[ed] two generations of the royal family of Pontus."[66] Brooke was also particularly attuned to the spectacular design of her play, adding elaborate stage techniques popular at the Opera House. For example, when Thamyris first enters in act 1, scene 2, the stage directions read: "*Scene draws to solemn music, and discovers the Inside of the Temple—the Pillars adorned with festoons of flowers—an Alter burning, crowned with Wreathes of Olive*—Orontes, *Priests, and Virgins in white, ranged on each side*—Thamyris *standing by the Alter*."[67] Brooke is clearly aware of the powerful effect of sound, lighting, and music, as the directions for the conclusion of the same scene reveal: "*As* Orontes *approaches the alter, and the orchestra begin the accompaniment, loud thunder is heard on the left—the temple shakes—the flames on the altar are suddenly extinguished, and the whole scene darkened.*"[68] Building on her knowledge of producing opera, Brooke took advantage of the playhouse's potential for spectacular entertainment. She wove together a large ensemble cast, glamorous costumes, powerful music and sound, and beautiful set design as key elements of the play. Her strategy appears to have been successful, as the *Morning Chronicle* wrote: "The scenery and decorations were various, and splendid, more so than those of any play lately presented at the theatre."[69]

Apart from consistent praise of the play's scenography, however, reviews of *Sinope* were mixed. Some felt that the play too obviously revolved around Yates; the *Universal Magazine of Knowledge and Pleasure* wrote, "Thamyris is the only character of importance among the Dramatic Personae; all the rest . . . are very insignificant, and have little to do."[70] Another reviewer disliked the play's similarity to opera: "We expected something of more importance than a meagre imitation of an Italian opera."[71] Still others were dissatisfied by the relatively light action in the play: "The language and sentiments being admirable, the plot is too barren of incidents and variety for theatrical exhibition."[72] Despite these tepid reviews, *Sinope* ran for a respectable ten performances from January 31 to February 19, 1781. Brooke received the standard author's benefit on the third, sixth, and ninth night, and receipts from the production suggest that she made a good profit.[73] The play was not revived in consequent seasons, but it was published during its performance run by Brooke's publisher, Thomas Cadell, on February 8, 1781.

Rosina *and* Marian

Following the moderate success of *Sinope*, Brooke finally achieved mass critical and financial success with her next play, *Rosina*, which the *Lady's Magazine* called "one of the best pastoral operas in possession of the stage."[74] Musical pastoral plays were popular on the eighteenth-century stage, often as afterpieces, and as Leslie Ritchie writes, "The pastoral, as a poetic mode, a musical style and as a comic theatrical form, was highly favoured by women."[75] Terry Gifford defines the pastoral as "any literature that describes the country with an implicit or explicit contrast to the urban" and "[a] delight in the natural."[76] Though the pastoral genre is often thought of as strictly generic—featuring rural utopia, peaceful shepherds, and happy young couples—Ritchie argues that the genre appealed to women because of "its potential for generating ironic, parodic, or allegorical meanings; its involvement (or lack thereof) in rural social change; and its contributions and debts to literary and musical pastorals' critical heritage."[77] Overlooked by scholars in terms of their dramatic value, Brooke's *Rosina* and *Marian* contain layered critiques of gender, class, and power.

The draft of *Rosina* that Brooke had begun in the early 1770s had lain neglected until Harris agreed to stage the play at Covent Garden following the production of *Sinope*. Harris's faith in Brooke proved to be a savvy financial decision, as *Rosina* became an instant sensation. After its debut on December 31, 1782, *Rosina* became one of the most popular afterpieces of the century, performed at least 201 times by 1800, according to *The London Stage*. In fact, the only afterpiece to receive more performances than *Rosina* in the final quarter of the century was John Dalton and Thomas Arne's *Comus* (1738), based on John Milton's 1634 masque of the same name, which was performed 215 times in the years 1775 to 1800.[78] In print, *Rosina* reached its fourteenth edition before the end of the century, suggesting that it was widely read as well as performed. While *Rosina*'s success was credited to a combination of factors—its romantic plot, musical accompaniment by William Shield, and theatrical effects—audiences warmly embraced Brooke's comic libretto. The *Public Advertiser* wrote, "No Piece on the Stage can boast a more beautiful Picture of Nature and Simplicity, and the Audience with the warmest Applause acknowledged its Merit," and correctly predicted that the play would have "a very long Run."[79] *Rosina* also raised Brooke's critical standing as a playwright. Shortly after the debut, the *British Magazine and Review* published a biography of Brooke in February 1783, placing the author in "the very first class of female literature."[80] Decades later, in 1806, the actress Anna Crouch wrote that *Rosina* "went off *then* amidst universal plaudits, and *still* maintains a powerful influence over the public whenever it is performed."[81]

Rosina is set in an English village, and, as in *Sinope*, the events of the plot span a single day. The protagonist, Rosina, an orphan, is cared for by the elderly Dorcas and her granddaughter Phoebe. This family of women survive by gleaning corn during the harvest season on an estate belonging to the Belville brothers. Phoebe is in love with a laborer named William, and Rosina has fallen in love with the landowner Belville, but she hides her true feelings from him. In turn, Belville notices Rosina's beauty and lets her glean extra corn. Unfortunately, Belville's rakish brother, Captain Belville, has also noticed Rosina and wants to take her as his mistress. He attempts to negotiate with Dorcas to allow him to bring Rosina to London. When Dorcas refuses his offer, the Captain leaves a purse of gold for Rosina in exchange for sexual favors. The Captain then hides in Dorcas's cottage and tries to rape Rosina, who manages to escape and finds solace in the arms of Belville. The Captain arranges to have his men kidnap Rosina, who is rescued just in time by a band of Irish farmhands. The Captain's villainy is revealed—and quickly forgiven—and Belville and Rosina (pictured in figure 2.2) confess their love for each other. They plan to marry, as do Phoebe and William, and the play ends in a celebratory dance.

Rosina is a simple moral tale in which virtue reaps reward: Rosina and Belville are rewarded in marriage, the farmhands receive financial gain for

Figure 2.2. W. Grainger, "Rosina & Belville," *The New Lady's Magazine; Or, Polite, Entertaining, and Fashionable Companion for the Fair Sex* (London) 5 (1790): 553.

their heroism, Dorcas finds protection in her old age, and a penitent Captain Belville is reformed and forgiven. However, the play also contains surprisingly complex characters, layered intrigue, and action with two romantic plotlines, an attempted rape, a kidnap, and rescue mission. Indeed, *Parker's General Advertiser and Morning Intelligencer* wrote that their only complaint was that the play was "cooped in an after piece, when it might have been with propriety, and, we think, with success, extended to a full piece."[82] Perhaps, in creating *Rosina*, Brooke was responding to the criticism that her play of the previous year, *Sinope*, had lacked action.

Though the 1772 draft of *Rosina* that Garrick and Colman had rejected no longer survives, we can confidently assume that Brooke made significant changes to the piece following her tenure as manager of the Opera House. As in *Sinope*, Brooke incorporated three paragraphs of highly detailed directions for the opening scene of *Rosina* that indicate her in-depth knowledge of stage design:

> SCENE opens and discovers a rural prospect: on the left side a little hill with trees at the top; a spring of water rushes from the side, and falls into a natural basin below: on the right side a cottage, at the door of which is a bench of stone. At a distance a chain of mountains. The manor-house in view. A field of corn fills up the scene.
>
> In the first act the sky clears by degrees, the morning vapour disperses, the sun rises, and at the end of the act is above the horizon: at the beginning of the second he is past the height, and declines till the end of the day. This progressive motion should be made imperceptibly, but its effect should be visible through the two acts.[83]

Though no new scenery appears to have been designed or painted for the debut, Brooke's directions reveal that she knew how to take full advantage of the theatrical effects that Covent Garden had to offer. In testament to the unique detail of Brooke's stage directions, John Dalton's libretto for *Comus*, the only afterpiece to eclipse *Rosina* in popularity in the late eighteenth century, contains brief opening scene directions: "*The first scene discovers a wild Wood.*"[84] Audiences were understandably entranced by the sound, lighting, and set design of *Rosina*, as well as the musical accompaniment.

Though the papers praised the set design and Shield's music alongside Brooke's libretto, in an advertisement appended to the first published edition of the play, Brooke is careful to claim *Rosina*'s success for herself. She begins by complimenting the performers and music, but positions Shield as a secondary, not equal, collaborator, writing that his music is "admirably adapted to the words."[85] Brooke also acknowledges that the plot of

Rosina is adapted from three different sources—the biblical story of Ruth, James Thomson's four-part poem *The Seasons* (1726–30), and Charles Simon Favart's opera *Les Moissonneurs* (1768)—but she also makes a point of distinguishing her own interpretation from her source texts, writing: "We are not, however extraordinary as it may appear, so easily satisfied with mere sentiment as our sprightly neighbours the French, I found it necessary to diversify the story by adding the comic characters of William and Phoebe, which I hop'd might at once relieve, and heighten, the sentimental cast of the other personages of the drama."[86] By adding an additional comic subplot featuring lower-class characters to *Rosina*, a distinctly Shakespearean feature, Brooke sought to elevate her role as librettist and distinguish English opera from the French. She ends the advertisement by noting that sections of her original libretto were cut from the performance text to make the opera an appropriate length for an afterpiece. Therefore, she takes advantage of the printed edition of the play to reinstate her abridged text, using inverted commas to note the dialogue missing from the production. According to Ritchie, in publishing her complete play in this manner, Brooke "distinguishes her libretto as an independent artwork, complete prior to staging."[87] After years of Garrick painting her as unworthy of the stage, Brooke was determined to claim sole responsibility for her success.

Five years after the smash success of *Rosina*, Brooke released a similar comic opera, *Marian*. The music was once again by Shield, and this time, new scenes were painted specifically for the debut.[88] The first scene featured "*a River; beyond which is a Road winding up the side of a Hill*," and the second, "*[a] different and more distant view of the River, with the Bridge over.*"[89] Like *Rosina*, *Marian* is a pastoral that follows the classical unities in spanning a single day in a rural village. Marian, the daughter of local farmer Oliver Meadow, is saddened because her father will no longer allow her to marry the poor laborer Edward since she received an unexpected inheritance from her godmother. Instead, her father wants her to marry Robin, a landowner. Sir Henry, the local squire, inquires after Marian's sadness and decides to help the couple. Sir Henry flirts with the local village girls, who find his attention discomfiting and encourage him to marry a woman of his own status. The scene changes to a country fair where Robin flirts with Patty, and Jamie—a Scottish peddler—flirts with Peggy. Oliver arrives to tell his daughter that he has seen Edward kissing the picture of another woman to whom he has sent money. Furious, Edward defends himself, explaining that it is a picture of his mother, a gentlewoman, who was wrongfully disinherited by a relative. Sir Henry offers to give Edward a small farm so that he may make a suitable match for Marian and soothe Oliver's concerns. However, Jamie the Scotsman reveals that he has been sent to find

Edward to tell him that his mother has inherited her estate and 1,000 acres of land. Edward and Marian decide to marry and live with Edward's mother. Sir Henry gives the farm to Oliver.

Marian did not receive the same unreserved adulation as *Rosina* following its debut at Covent Garden on May 22, 1788. The music by Shield was praised unreservedly, but the libretto by Brooke was widely deemed lacking. The *Gazetteer and New Daily Advertiser* assessed *Marian* as a "a simple representation of pastoral manners, without plot and almost without dialogue," and the *London Chronicle* similarly wrote that the libretto was "so light and so thin of incident that it scarcely contains business enough to entitle it to the character of dramatic action."[90] These reviews must have been frustrating for Brooke, who had been criticized for including too much action in *Rosina*, and now too little in *Marian*. Despite these negative assessments of the libretto, *Marian* was, in fact, popular, and it remained so for many years. Shield's music was deemed "excellent" by the *Morning Post*, and the stage design was considered superb by the *Morning Chronicle*: "The stage presents one of the most picturesque landscapes we ever saw exhibited by scenery."[91] The *World* praised *Marian* and predicted that the piece would "repay the pains that have been given to it," suggesting that the manager was certain the play would succeed and spared no expense in production.[92] *Marian* was performed at least forty times by the end of the century, according to *The London Stage*. Though it was not comparable to the overwhelming success of *Rosina*, *Marian* had impressive longevity. The libretto was not published until 1800, twelve years after the play's debut and eleven years after Brooke's death in 1789. Perhaps it was deemed that the libretto would not sell well at the time of the play's opening; however, its late publication indicates that the play had enduring marketability. *Marian* was revived for the Turkish ambassador, Ismail Ferrouh Effendi, in 1800, coinciding with the publication of the libretto.[93]

Both *Marian* and *Rosina* are best contextualized within their historical moment—namely, the theater's efforts to mediate public dismay following the disruption caused by Britain's recent loss of the American colonies. *Rosina* was performed at the beginning of 1783, after the British surrender at Yorktown, Virginia, that effectively ended the Revolutionary War, and before the signing of the Treaty of Paris on September 3, 1783. Though *Marian* was produced five years after the end of the American Revolution, Britain was still navigating these devastating colonial losses, and as Daniel O'Quinn has shown, the theater played a key role in affirming British imperial identity.[94] While *Rosina* and *Marian* make no mention of the disruption the war wreaked on English life, both plays depict the English working-class laboring happily on the farms belonging to the benevolent aristocracy. In each play, peace is made with the Scottish and the Irish as English characters overcome their prejudices. While there is a suggestion that cross-class relations may disrupt the utopias presented, each play ultimately reveals that the couples—Rosina and Belville, and Marian and Edward—were equal in status all along. Both plays soothe the battle wounds of defeat by celebrating a nation whose people are content and whose hierarchical social structure appears to please everyone. On the surface, the plays are conventional and appealing, easily grouped with pastorals like Garrick's *Florizel and Perdita* (1756) and Macnamara Morgan's *The Sheep-Shearing* (1754), which similarly feature women's rags-to-riches narratives.

Yet, within this construction of an English paradise, *Rosina* and *Marian* contain surprisingly blunt critiques of the challenges women face within England's social and economic systems. Both Rosina and Marian are working women who are at a significant gendered disadvantage as they attempt to meet their basic needs and lead fulfilling lives. Like Mariana in Shakespeare's *Measure for Measure* (1604), Rosina was meant to have inherited a fortune, but it was lost in the shipwreck that killed her parents. Without family or fortune, she is taken in by the generous but poverty-stricken Dorcas and her granddaughter Phoebe. As in Clive's gendered inversion of Buckingham's *The Rehearsal* in *Bayes in Petticoats*, Brooke inverts the pastoral elements of Shakespeare's *The Winter's Tale* (c. 1610–11), in which Perdita is raised by a shepherd and his son. The small family of women—Rosina, Dorcas, and Phoebe—face gendered challenges in surviving without the support of a husband, father, or son to offer them legal status, financial stability, and physical protection. The women have no means of earning a living and survive on Belville's charity during the harvest. Dorcas is ashamed that Rosina has joined her in poverty and wants to ask Belville to provide for Rosina, but Rosina resists: "Not for worlds, Dorcas, I want nothing: you have been a mother to me."[95] In another echo of *The Winter's Tale*, in which Florizel's father suggests that his son take the supposedly low-born Perdita as a mistress rather than a wife, the Captain suggests that Rosina come to London with him and be his paramour. The Captain even attempts to negotiate this arrangement with Dorcas:

CAPT. BELVILLE. You have a charming daughter—
DORCAS. [*aside*] I thought as much. A vile, wicked man!
CAPT. BELVILLE. Beauty like hers might find a thousand resources in London: the moment she appears there, she will turn every head.
DORCAS. And is your honour sure her own won't turn at the same time?

CAPT. BELVILLE. She shall live in influence, and take care of you too, Dorcas.[96]

Dorcas rejects the Captain's offer, saying, "If I must be a trouble to the dear child, I shall rather owe my bread to her labour than her shame," but, without the protection of a male family member, Dorcas and Rosina have little power to deny the Captain's desires.[97] Indeed, in the following scenes the Captain attempts, and fails, to rape Rosina. However, Rosina is no passive victim. Linda V. Troost calls her an "active agent" who negotiates the terms of her survival.[98] Eventually, Rosina's problems are resolved when she marries Belville, and, in doing so, attains status, safety from sexual violence, and financial security. The play celebrates Rosina's marriage while simultaneously drawing attention to the extreme precarity of women's lives in a patriarchal society.

The complex gendered politics of class, marriage, and economy are also overt in *Marian*. Peaceful rural life is disrupted when Marian inherits money from her godmother, but instead of establishing her independence, the money causes her father to want to improve his own social status. As Marian explains to Edward, "My father wants me to marry Robin, because he has ten acres of land, besides the ferry, and a cot in the country, and milks four cows; but I won't marry Robin, nor anybody but Edward."[99] Edward, in a show of masculine virtue, argues that he will not allow Marian to lower herself for him, saying, "How could I be so unjust, Marian?"[100] Marian loves Edward and wants to marry him, but her father's and Edward's pride obstruct her autonomy. Notably, it is another woman's inheritance that ultimately resolves Marian's problem. When Edward's mother is restored to her estate that was wrongfully withheld from her, Oliver is appeased that his daughter is marrying upwardly, and Edward is content that he can appropriately provide for Marian. Though Marian's position never changes, male ego must be soothed before she can make her own decisions.

The original manuscript of *Marian* submitted for licensing to the Lord Chamberlain's Office includes a line that clarifies the injustice of Marian's situation. In act 2, Sir Robert (whose name was changed to Sir Henry in the performance and printed versions of the play) is trying to convince Marian's father to allow her and Henry (whose name was later changed to Edward) to marry:

OLIVER. It's very hard, your Honor, if a freeborn Englishman may not dispose of his own Daughter.—
SIR ROBERT. It would be much harder if a freeborn Englishwoman might not dispose of herself.[101]

Though this line is cut from the printed edition of the play (it may have been performed, as it is not excised on the licensing copy), it illuminates Brooke's critical intervention. She emphasizes English women's lack of autonomy by comparing their condition to slavery—Elizabeth Inchbald does something similar in *The Mogul Tale* (1784), as does Hannah Cowley in *A Day in Turkey* (1791). Thus, like *Rosina*, the play argues that women ought to have better access to self-determination.

As in *Rosina*, *Marian* offers a critique of the sexual threat that aristocratic men pose to working-class women. The Captain in *Rosina* is openly predatory toward the women who work for him and his brother. When he first appears in the play, he decides to eat in the field with the laborers to watch the women, saying, "Pray let me be of your party, your plan is an admirable one, especially if your girls are handsome."[102] His predatory gaze becomes fixated on Rosina. A similar threat is embodied by Sir Henry in *Marian*. Like Captain Belville, Sir Henry is unmarried, and he likes to watch and flirt with the women of the village. An Irish woman named Peggy confronts him about his behavior:

> SIR HENRY. Why do you fly me my pretty lassie? I mean you no harm.
> PEGGY. I donna know that—I donna laike when great lairds are sa free wi' poor lassies; I wonna be woo'd; I'se Jamie's bride, and my gude will is a' for him—I ha' lov'd him lang; he's a neighbour's bairn, and I ken his bringing up.
> SIR HENRY. Only take this ribbon, my pretty lassie, to tie on your bosom.
> PEGGY. I'se none o' your gear, gude Sir.[103]

Peggy is not the only character who finds Sir Henry's behavior alarming. Other characters encourage him to marry, including Edward, who says, "Your tenants have but one wish, that you wou'd bring down a lady to replace your honor'd mother."[104] But Sir Henry has no interest in marrying, and responds, "I shall marry the moment I am tired of being a bachelor: in the meantime, my tenants may be perfectly easy:—pleasure without remorse, the rose without the thorn, is my pursuit.—Yet I cannot convince the girls of this; even the lively Patty, whom I shou'd think less apprehensive, if she meets me alone, darts from me with the swiftness of a lapwing."[105] Sir Henry's plotline is never resolved in *Marian*; he does not marry, nor does he reform his behavior. Though Ritchie argues that Sir Henry is not a real threat, merely "an effeminate fop who only poses as a rake," I contend that there is a darker element to his character.[106] While he never acts on his flirtations, there is nothing to stop Sir Henry from harassing or coercing the women who work on his property, just as the Captain does in *Rosina*. Both men's total sexual power is juxtaposed against the women characters' sexual precarity.

Performance records show that Thomas Harris regularly produced both *Rosina* and *Marian* alongside full-length comic plays by other women, suggesting that he identified the feminist politics at the heart of Brooke's plays and realized a marketing opportunity. For example, on May 29, 1784, Harris paired *Rosina* with Susanna Centlivre's *The Busy Body* (1709), and on December 21, 1784, with Cowley's *The Belle's Stratagem* (1780). Over the years, he continued to stage *Rosina* with other comedies by Centlivre, Cowley, and Inchbald. When *Marian* debuted in 1788, Harris chose to have it performed with Inchbald's *Animal Magnetism* (1788). *Marian* continued to be paired with other Inchbald comedies including *The Child of Nature*, *Such Things Are*, and *The Midnight Hour*. Backscheider has shown that when Harris staged *Rosina* and *Marian* with other women's comedies, the house made more money than when he paired the works with plays by men, indicating the significant popularity and influence of women's comedies.[107]

Brooke's theatrical career and contributions as a comic playwright are remarkable. Her perseverance in staging her work despite Garrick's blacklisting, her pioneering experience as a woman manager of the London Opera House, and the consequent commercial success of her comic operas make her one of the most influential theatrical women of the century. The narrative of her career reveals both the entrenched sexism of the theater industry during the period and her own extraordinary grit in navigating, scheming, and circumventing that sexism. As a manager, she labored for years to bring more comic opera to London, and as a playwright, she capitalized on the demand for comic opera to optimize her own playwriting career. The extent to which Brooke encouraged other women playwrights of the period is difficult to ascertain precisely, but the influence of *Rosina* lasted into the Victorian era. While popular in London and the provinces, the play was also performed in Scotland, Ireland, Jamaica, and America. The fact that Brooke's comic operas were staged for decades alongside the comedies of other women indicates her ongoing influence on the growing number of women playwrights in the 1780s, including her young friend, Frances Burney.

3

Laughter and Femininity

Frances Burney

A central theme of Royall Tyler's 1787 comedy of manners, *The Contrast*, is the nature of laughter as is relates to reputation, class, and femininity. Anxiety over women's laughter culminates in the character of Charlotte Manly and her foil, Maria Van Rough. Charlotte is a giggling coquette who seeks a rich husband and Maria is a "sentimental grave girl" who wants to marry for love.[1] "The heart," says Charlotte sarcastically of her more reserved friend, "is one of the last of all laughable considerations in the marriage of a girl of spirit."[2] However, in the final act of the play, it is the serious Maria who is rewarded with love and marriage, while Charlotte the jokester is assaulted by Dimple and repents her jocular ways: "If repentance can entitle me to forgiveness, I have already much merit; for I despise the littleness of my past conduct. I now find, that the heart of any worthy man cannot be gained by invidious attacks upon the rights and characters of others;—by countenancing the addresses of a thousand;—or that the finest assemblage of features, the greatest take in dress, the genteelest address, in the most wit, cannot eventually secure a coquet from contempt and ridicule."[3] In the end, Charlotte is no longer laughing after she learns a violent lesson about women and humor, while her sentimental counterpart Maria is celebrated as the epitome of femininity.

This chapter investigates the gendered politics of comedy in Frances Burney's unperformed 1779 play, *The Witlings*. Following the surprise success of her debut novel *Evelina* in 1778, Burney (later Madame d'Arblay; 1752–1840) was befriended by one of her father's patrons, Hester Thrale, who ran a literary salon at her estate, Streatham Park. Arthur Murphy, London's premier playwright of comedy, was a frequent visitor at Streatham and, according to Burney's journals and letters, an encouraging adviser. He read the first two acts of *The Witlings*, and possibly others, while offering Burney critical advice about comedy, stagecraft, and live performance. Perhaps if *The Witlings* had been published or performed, Murphy's mentorship of

Burney would be better known today, but his relationship with Burney waned following the suppression of the piece, and the connection between these two famous eighteenth-century writers has been overlooked.[4] In Jesse Foot's *The Life of Arthur Murphy* (1811), for example, the relationship is not once mentioned.[5] Modern biographers of Burney generally gloss over Murphy as one of a "bevy of consultants" who encouraged Burney to write for the stage.[6] Margaret Anne Doody, for instance, notes Murphy's encouragement and writes that he "thought well" of *The Witlings*, and Kate Chisholm states that Murphy "was impressed" by the play.[7]

This chapter turns to a little-known manuscript held by the Beinecke Rare Book & Manuscript Library that offers new evidence of the significance of Murphy's influence on Burney's playwriting. The manuscript comprises adapted scenes written by Burney of Murphy's play *All in the Wrong* (1761). As nearly all of Burney's extant correspondence, journals, and manuscripts are now published, this neglected manuscript provides an exciting new perspective on Burney's identity as a playwright and her interest in comic trends of the 1770s, particularly laughing comedy. This chapter will draw on the manuscript, evidence from Burney's journals and letters, and a comparative analysis of *All in the Wrong* and *The Witlings* to argue that laughing comedy was foundational to the creation of *The Witlings* and the development of Burney's comic voice. I argue that while Burney was attracted to laughing comedy, encouraged by her mentor Murphy, she also harnessed the style for her own purposes, avoiding sexual intrigue and focusing instead on the experiences and relationships of women characters. Sadly, Burney's foray into comic playwriting provoked the ire of her father, the musicologist Charles Burney (hereafter Dr. Burney), and family friend Samuel Crisp, a failed playwright whom Burney regularly referred to as her second "Daddy." The final parts of this chapter consider Crisp's correspondence with Burney from 1778 to 1779 and argue that Crisp identified laughing comedy as antithetical to femininity, which ultimately motivated his suppression of the play.

Burney is unique among the women playwrights of this study because none of her comedies ever appeared on the stage. Nonetheless, she aspired to become a professional playwright, and the creation of *The Witlings* reveals that she identified comedy as the best genre with which to break into the industry. She made strides toward negotiating the staging of her play, and she took part in a women's tradition of comic playwriting by writing a self-referential, women-centric play. *The Witlings* is a fascinating social satire that displays all the features of a professional production; Murphy believed it would be a commercial success. This chapter highlights the gendered barriers women faced in writing and producing comic plays, particularly the association between comedy and masculinity. The events surrounding the suppression of *The Witlings* offer valuable insight into the vexed gendered politics of women's comic playwriting in the mid-eighteenth century.

Burney and Murphy at Streatham Park, 1779

Burney's father's career as a musician, musicologist, and music tutor provided Burney with formative exposure to the theater. As a child, she met various figures from the London theater scene, including musicians, playwrights, and performers. Dr. Burney himself worked in the theaters: he performed in the orchestra at Drury Lane and wrote commissioned scores for David Garrick. As a friend and colleague of Garrick, Dr. Burney attended many performances with his family in Garrick's own box.[8] Evidence of Burney's love of the theater is scattered throughout her journals and correspondence in detailed descriptions of plays that she either saw or read. She even tried writing her own plays as a child, among other literary experiments. She wrote "Elegies, Odes, Plays, Songs, Stories, Farces—nay Tragedies and Epic Poems," which she later burned in a fit of adolescent passion at the age of fifteen in 1768.[9] Ten years later, Burney published her first novel. With the clandestine assistance of her brother and her cousin, Charles Burney and Edward Francesco Burney, she secretly wrote and anonymously published *Evelina*. Despite her best efforts to keep her authorship a secret—even writing the manuscript in a disguised hand—*Evelina* was an instant critical success, and her identity soon became public knowledge. Thus, at the age of twenty-five, Burney (pictured in figure 3.1) was catapulted into literary fame with "remarkable speed."[10]

After taking the young novelist under her wing, the *salonnière* Hester Thrale was quick to advise Burney that her next project ought to be a stage comedy, as this would be her best route to professionalization, "the Road both to Honour & Profit."[11] Thrale had been disturbed to learn that Burney had been paid almost nothing by the publisher of *Evelina*, and she thought the young writer deserved more. During her first sojourn at Streatham in August 1778, Burney records Thrale's advice in a letter to her sister Susanna: "She proceeded to give me her serious advice to actually set about [a Comedy]; she said it was her opinion I ought to do it the moment she had finished the Book; she stated the advantages attending Theatrical writing, & promised to ensure me success."[12] Thrale enlisted the help of her house guests to further encourage Burney in the direction of playwriting. At a dinner party at Streatham in January 1779, Burney was introduced to Richard Brinsley Sheridan, the manager of Drury Lane: "He is Tall & very

Figure 3.1. Charles Turner after Edward Francisco Burney, *Frances "Fanny" Burney* (1840), © National Portrait Gallery, London.

upright, & his appearance & address are at once manly & fashionable, without the smallest tincture of foppery or modish graces."[13] At this dinner, Sheridan and Sir Joshua Reynolds, a famous painter, flirted with Burney about becoming a playwright—an encounter which she records in her journal as a theatrical dialogue:

> SIR JOSHUA. *Any* thing in the *Dialogue* way, I think, she *must* succeed in,—& I am sure *invention* will not be wanting,—*Mr. Sheridan* No, indeed;—I think, & say, she should write a *Comedy.*
> Lord, Susy, I could not believe my own Ears! *This* from Mr. *Sheridan!*
> SIR JOSHUA. I am sure *I* think so; & I hope she *will.*
> I could only answer by *incredulous* exclamations.

> 'Consider, continued Sir Joshua, you have already had all the applause & fame you *can* have given you in the *Clozet,*—but the Acclamation of a *Theatre* will be *new* to you.'
>
> And then he put down his Trumpet, & began a violent clapping of his Hands.
>
> I actually shook from Head to foot! I felt myself already in Drury Lane, amidst the *Hub bub* of a first Night.[14]

Sheridan delighted Burney by offering to stage any comedy she wrote "*sight unseen,*" a stunning promise considering her lack of experience and the number of new playwrights regularly seeking to have their work produced.[15] Ellen Donkin observes that Sheridan's interest was shrewd, considering that Burney's name was now a "valuable commodity."[16] Thrale, realizing that Burney would need the support of an insider to succeed in this new venture, enlisted her husband's best friend, Murphy, for assistance.

Burney's journals and letters confirm that she was already familiar with Murphy's large oeuvre of farces and comedies—including *The Upholsterer* (1757), *The Way to Keep Him* (1760), *All in the Wrong* (1761), *The Citizen* (1761), and *Know Your Own Mind* (1777)—long before the two ever met, causing Francesca Saggini to assert that Murphy was "one of Burney's favourite playwrights."[17] In December 1775, Burney had even copied the part of the Widow Belmour from Murphy's *The Way to Keep Him* for her friend, the actress Jane Barsanti, to prepare for the role.[18] The following year, in 1777, the Burney family staged the same play in a private performance at Burney's uncle's estate, Barborne Lodge, with Burney playing the role of Mrs. Lovemore.[19] Thus, when Murphy and Burney first met at Streatham on February 11, 1779, Burney was excited to meet the popular playwright, writing to her sister that he was "the man of all other *strangers* to me whom I most longed to see."[20]

On meeting Murphy, Burney was starstruck, and Thrale had to pull her aside and instruct her to "*make myself agreeable* to Mr. Murphy,—He may be, of *use* to you, she said,—he knows stage Business so well,—& if you will but take a fancy to one another, he may be more able to serve you than all of us put together."[21] Murphy was kind, complimentary, and immediately offered his support to the young playwright. Though he knew that Burney was the anonymous author of *Evelina*, he soothed her discomfort at being named its creator by feigning ignorance: "I speak what I really think;—Comedy is the *forte* of that Book,—I Laughed over it most violently;—I lent it to two young ladies, very sensible Girls, of my acquaintance, & they could not go to Bed while it was in reading, *that* seems to me as good a testimony as a Book can have. And if the Author—I won't say *who.*—(all the Time looking away from me) will write a *Comedy*, I will most readily, & with great pleasure, give any advice or assistance in my power."[22] At this initial meeting, Burney and Murphy solidified their mentorship arrangement. Murphy agreed to examine the "*Plan*" for Burney's comedy, suggesting that she already had an outline of the play in mind, and he provided her with "several *rules*" about writing a comedy.[23] His knowledge of comedy and the theater business and his willingness to advise Burney on matters of performance made him an exceptional mentor. He assured her, saying, "I have had so much experience in this sort of Work, that I believe I can always tell what will be *Hissed* at least."[24] Murphy's offer to support her was so momentous that Burney later gushed to her sister Susanna, "Think but of encouragement like this from so experienced a Judge as Mr. Murphy! how *amazing*, that this idea of a *Comedy* should strike so many! And how very kind is this offer of service!"[25]

Over the next several months, Murphy kept his promise to mentor Burney. On May 21, 1779, he returned to Streatham to read the first act of *The Witlings*, and Burney wrote that "he was pleased to commend it very liberally; he has pointed out 2 places where he thinks I might enlarge, but has not criticised one *Word*, on the contrary; the Dialogue he has honoured with high praise."[26] On May 27, Murphy again visited Streatham and read the second act: "He made me many very flattering speeches of his eagerness to go on with my Play,—to know what became of the several Characters,—& to what place I should next conduct them, assuring me that the first Act had run in his Head ever since he had read it."[27] After one of these visits, Thrale told Burney that "[Murphy] calls you a *sly, designing body*,—& says you look all the people through most wickedly. He watches You—& Vows he has caught you in the act:—nobody and nothing, he says, escapes you, & you keep looking round for Characters all Day long."[28] Following Burney and Murphy's May meetings, she went on to significantly revise the play, writing on July 30, 1779, that the draft was "an enormous length, though half as short again as the original."[29]

The Debate over Laughing and Sentimental Comedy

Even without more detail from Burney's own journals and letters, the nature of Murphy's advice to her can be confidently deduced. Murphy held strong beliefs about the nature and purpose of comedy and was an outspoken proponent of Restoration-style comedy, which was characterized by a reliance on wit, mockery, and sexual intrigue and known in the eighteenth century as laughing comedy.[30] Following the emergence in the early eighteenth century of sentimental comedy, which "highlighted sentiment, exemplary displays of virtue, and ... the more emotive forms of sensibility," debate erupted over the fundamental purpose of comedy: should comedy provide moral instruction amplified by displays of affect, or should it seek to incite laughter and amusement through satire, mockery, and intrigue?[31] Robert D. Hume and other scholars have argued that in practice, the dichotomy between laughing and sentimental comedy was not as definitive as those debating the topic at the time made it seem, and plays from the period often contained elements of both subgenres mixed with others.[32] But as Lisa Freeman writes, "Two distinct strains in comedy did emerge in this period," and playwrights, critics, and audiences regularly positioned themselves in one of the two camps.[33] Murphy himself was a major voice in these debates.

Over his lengthy career in the theater, Murphy established himself as a strict proponent of laughing comedy, and his oeuvre contributed to a so-called revival of the style in the 1770s, famously marked by Oliver Goldsmith's essay "A Comparison between Laughing and Sentimental Comedy" (1773). While Goldsmith is often credited with spearheading the campaign against sentimental comedy in his essay, Murphy had already been writing sustained criticism on the topic for decades. He wrote multiple essays on comedy in his periodical the *Gray's-Inn Journal* (1752–54) under the pseudonym Charles Ranger, a character from Benjamin Hoadly's *The Suspicious Husband* (1747) famously played by Garrick.[34] In his theatrical criticism, Murphy praised the plays of Plautus and Terence, whose clever satires had inspired Restoration comic playwrights like William Congreve and William Wycherley; on September 29, 1753 he wrote, "The last Century was remarkable for a comic Genius, which sometimes run out into unwarrantable Luxuriancies, and a Breach of Manners; the present Times have a politer taste but cannot produce any Work of Theatrical Humour."[35] Nostalgic for Restoration comedy and contemptuous of the more sentimental comedy, Murphy argued that the ultimate purpose of comedy must be, at all costs, to induce laughter: "It is not enough to display Foibles and Oddities; a fine Vein of Ridicule must run through the whole, to urge the Mind to frequent Emotions of Laughter; other wise there will be danger of exhibiting disagreeable Characters without affording the proper Entertainment."[36]

When Murphy finally began to write his own comedies, they reflected the values laid out in his essays. J. Homer Caskey confirms that Murphy was "as unsentimental in his practice as in his theory," and Robert Spector describes Murphy's first farce, *The Apprentice* (1756), as a "blend of Restoration comedy of manners and Augustan satire."[37] Murphy's first full-length comedy, *The Way to Keep Him*, staged at Drury Lane in 1760, was a great critical and commercial success, and it was followed by similarly popular productions of *All in the Wrong* (1761) and *Know Your Own Mind* (1778).

Burney's journals and letters confirm that she enjoyed the laughing comedies of Goldsmith, George Colman the Elder, Samuel Foote, Garrick, and, of course, Murphy himself.[38] Moreover, Sheridan, who had promised to stage *The Witlings* at Drury Lane, was the author of one of the most iconic laughing comedies of the century, *The School for Scandal* (1777), and she was eager to please him. Thus, when Burney began writing *The Witlings* in the late 1770s, laughing comedy was in high demand and she was being mentored by its greatest advocate.

Burney's Interest in Murphy's Laughing Comedy

An overlooked manuscript reveals Burney's particular interest in one of Murphy's most popular laughing comedies, *All in the Wrong*. The manuscript, which was unavailable to scholars in the private collection of Paula Peyraud until 2009, when it was acquired by the Beinecke Library, comprises a series of adapted scenes featuring Lady Restless and her maid Tattle from acts 1, 2, and 3 of *All in the Wrong* and an additional original scene. Though there are no legible watermarks or dates on the four-page bifolium manuscript, both Peyraud and the Beinecke tentatively date it to 1779, aligning the manuscript's creation with Burney and Murphy's meeting at Streatham and his promise to assist her in writing a comedy. On the fourth leaf of Burney's adaptation, the dialogue ends abruptly at the foot of the page, with no markings to indicate the scene's completion. Since the scenes are arranged chronologically and include all of Lady Restless and Tattle's scenes from the original play, except for their final scene together in act 4, it follows that Burney's adaptation likely continued onto additional pages that are now lost. The top right corner of the first page bears a note written in different ink, "The Writing of Madame D'Arblay, late Miss Burney."[39] This inscription was possibly added by a previous owner of the manuscript. Notably, the formatting of the manuscript is quite like Burney's only surviving copy of *The Witlings*, held in the Berg Collection at the New York Public Library. The lines of dialogue are written in neat, uncrowded rows, stage directions are centered and underlined, and each character's departure is marked by a right-justified "Exit."

The result of Burney's adaptation of scenes from *All in the Wrong* is a series of comic vignettes between Lady Restless and Tattle evocative of a vaudevillian double act. The two characters are perfect foils to one another. Lady Restless is mistakenly convinced that Tattle's friend Marmalet, maid to Lady Conquest, is having an affair with her husband, Sir John Restless. She constantly harasses Tattle to reveal Sir John's whereabouts and liaisons. In fact, Tattle has no knowledge of such escapades because Sir John is entirely faithful to Lady Restless and is himself convinced that his wife is having an affair. Burney does not alter the overall plot of the scenes that take place between Lady Restless and Tattle, but she quickens the comic pacing by removing unnecessary characters—apart from a single line from Sir John—and altering the dialogue. Indeed, Burney's scenes are roughly half the length of Murphy's, and characters that appear in Murphy's scenes—Marmalet, a valet named Robert, and another servant—are cut entirely from Burney's adaptation. Burney uses the new two-hander scenes to emphasize the differences between the women: Lady Restless's irrationality becomes more farcical when paired exclusively with Tattle's bewilderment.

For example, in Murphy's original, Lady Restless directs her anger at both Tattle and Marmalet, dispersing her rage on multiple characters, but in Burney's adaptation, the weary Tattle must bear the brunt of Lady Restless's tyranny as she is accused of assisting Marmalet and Sir John's liaison: "You favoured her escape, I find." Tattle, justifiably perplexed, replies, "I favoured her escape, Madam?" Tattle's confusion seems to only ignite Lady Restless's suspicions. In Burney's original scene—placed last in the manuscript and marked by the subheading "Scene"—she further emphasizes Lady Restless and Tattle's dispute. Tattle comes running at Lady Restless's call, apologizing for her delay as she was putting on her cap. Lady Restless has become so crazed that she accuses Tattle of wanting Sir John for herself and threatens to dismiss the long-suffering maid. Tattle cries: "As I hope to live and breath, ma'am, I had not such a thought." Lady Restless's unfounded accusation in Burney's version functions to highlight her absurdity, as does Tattle's bafflement about why an act so mundane as putting on her cap would cause such outrage.

Though it is unclear why Burney adapted these scenes, it is possible that the adaptation was meant for a private theatrical like the Burney family's performance of *Know Your Own Mind* in 1777. The manuscript, at times, appears to be a cue script for the part of Tattle, as Lady Restless's dialogue is more heavily altered than Tattle's and often includes only the final line of her speech. Take, for example, a scene in act 2 in which Lady Restless accuses Tattle of orchestrating Sir John's affair. In Murphy's play, the scene reads:

> LADY RESTLESS. Oh! very well, Mrs. Busy-Body—you have been there, have you?—You have been to frame a story among yourselves, have you, and to hinder me from discovering?—But I'll go to my Lady Conquest myself—I have had no answer to my letter, and 'tis you have occasioned it—
> TATTLE. Dear, my lady, if you will but give me leave—I have been doing you the greatest piece of service—I believe, in my conscience, there is something in what you suspect about Sir John.[40]

Alternatively, in Burney's version only the final line of Lady Restless's dialogue is provided, but Tattle's response is intact with slight alterations:

> LY. REST: = 'tis you have occasioned it.
> TATTLE: = Dear my lady, if you will but give me leave to speak!—I have been doing your ladyship the greatest piece of service:—I believe in my conscience there is something in what you suspect about Sir John![41]

Whatever the intended purpose of Burney's adaptation, she was clearly attracted to the play's bright dialogue and the dynamic between the weary servant and her tyrannical mistress. Her adaptation, though brief, displays many of the features that reoccur in her plays and novels: lively comic dialogue, relationships between women, and social satire.

The Witlings *and* All in the Wrong

Comparing Burney's *The Witlings* to Murphy's *All in the Wrong* reveals many structural and stylistic similarities, including traits of laughing comedy undergirding both plays, as well as meaningful ways in which Burney deviates from the conventions of the style. As is standard in laughing comedies, characters' names in both plays are references to their personalities and foibles—a practice that harkens back to Restoration comedies. In *All in the Wrong*, Sir John and Lady Restless are an aristocratic couple each obsessed with the other's perceived infidelity, Tippet and Tattle are clever and gossipy servants, and Bellmont is the handsome lover besotted with his best friend's sister. The characters in *The Witlings* are similarly named: Lady Smatter has a scattered knowledge of literature, Codger is old and long-winded, Mrs. Sapient pretends to be wise, and Beaufort is the handsome, romantic lead. The plots of both plays focus on a young couple who must overcome parental resistance and their own miscommunication to be married. In *All in the Wrong*, Bellmont's father opposes his son's marriage to Clarissa; in *The Witlings*, Lady Smatter stands in the way of the marriage of her nephew Beaufort to Cecilia.

While Burney's *The Witlings* adopts many features commonplace in laughing comedies of the period, these elements are not necessarily indicative of the specific influence of Murphy's *All in the Wrong*, although the similar antagonists of both plays, Lady Restless and Lady Smatter, do suggest a more direct line of influence, especially considering Burney's particular interest in Lady Restless in her adaptation of Murphy's play. Both characters are elitist, narcissistic, and controlling, and both comically destabilize the idea that class indicates moral superiority. In *All in the*

Wrong, Lady Restless is consumed by jealousy. She terrorizes Tattle with questions about her own husband's infidelity and is constantly monitoring her husband's activities: "I'll follow him thro' the world, or I'll find him out.... The cruel, false, deceitful man!"[42] Likewise, Burney's Lady Smatter carefully monitors and controls the behavior of her nephew, but her narcissism takes a different form. Lady Smatter is a pseudo-intellectual. She professes to be an expert on Shakespeare, Pope, and Swift and she hosts a literary club, the Esprit party, but she has only a smattering of knowledge, as her name suggests. Her key flaw is not that she reads literature, but that she only does so to receive admiration from others: "I declare, if my pursuits were not made public, I should not have any at all, for where can be the pleasure of reading Books, and studying authors, if one is not to have the credit of talking of them?"[43] Like Lady Restless, Lady Smatter is entirely selfish and emotionally shallow. No sooner has Jack announced to the Esprit club that Cecilia's guardian and banker has gone bankrupt than Lady Smatter cries, "I can't think what the poor Girl will do! for here is an End of our marrying her!"[44]

Eventually, both Lady Restless of *All in the Wrong* and Lady Smatter of *The Witlings* receive their comeuppances in the final scenes of each play through the deployment of a screen scene, a comic device popular in laughing comedies in which characters conceal themselves behind a set piece to hide from, or to spy on, another character. The attempt is often unsuccessful and results in the hidden character's true identity being revealed to the other characters and the audience. A screen is famously deployed in the fourth act of William Wycherley's Restoration comedy *The Country Wife* (1675), when Horner tells the doctor Quack to hide behind a screen as he exhibits the success of his sexual ploys. The most famous eighteenth-century screen scene takes place in Sheridan's *The School for Scandal* when Lady Teazle hides from her husband behind a screen, and he in turn hides in a cupboard. Lady Teazle has grown tired of her older husband, Sir Peter Teazle, and she confides her feelings to a young rake, Joseph, at his home. The two are flirting when Sir Peter arrives at the house, and Lady Teazle screams, "Oh, I'm quite undone! What will become of me now, Mr Logic? Oh, he's on the stairs. I'll get behind here—and if ever I'm so imprudent again—(*Goes behind the screen*)."[45] Joseph hides Lady Teazle and pretends to read a book as Sir Peter walks in the door:

> JOSEPH. Oh, my dear Sir Peter, I beg your pardon. (*Gaping, and throws away the book*) I have been dozing over a stupid book. Well, I am much obliged to you for this call. You haven't been here, I believe,

>since I fitted up this room. Books, you know, are the only things I am a coxcomb in.
>
>SIR PETER. 'Tis very neat indeed. Well, well, that's proper; and you make even your screen a source of knowledge—hung, I perceive, with maps.
>
>JOSEPH. Oh, yes, I find great use in that screen.
>
>SIR PETER. I dare say you must. Certainly when you want to find anything in a hurry.
>
>JOSEPH. (*Aside*) Aye, or to hide anything in a hurry either.[46]

Sir Peter confesses to Joseph that he loves his young wife, but he believes that she is having an affair with Joseph's brother Charles. When Charles also arrives at the house, Sir Peter tries to hide behind the same screen that his wife currently occupies so that he might overhear Charles confess to the affair. Eventually, both Sir Peter and Lady Teazle are revealed and must acknowledge one another's absurdity.

Similarly, the screen scene in Murphy's *All in the Wrong* is used to mock the misplaced jealousy of a married couple and force a resolution to the play. The maid Tattle allows a young man, Beverley, to hide in a closet, as he suspects that his love, Belinda, is having an affair with Sir John. While Beverley hides, Sir John allows a distressed, masked woman to take shelter in his home. The masked woman reveals herself to be his wife, Lady Restless, seeking to trap him in an act of infidelity. Thinking herself successful, she cries, "Oh, Sir John! Sir John!—what evasion have you now, Sir?—Can you deny your guilt any longer?"[47] Lady Restless's triumph is cut short when Beverley is then revealed in the closet and Sir John believes that he has found proof of her infidelity: "Oh madam! you know his business—and I know his business—and the gentleman knows his business—There he is . . . waiting for you."[48] The tables are turned and Lady Restless becomes the subject of false accusation and suspicion.

Burney's screen scene in *The Witlings* is more like Murphy's in *All in the Wrong* than Sheridan's in *The School for Scandal*, as both Burney and Murphy use the device to bring their antagonists, Lady Smatter and Lady Restless, to task. Unlike Lady Teazle, neither woman is actually the character in hiding. Rather, Burney uses the premise of a screen to reveal Lady Smatter's hypocrisy. At the end of *The Witlings*, Mrs. Sapient, a member of Lady Smatter's Esprit Club, arrives at the home of the poet Dabler, with whom she is infatuated. On finding that Dabler is away, Mrs. Sapient jumps at the opportunity to go through his room and "discover whether any of his private papers contain [her] name."[49] Mrs. Voluble is eager to assist, but when Dabler arrives home, Mrs. Sapient must hide in the nearest cupboard. Dabler confronts Mrs. Voluble about his missing papers, and Mrs. Voluble quickly betrays Mrs. Sapient's secret, whispering, "She came to me, and—and—and begged just to look at your Study, Sir—So, Sir, never supposing such a lady as that would think of looking at your papers, I was persuaded to agree to it,—but, Sir, as soon as ever we got into the Room, she fell to Reading them without so much as Saying a Word!—while I, all the Time, stood in this manner!—staring with stupefaction. So, Sir, when you knocked at the Door, she ran down to the closet."[50] Dabler, secretly thrilled by Mrs. Sapient's devotion, leaves her in the cupboard undiscovered as other characters in the play congregate at the house. First, Mrs. Wheedle arrives to offer a servant's job to Cecilia. Just as she is about to accept the offer, Beaufort arrives on scene to proclaim his undying love for his "adored Cecilia!"[51] He is soon interrupted by the arrival of a horrified Lady Smatter: "How, Beaufort here—and kneeling, too?"[52] Finally, Censor arrives to blackmail Lady Smatter into condoning her nephew's marriage, threatening to reveal her as a literary fraud. It is only in the concluding moments of the play that Mrs. Sapient finally bursts forth from the closet to interrupt Lady Smatter, who has been gossiping about her. Mrs. Sapient is comically indignant, exclaiming, "Those who speak ill of people in their absence, give no proof of a Sincere Friendship."[53] Mrs. Sapient looks ridiculous, and Lady Smatter's insincerity and false kindness is exposed to all.

Notably, Burney's screen scene differs from Sheridan's and Murphy's in one obvious way: it is defanged of sexual intrigue. Both Sheridan and Murphy rely heavily on sexual innuendo and double entendre to heighten the comic potential of their screen scenes. In *All in the Wrong*, Lady Restless and Sir John are consumed by sexual jealousy, and, in *The School for Scandal*, Lady Teazle nearly cheats on her suspicious husband. Alternatively, in *The Witlings*, Burney uses the screen scene to relay a moral message about women's friendships, unrelated to sexual behavior. While Mrs. Sapient does display illicit desire when she breaks into Dabler's rooms to go through his papers, her behavior breaks social rules more so than sexual ones. Burney's play ends by mocking upper-class women who behave cruelly to those with less power.

The lack of sexual intrigue in Burney's screen scene, and in *The Witlings* more generally, is one of the most significant differences between Burney's play and other laughing comedies of the period. It points to Burney's preference for portraying relationships between women, rather than between women and men, but it also alludes to the limitations she faced as a woman writing a laughing comedy. The lack of sexual content cannot be explained by Burney's own sexual inexperience, because she had proved in *Evelina* that she could write a joke about sex. In one risqué scene, Evelina is accosted by a rapacious soldier in a pleasure garden and is rescued by two cheerful sex workers who tell her she "should not want for friends, whilst [she is] with them."[54] Burney's reluctance to make similar sexual jokes in *The Witlings* speaks to the public nature of playwriting and the fact that the playwright could not remain anonymous.

Additionally, Burney's play, unlike Murphy's, is entirely women-centric. Not only is the rivalry and unbalanced power dynamic between Lady Smatter and Cecilia at the heart of the plot, but Burney also pays particular attention to the lives of working women. The first act of *The Witlings* takes place in a milliner's shop run by Mrs. Wheedle, as the shop-girls Miss Jenny, Miss Sally, and Miss Polly gossip about the upcoming marriage of Beaufort and Cecilia. The final act of the play takes place in the boardinghouse of Mrs. Voluble, another working woman. These interfering and gossipy women are not merely a comic foil to the poised and reserved Cecilia. Rather, their interference is vital to the plot's development and their gossip is crucial to the circulation of information in the fictional world of the play. Burney's knowledge of women as conduits of London's social and economic life was no passing fancy. Her mother, Esther Sleepe Burney, was a businesswoman who ran a successful fan-making shop in Cheapside with a workforce made up primarily by women.[55] Burney draws on her insider knowledge to provide a unique representation of working women within the comic oeuvre of the eighteenth century—one that is not derogatory, but celebratory. She even identifies herself as one of these women, claiming authorship of the play not by name but as "a Sister of the Order."[56]

Crisp's Gendered Censorship

The Streatham set, including Murphy, agreed that *The Witlings* would be a success on the stage, but they failed to predict Burney's family's negative reception of the play. Earlier manifestations of *The Witlings* had been warmly approved by Murphy, Thrale, Johnson, and, according to Thrale's journal entry of May 1, 1779, Dr. Burney himself, who "like[d] it vastly."[57] Yet, to Burney's complete surprise, in August 1779 the final manuscript was roundly condemned by her father and Crisp, who ordered her to abandon the work. Dr. Burney and Crisp's sudden and total opposition to the comedy shocked Burney, who wrote, "I expected many Objections to be raised, a thousand errors to be pointed out, & a million of alterations to be proposed;—but—the suppression of the piece were words I did not expect,—indeed after the warm approbation of Mrs. Thrale, & the repeated commendations & flattery of Mr. Murphy, how could I?"[58] Though Burney found the men's condemnation surprising, an analysis of Crisp and Burney's letters in the months leading to her completion of *The Witlings* reveal that Crisp had been hinting at his displeasure with Burney's theatrical ambition and her interest in laughing comedy for some time.

After learning of the Streatham group's desire that Burney write a comedy, Crisp deployed various strategies to deter her from following their advice. In a letter of December 8, 1778, he warns her about the trauma of a public failure, writing, "The Moment the Scene ceases to move on briskly, & business seems to hang, Sighs & Groans are the Consequence!—Oh dreadful Sound!"[59] Public disapproval was already a great concern for Burney, who had gone to such pains to hide her authorship of *Evelina*, and Crisp elevated these fears. He wrote that writing a comic play would reflect badly on Burney's character:

> I think You Capable, highly Capable of it; but in the Attempt there are great difficulties in the way; some more particularly, & individually in the way of a Fanny than of most people.... I need not Observe to You, that in most of Our successful comedies, there are frequent lively Freedoms (& waggeries that cannot be called licentious, neither) that give a strange animation, & Vig[our] to the same, & of which, if it were to be depriv'd, it would lose wonderfully of its Salt, & Spirit—I mean such Freedoms as Ladies of the strictest Character would make no scruple, openly, to laugh at, but at the same time, especially if they were Prudes, (And You know You are one) perhaps would Shy at being known to be the Authors of.[60]

This underhanded threat, that Burney ought to be ashamed to consider writing a comedy with sexual intrigue, is quickly followed by Crisp's warning that she must also steer away from sentimental comedy: "Of late Years (I can't tell why, unless from the great Purity of the Age) some very fine-Spun, all-delicate, Sentimental Comedies have been brought forth, on the English, & more particularly on the French Stage which, (in my Coarse way of thinking, at least,) are such sick things so Void Of blood & Spirits! that they may well be call'd *Comedies Larmoyantes!—and* I don't find that they have been greatly relished by the public in general, any more than by *my* vulgar Soul—moral, sublime to a degree!"[61] Ultimately, Crisp presents Burney with an impossible dilemma: if she writes a laughing comedy she will sacrifice her femininity and morality, but if she writes a sentimental comedy she will fail as a true comedian. Though Crisp claims that he is not "discouraging" Burney from writing a comedy, he presents her with a situation in which she cannot succeed.[62]

Crisp ends his letter with one final blow, cruelly suggesting that, as a novelist, Burney might be incapable of writing stage comedy at all:

> 'Tis certain, different Talents are requisite for the two species of Writing, tho' they are by no means incompatible;—I fear, however, the labouring oar lies on the Comic Author. . . . The exquisite touches such a Work [a novel] is capable of (of which, Evelina is, without flattery, a glaring instance) are truly charming.—But of these great advantages, these resources, YOU are strangely curtailed, the Moment You begin a Comedy: *There* every thing passes in Dialogue, all goes on rapidly;—Narration, & description, if not extremely Short, become intolerable.—The detail, which, in Fielding, Marivaux, Crebillon, is so delightful, on the *Stage* would bear down all patience.[63]

Instead of plays, Crisp encourages Burney to continue writing novels, which he patronizingly refers to as "little entertaining, elegant Histories."[64]

Over a span of many months, Crisp continued his relentless, multipronged attack on Burney's comic playwriting, always under the guise of care and support. In a letter of January 11, 1779, Crisp threatens to stop Burney from producing the play: "I have been ruminating a good deal on the Obstacles & difficulties I mention'd in my last, that lye directly across *YOUR* Path (as a Prude): in the Walk of Comedy—on the most mature Consideration, I do by no means retract the general Principle that produc'd those observations; I will never allow You to sacrifice a *Grain* of female delicacy, for all the Wit of Congreve & Vanbrugh put together."[65] By comparing her to male, Restoration-era wits, Crisp emphasizes the masculine tradition of laughing comedy. But either Burney did not fully comprehend the depth of Crisp's disapproval, or she chose to ignore it, because she continued to work on the play.

Beyond the obviously sexist and paternalistic nature of Crisp's attitude, he had personal reasons to deter Burney from playwriting. He himself was a failed playwright, and his efforts to steer Burney away from the profession may have been rooted in an attempt to save his protégée from similar embarrassment—or, more insidiously, to stop her from eclipsing him. In 1754, Crisp had published a tragedy, *Virginia*, and staged it at Drury Lane. Garrick thought poorly of the play but was pressured by Crisp's patrons, the Count and Countess of Coventry, to stage the work.[66] As discussed in chapter 2, Frances Brooke's play of the same title was consequently shelved. Crisp's production received a damning description in the *Monthly Review*: "There appears great want of invention, and little knowledge of the stage, in this author; the scenes are so uncemented, and so uninteresting, that, for four acts, we are hardly ever awakened to any feelings that employ our minds, or repay our patient waiting for the only affecting scene, that of *Virginius* with his daughter in the last act."[67] The anonymous critic holds back no reproach for Crisp, and the six-page condemnation must have haunted him, for he never wrote for the stage again.

Crisp was also jealous of Burney's new literary friends and her growing fame. Burney even wrote to Crisp that "Dr. Johnson [was] another Daddy Crisp to [her]."[68] His feelings of abandonment are made clear in a letter to his sister, Sarah Gast, on March 28, 1779:

> As to Fanny Burney, she now in a manner lives at Streatham; and when she was, not long ago, at home for a week, Mrs. Thrale wrote to her to *come home*. As you say, she is so taken up with these fine Folks, I imagine we shall see but little of her now. She is become so much the fashion, is so carried about, so fêted from one fine house to another, that if she wished it, it is now really almost out of her power to see her old Friends.... I know Dr. Johnson, Mrs. Thrale, Mrs. Montagu and some of the Wits are driving hard at her to write a Comedy; and ... I have reason to think she is actually at work.[69]

Burney never seemed to realize that Crisp's personal feelings toward her and toward the theater might bias his attitude toward *The Witlings*. In the end, it likely would not have mattered if Burney had tried to alter her play to appease Crisp. For various petty reasons, he was never going to approve.

In August 1779, Crisp made good on his threat to "never allow" Burney to sacrifice her delicacy by writing a comedy.[70] To her complete surprise, she received a resounding damnation of the final manuscript, signed jointly by Crisp and her father, who ordered her to abandon the play. This letter of suppression is now lost, but Burney's response gives some sense of its content: "You *have* finished it, now,—in *every* sense of the Word,—*partial* faults may be corrected, but what I most wished was to know the general effect of the Whole,—& as *that* has so terribly failed, all petty criticisms would be needless. I shall wipe it all from my memory, & endeavour never to recollect that I ever writ it."[71] Like Crisp, Dr. Burney seemed to identify something shameful about the play and told his daughter that "not only the Whole Piece, but the plot had best be kept secret, from every body."[72] Of course, Dr. Burney himself was no great champion of women comedians. He wrote, for example, multiple demeaning descriptions of Catherine Clive as an unfeminine, comic hack, as recorded in *A General History of Music* (1789), in Abraham Rees's *Cyclopaedia* (1802–20), and in *The Memoirs of Charles Burney* (1832).[73]

Though the two men had myriad reasons for suppressing *The Witlings*, a main source of their concern seems to have been Burney's perceived mockery of Elizabeth Montagu, the illustrious leader of a literary group known as the Bluestockings, which was made up primarily of educated, intellectual, and creative women. As Doody suggests, Dr. Burney was disturbed that the play was "satiric," and Chisholm agrees that the men were concerned that the play "would insult the very literary ladies on whom Fanny depended for her reputation as a writer," and, of course, on whom Dr. Burney relied on for patronage.[74] Though Burney refuted any connection between Montagu and Lady Smatter, the similarities are striking: like the character, Montagu had adopted her nephew and heir, and she was well known for her literary salon and her analysis of Shakespeare. In January 1780, Burney proposed altering the play to address her father and Crisp's concerns about Montagu:

> *My* Notions I will also tell you; they are:—in case I *must* produce this piece to the manager—
> To entirely omit all mention of the *Club*;—
> To curtail the parts of Smatter & Dabler as much as possible;—
> To restore to Censor his £5000—& not trouble him even to *offer* it;—
> To give a *new* friend to Cecilia, by whom her affairs shall be retrieved, & through whose means the Catastrophe shall be brought to [a] happy;—
> And to change the Nature of Beaufort's connections with Lady Smatter, in order to obviate the unlucky resemblance the *adopted Nephew* bears to our *Female Pride of Literature*.[75]

In response, Crisp deemed the proposal of major revisions "impossible," and Burney finally abandoned the play.[76]

Following the suppression of *The Witlings*, Crisp sought to pacify Burney by suggesting that she try writing a new comedy, but one that steered clear of the traits of laughing comedy. He writes that his "Fannikin" should trying writing a "witty, Moral, Useful Comedy without descending to the invidious, & cruel Practice of pointing out Individual Characters, & holding them up to public Ridicule."[77] He offers Burney a new comic topic instead, one that leans toward farce—considered a less significant genre—and away from laughing comedy:

> Your Daddy Doctor related to me something of an Account You had given him of a most ridiculous Family in your present Neighbourhood, which even in the imperfect manner he describ'd it, struck me most forcibly— the *Pitches*—he says You gave it him with so much humour, such painting, such description, such fun, that in your Mouth it was a perfect

Comedy—he describ'd (from You) some of the Characters, & a general Idea of the act—I was quite animated—there seem'd to me an inexhaustible Fund of Matter for You to worke on.... Nothing can be more general than the reciprocal Follies of Parents & Children—few Subjects more Striking—they, if well drawn, will seize the attention, & Interest the feelings of all Sorts, high & low—in Short I was delighted with the Idea.[78]

Crisp's proposed farce about the domestic life of a working-class family is completely out of touch with Burney's own biting satirical voice, interest in women, and current comic trends; while it would not offend, it could hardly have entertained. The proposed comedy would, however, fulfill Crisp's paternalistic desire to protect Burney's reputation and his jealous desire to corral her theatrical career. Burney wisely ignored Crisp's advice and there is no evidence that she ever tried writing his alarmingly ill-advised comedy, *The Pitches*.

Following the suppression of *The Witlings*, Burney and Murphy's mentoring relationship, so closely tied to the creation and production of the comedy, deteriorated. During their last recorded meeting, on January 22, 1780, exactly one year after Murphy had initially agreed to mentor her, Burney told him that she had decided to abandon the play: "I told him I had quite given it up,—that I did not like it now it was done, & would not venture to try it."[79] Murphy, convinced the play would be a success on the stage, was horrified: "He quite *flew* at this,—vowed I *should* not be it's judge;—'What!' cried he, 'condemn in *this* manner!—give up such writing!—such Dialogue! such Character!—No; it *must not* be,—shew it *me*, you *shall* shew it me,—if it wants a few Stage Tricks, trust it with me, & I will put them in,—I have had a long experience in these matters, I know what the Galleries will & will *not* bear—I will promise not to let it go out of my Hands without *engaging* for it's success.'"[80] Interestingly, Burney chose not to tell Murphy about her father and Crisp's opposition to the play. Instead, she insisted the distaste for *The Witlings* was purely her own, a claim that undoubtedly confused Murphy, who had been prepared to accept Burney as a colleague. Eight years later, while Burney was living at court as Queen Charlotte's keeper of the robes, Murphy tried to arrange a meeting with her, but she declined. In an oddly cruel summation of Murphy's character at that time, Burney wrote in her journal:

He is an extremely agreeable & entertaining man, but of so light a character, in morals, that I do not wish his *separate notice*, though, when I met with him at Streatham, as associates of the same friends, I could not but receive much advantage from his notice: amusement, rather, I should perhaps say:—though there was enough for the higher word *improvement*, in all but a *serious* way. However, where, in that serious way, I have no opinion, I wish not to cultivate,—but rather to avoid, even Characters in other respects the most captivating. It is not from fearing contagion,—they would none of them attack me; it is simply from an internal draw back to all pleasure in their society, while I am considering their talents *at best* as useless.[81]

In this passage, Burney's negative assessment of Murphy must be contextualized by her own "wretched" life at court rather than her true feelings toward him, and her intense wariness about his morality seems to be a reference to his infamous affair with the actress Ann Elliot.[82] However, in later recollections of Murphy, written intermittently throughout her life, she remembers him fondly. The two never met again after their last encounter in 1780.

Lady Smatter Returns

While Burney and Murphy did not maintain a relationship following the suppression of *The Witlings*, Murphy's mentorship in 1779 continued to influence Burney throughout her career. Twenty years after Dr. Burney and Crisp suppressed *The Witlings*, Burney renewed her efforts to become a comic dramatist. During this period, Burney wrote three new comedies: *Love and Fashion* (1799), *A Busy Day* (1802), and *The Woman-Hater* (1802). *Love and Fashion* was even arranged for production by Thomas Harris, the manager at Covent Garden Theatre, in early 1800.[83] This time, Burney kept the writing process a secret from her father. Her brother Charles acted as her emissary, as he had when she published *Evelina*, and he exchanged letters with Harris on her behalf. Burney and her siblings even adopted a code when discussing *Love and Fashion*, referring to Harris as the "Upholsterer."[84] Tara Ghoshal Wallace has posited that this code was a reference to Murphy's play of the same name, *The Upholsterer* (1758), suggesting that, unsurprisingly, Murphy was on Burney's mind as she wrote her second comedy.[85]

In a painfully ironic turn of events, Dr. Burney once again suppressed Burney's comic play, arguing that Burney should withdraw *Love and Fashion* from production out of respect following the sudden death of her sister Susanna. Burney acquiesced, entreating Harris to stop preparations for the production at Covent Garden. Now a celebrated and independent author, she had the confidence to confront her father about his censorship, writing:

> This release gives me present repose which indeed I much wanted—for to combat your—to me—unaccountable but most afflicting displeasure, in the midst of my own panics & disturbance, would have been ample

punishment to me, had I been guilty of a crime in doing what I have all my life been urged to, & all my life intended, writing a Comedy. Your goodness, your kindness, your regard for my fame, I know have caused both your trepidation, which doomed me to *certain* failure; & your displeasure that I ran, what you thought, a wanton risk. But it is *not* wanton, my dearest Father. My imagination is not at my own controll, or I would always have continued in the walk you approved. The combinations for another long work did not occur to me. Incidents & effects for a Dramma did. I thought the field more than open—inviting to me. The chance held out golden dreams.[86]

This passage reveals the depth of Burney's desire to become a comic playwright and her realization that Crisp and her father had done her a disservice by suppressing that instinct. She challenges her father's characterization of her playwriting as a "wanton risk," his gendered language harkening back to Crisp's fears about *The Witlings*.[87] Burney now saw those fears for what they were: sexist and manipulative.[88]

Following this second suppression, Burney went on to resurrect parts of *The Witlings* in a new comedy titled *The Woman-Hater* (c. 1802). *The Woman-Hater* maintains aspects of the laughing comedy at work in *The Witlings*, especially through its characterization. The most overt connection is the reintroduction of Lady Smatter, who maintains her original iteration's habit of misquotation and literary pretension: "My soul, as Parnel somewhere says, is the soul of poetry."[89] However, this new iteration of Lady Smatter is also rehabilitated as a kinder and more self-aware figure, which, as Hilary Havens argues, is likely indicative of Burney's own maturity and increased appreciation for the Bluestockings.[90] Of all the characters in *The Witlings*, Dr. Burney and Crisp had found Lady Smatter to be the most offensive. It is notable, therefore, that Burney returns to the character and that this is the only original character name that Burney maintains.

Hints of other characters endure, however: Bob Voluble becomes Bob Sapling, an illiterate bumpkin dominated by his sister Henny, and Codger becomes Old Waverly, the well-intentioned but doddering father. Cecilia and Beaufort are replaced by a slightly more dynamic couple, Sophia and Young Waverly. New, farcical characters are introduced. Sir Roderick—the woman-hater—who has never recovered from being jilted by Lady Smatter twenty years prior, turns his anger on those around him. He lectures his servants at length about the ills of women and, during one particularly extreme tantrum, pelts them with pieces of his backgammon board whilst screaming, "I'll teach you to throw dice! There! There! There!"[91] Young

Waverly, Sir Roderick's heir, also takes on a farcical quality. Barred by Sir Roderick from marrying, Young Waverly finds himself obsessed with women: "He has kept me at such an unnatural distance from the Women, that I have hardly ever seen a laundress, but I have become enamoured of her."[92] Consequently, Young Waverly decides to cast off Sir Roderick's yoke and tells his servant Stephanus that he will "search out some pliant old Dowager, worth fifty thousand pounds—and invite Sir Roderick to my wedding."[93]

Though many of the characters in *The Woman-Hater* are conceived in the tradition of laughing comedy, overall, the plot of *The Woman-Hater* is more sentimental than that of *The Witlings*. Shortly after their marriage, Eleonora and Wilmot separate in the West Indies after Wilmot mistakenly accuses Eleonora of having an affair. In fear for her safety, Eleonora takes their young daughter Sophia and leaves him. Succumbing to the ruse of a crafty nurse, Wilmot believes that a different young woman, whose real name is Joyce, is his own daughter. Two decades later, both Wilmot (with the fake Sophia) and Eleonora (with the real Sophia) travel to England to beg favor of the girl's wealthy uncle, Sir Roderick. As the plot unfolds, various characters make sincere and impassioned soliloquies, indicative of sentimental comedy, meant to induce the sympathy of other characters and the audience. At one point, terrified that her estranged husband will take Sophia away from her, Eleonora exclaims, "She comes not! My poor Sophia! What can thus detain thee? I tremble at every step; yet can rest inactive no longer.—Should accident make her known—or Me!—I must not proceed,—I dare not!—He will demand his daughter—he will unbraid my carrying her off—All the courage that rises when I think upon what I have suffered, dies away when I meditate upon what I may have inflicted."[94] Eleonora's fears are soon proved unfounded when she confronts Wilmot and the two are reconciled. Young Waverly falls in love with Sophia, Joyce reveals her true identity, and Sir Roderick recognizes his own foolishness.

Sabor and Sill write that in creating *The Woman-Hater*, Burney displays her knowledge of current comic trends.[95] As the eighteenth century ended, a "flood of sentimental drama" swept London.[96] Burney was clearly attuned to this and adapted her comic techniques appropriately. It follows that *The Woman-Hater* likely would have succeeded alongside sentimental comedies like Elizabeth Inchbald's *Lovers' Vows* (1798)—which similarly features a couple reunited after many decades, as I discuss in chapter 5—just as *The Witlings* likely would have succeeded among the laughing comedies of the 1770s. Burney even wrote a cast list of actors from Drury Lane for

The Woman-Hater, suggesting that she hoped the play would be produced.[97] Sadly, *The Woman-Hater* was never staged, as Burney departed for France in 1802 with her husband and young son, and they would remain there for the next decade.

While there are surprisingly no mentions of *The Woman-Hater* in Burney's journals or letters, there is one rare mention of Murphy, written during the period when she was working on the comedy, suggesting that Murphy continued to be a creative influence on her. In her French exercise book, Burney copied out an entry from April 1802, likely around the time she was finishing *The Woman-Hater*. She reminisces fondly about her time spent at Streatham and about Murphy specifically. She even praises a handful of his plays, including *All in the Wrong*: "Il se donna alors à écrire pour le théatre, et il avoit un succès le plus flatteur possible. Un de ses pièces, Comment il faut le garder, est toujours jouée encore toutes les fois où il y a des acteurs qui meritent de jouer les roles celebres et distingués qui en composent la dramatis personae. . . . All in the Wrong, Know your own mind, (pris de l'Irresolu de Destouches,) et d'autres pieces, ont aussi été reçues à merveille" (He gave himself up to writing for the theater, and he had the most flattering success possible. One of his plays, *The Way to Keep Him*, is always played whenever there are actors who deserve to play the famous and distinguished roles that make up the dramatis personae. . . . *All in the Wrong, Know Your Own Mind* [taken from Destouches's *L'Irresolu*], and other pieces have also been received wonderfully).[98] Burney's recollection of Murphy alludes to her ongoing regard for his plays and the significance of his influence.

Though he played only a supporting role in the drama of Burney's literary life, Murphy was an important influence on *The Witlings*. Burney's journals and letters reveal that he gave her formative input on her original outline of the play, and that he read and offered encouragement on the first two acts and possibly others. As Burney's only mentor who was a playwright by profession, Murphy gave advice that was critical to the aspiring dramatist, and his confidence that the play would succeed carried weight. Perhaps Murphy's most important contribution was his unequivocal support of the playwright herself. When Burney abandoned *The Witlings* following Dr. Burney and Crisp's condemnation, Murphy refused to agree that the play was not good enough to stage and expressed distress at her abandonment of a fine work. Burney drew on Murphy's confidence in her later in life when she once again renewed her efforts to become a comic playwright. Though her dream did not come to pass, Burney never forgot the support of Murphy, and in her final publication before her death, a memoir of her father, she reflects affectionately on the "gaiety of spirits" and "convivial hilarity" of her mentor.[99]

Though Burney's career as a comic playwright was stalled following *The Witlings* debacle, she became one of the most recognized and influential comic women writers of the late eighteenth century in the novel form. She certainly had a significant impact on other women playwrights, especially one of the most prolific women playwrights of the final decades of the century, Hannah Cowley. Reflecting on the subtle character development, insightful wit, and nuanced writing in Burney's novels, Cowley authored a poem paying homage to her sister writer shortly after the publication of *Evelina*:

> What pen but Burney's then can sooth [sic] the breast
> Who draws from nature with a skill so true
> In e'vry varying mode it stands confest
> When brought by her before th'enquirers view
> A power-peculiar, all her portraits fill:
>
> . . .
>
> Burney detects, drags it to open day,
> Makes evident what slipp'd the unmasking eye
> And bids it glare, with truth's pervading ray.
>
> . . .
>
> And sure 'tis this is keen-ey'd Burney's forte
> Touch'd by her spear, they sudden spring to sight
> But not new form'd—she shows them as they are
> She molds no character, but gives the light
> Which makes them clear, as Herschel sees a star![100]

Like Burney, Cowley was drawn to the biting wit and powerful social criticism of laughing comedy, but with an additional feminist twist that elevated women's perspectives on friendship and romance. Cowley was clearly impressed by Burney's writing, and several scholars have confirmed the theatrical influence that *Evelina* had among women writers of the day.[101] The next chapter turns to Cowley's remarkable career and her production of over a dozen comedies between 1776 and 1794.

4

The Satirical Seraglio
Hannah Cowley

Hannah Gadsby's breakthrough comedy special *Nanette* (2018) is premised on Gadsby's announcement that they will quit comedy because of their deep concerns with the oppressive and patriarchal nature of the genre. Citing homophobia, sexism, and gender-based and sexual violence, Gadsby argues that men experience more freedom in writing and performing comedy, while gendered expectations limit women and gender-diverse people: "Look, I am angry. . . . It's not my place to be angry on a comedy stage. I'm meant to be doing self-deprecating humor. People feel safer when men do the angry comedy. They're the kings of the genre. When I do it, I'm a miserable lesbian, ruining all the fun and the banter. When men do it, heroes of free speech."[1] Two hundred and fifty years earlier, another angry comedian named Hannah made a similar critique of the gender politics of stage comedy in a preface to her new play, *A School for Greybeards* (1786). Women, Hannah Cowley (née Parkhouse; 1743–1809) wrote, take on disproportionate risk when they write comedy: "The Novelist may use the boldest tints;—seizing Nature for her guide, she may dart through every rank of society, drag forth not only the accomplished, but the ignorant, the coarse, and the vulgar-rich; display them in their strongest colours, and snatch immortality both for them, and for herself! I, on the contrary, feel encompassed with chains when I write, which check me in my happiest flights, and force me continually to reflect, not, whether *this is just*? but, whether *this is safe*?"[2] Notably, neither Gadsby nor Cowley abandoned the stage after publicly voicing their displeasure with stage comedy. In a 2019 TED Talk, Gadsby joked good-naturedly that "quitting launched my comedy career";[3] Cowley went on to solidify her identity as one of the most popular and respected comic playwrights of the late eighteenth century. For both, comedy is the vehicle they chose to deliver their most powerful feminist critiques while also critiquing the genre itself (see figure 4.1).

Figure 4.1. James Heath after Richard Cosway, *Comedy Unveiling to Mrs. Cowley* (1783), Harry R. Beard Collection, given by Isobel Beard, © Victoria and Albert Museum, London.

An 1813 biography of Cowley characterized the late playwright as an "unassuming," "domestic," and anti-theatrical woman: "Neither before nor after she wrote did she take pleasure in viewing, nor was she accustomed to be present at, a theatrical representation. She never witnessed a first performance of her own plays. Successive years elapsed without her being at a Theatre once. Though her writing gave public celebrity to her Name, her mind always retreated to the shades of private life."[4] This sexist depiction of Cowley is decidedly false. In reality, Cowley had a great passion for live theater, fierce professional ambitions, and, like Gadsby, she was publicly outspoken, even brazen, about the sexism she experienced writing for the stage. She tenaciously and consistently defended her creative autonomy over a twenty-year career. This chapter evaluates Cowley's career as a comic playwright, with particular attention paid to her penultimate comedy, *A Day in Turkey; Or, The Russian Slaves* (1791), to illuminate the feminist theatrical critique that defined her professional identity.

A Day in Turkey is unique among Cowley's comic oeuvre; it deviates from her more conventional comedies of manners that feature feisty English heroines pursuing the men they love within London's competitive marriage market. While *The Belle's Stratagem* is considered emblematic of Cowley's career and a canonical example of an eighteenth-century woman's comedy, *A Day in Turkey*, in contrast, is irreverent, political, and experimental. Instead of foregrounding English social life, *A Day in Turkey* features a host of Turkish, Russian, French, and Italian characters imprisoned in the harem of a Turkish pasha (anglicized in the play as "bassa"). The play is set during the Russian-Turkish War of 1787–92 and the French Revolution, and it contains critiques of the slave trade, gender inequality, and colonialism. These controversial topics and themes are presented in a play that contains multiple comedic genres including farce, pantomime, and sentimental and musical comedy. Cowley's contemporaries were puzzled by the play. They found the genre mixing and political allusions discomfiting. A reviewer for the *Oracle*, for example, wrote, "This piece is by no means a Comedy, for the Songs make a part of the communication of opinions; besides, the tragic incidents predominate.... It is an Opera, like many extremely popular, with incidents of the serious and the comic kind."[5] The *Public Advertiser* complained about the play's political allusions, deemed "equally reprehensible whether they allude to this country or any other."[6] Despite the evident anxiety surrounding the play, it was a moderate commercial success, performed fourteen times throughout the 1791–92 season and revived in 1794.[7]

Modern critics of *A Day in Turkey* have been intrigued by Cowley's political commentary and generic experimentation in the play. Betsy Bolton argues that mixing farce and sentiment allowed Cowley a certain freedom to engage in public political debate that might otherwise have been impossible.[8] Similarly, Daniel O'Quinn reads *A Day in Turkey* as an explicit political allegory. He argues that Cowley "examin[es] what constitutes acceptable proximity between women and political power."[9] Anne K. Mellor finds that the play proposes an "embodied cosmopolitanism" that places women at the heart of international diplomacy, and Greg Kucich echoes this idea in describing the play as "a new kind of women's cosmopolitanism."[10]

Building on this body of scholarship but moving away from Cowley's macro vision of gender and global politics, this chapter focuses on Cowley's criticism of theatrical politics in the play. By the late stages of her career, Cowley had become embittered by the sexism and censorship of the London theaters and changing theatrical tastes, including the demand for spectacular entertainment.[11] In *A Day in Turkey*, Cowley draws on her experiences as a professional woman playwright to create a biting metatheatrical critique of gender politics in the theater. She draws on the pressing political issues of war, imperialism, and slavery to articulate her experience as a woman playwright subjected to the audiences', critics', and managers' tyrannical demands. By portraying the harem as a women-run theatrical playing space, Cowley reveals the disparate power dynamics between men and women in London's theatrical establishment. The play simultaneously exposes the theater as a source of empowerment *and* oppression for women, a space in which they may exercise their power but only under precarious conditions.

Cowley's Theatrical Career

The details of Cowley's professional struggles with managers, critics, and audiences provide critical context to understanding her identity as a playwright and the critique at the heart of *A Day in Turkey*. Cowley was not born into a theatrical family, nor did she work as an actress before trying her hand at playwriting. However, like Frances Brooke, she received an unusually good home education. Cowley's father, Philip Parkhouse, was a bookseller and local politician in Tiverton—a town in Devon, far from London's bustling theater scene—and his trade provided his young daughter with endless reading material. As a young woman, Hannah Parkhouse married Thomas Cowley, a Stamp Office clerk and theater critic for the *Daily Gazetteer*, and relocated to London.[12] After attending the theater with her husband, Cowley was inspired to launch her own playwriting career, saying, "Why I could write as well myself!"[13] She was also likely financially motivated, as the young couple had children and Thomas did not earn a high wage.[14]

Cowley's first comedy, *The Runaway*, was accepted by David Garrick for production at Drury Lane and debuted on February 15, 1776. As I discussed in previous chapters, Garrick staged the plays of many women, but he also acted as a gatekeeper. Cowley was the last woman whose work Garrick produced before his retirement in 1776, and *The Runaway*, according to Ellen Donkin, was "the biggest success of them all," helping cement Garrick's legacy, problematically, as an ally of women playwrights.[15] Cowley was grateful to Garrick for his support of her play, and she included a letter of praise to him in the first published edition: "Unpatronized by any *name*, I presented myself to you, obscure and unknown. You perceived *dawnings* in my Comedy, which you *nourish'd* and *improved*."[16] Self-deprecating and ingratiating, the letter reveals the sort of dynamic common among Garrick's women mentees. Cowley, however, also leveraged the relationship to her own advantage. She emphasized her association with Garrick, the most important theater professional of the century, while also highlighting Garrick's approval of her work. Clearly aware of her gendered disadvantage as a woman playwright, Cowley paints herself as a humble woman, unthreatening to the existing status quo: "The RUNAWAY has a thousand faults, which, if written by a Man, would have incurred the severest lash of Criticism—but the Gallantry of the English Nation is equal to its Wisdom—they beheld a *Woman* tracing with feeble steps the borders of the Parnassian Mount—pitying her difficulties (for 'tis a thorny path) they gave their hands for her support, and placed her *high* above her level."[17] Cowley's self-effacing statement should not be misread as an admission of her inferiority; rather, it is an example of the maneuvering women playwrights adopted regularly to appease the male-dominated industry and defang any threat their work might pose.

Cowley similarly emphasizes her feminine modesty in her prologue to the play, in which she portrays *The Runaway* as merely trivial and lighthearted:

> Our Poet of to-night, in faith's a—Woman,
> A woman, too, untutor'd in the School,
> Nor Aristotle knows, nor scarce a rule
> By which fine writers fabricate their plays,
> From sage Menander's, to these modern days:
> . . .
> Now for a hint of her intended feast:
> 'Tis rural, playful,—harmless 'tis at least;
> Not over-stock'd with repartee or wit,
> Tho' here and there *perchance* there is a hit.[18]

Cowley's strategy of feminine demurral was effective. *The Runaway* was celebrated by the public and was performed an impressive twenty times in the year of its debut and thirty-nine times by the end of the century. The play featured a plot that would become the foundation of Cowley's comic oeuvre. Writing in the comic tradition of women playwrights since the Restoration, Cowley was familiar with the works of Aphra Behn and Susanna Centlivre, even adapting Centlivre's *The Stolen Heiress* (1702) and Behn's *The Lucky Chance* (1686).[19] As in her foremothers' plays, Cowley's opinionated and independent women characters successfully pursue companionate and egalitarian marriages in the face of patriarchal opposition, or do not marry at all. Indeed, Cowley paid conscious homage to Behn and Centlivre in several plays, linking her work to a women's comic lineage from the Restoration to the present day.

With such promising beginnings, Cowley's career should have progressed smoothly, but, like Brooke, she quickly found herself entangled in the disingenuous web of the theater's managerial boys' club. When the playwright Richard Brinsley Sheridan took over Drury Lane following Garrick's retirement in 1776, Cowley felt that he purposefully blocked *The Runaway* from being revived in order to stage his own plays.[20] Such sabotage was not limited to Garrick, who had blocked Brooke's plays, and theatrical record shows that Cowley's accusation against Sheridan was credible. His own comedy, *A Trip to Scarborough*, debuted later that season on February 24, 1777, and his *The School for Scandal* on May 8, 1777. Additionally, Sheridan brought his comedy, *The Rivals*, which had first played at Covent Garden in 1775, for its debut performance at Drury Lane on January 16, 1777. Though Cowley's *The Runaway* had done very well the previous season, Sheridan produced it only four times in 1777, clearly making room for his own works. Possibly realizing that Sheridan, a comedian, had the power to quash any rival playwright, Cowley next tried writing a tragedy, *Albina*. Unfortunately for Cowley, neither Sheridan nor Thomas Harris at Covent Garden was interested in *Albina*. Both men read the play and declined to produce it.[21] Cowley did not know that the two men had a pact at the time not to produce any plays declined by the other.[22] In the meantime, Sheridan accepted Cowley's afterpiece *Who's the Dupe* in 1778, but then delayed staging it until the very end of the season, in April 1779, much to Cowley's annoyance.[23]

Adding to Cowley's frustration with the managers was the production of two tragedies by a less experienced woman playwright. In 1777, Hannah More succeeded in staging her tragedy *Percy* at Covent Garden, followed by *The Fatal Falsehood* in 1779. Cowley felt that both plays, but especially *Falsehood*, shared striking similarities with her manuscript of *Albina*, as she wrote in her preface to the printed play: "Should it, after all, appear to the Public, that there is nothing more in these repeated resemblances, than what may be accounted for supposing a similarity in our minds; and that, by some WONDERFUL coincidence, Miss More and I have but one common stock of ideas between us, I have only to lament that the whole misfortune of this similarity has fallen upon me."[24] Cowley realized that there would never be a production of *Albina* at either of the more prestigious winter playhouses, so she offered the play instead to George Colman the Elder, the manager of the Haymarket. The Haymarket primarily staged comedies during the summer season and *Albina*, a tragedy, was not a good fit; it was performed a meager seven times, beginning July 31, 1779.

The entire situation struck Cowley as exceedingly unjust, but she hoped that the performance and publication of the play would prove that More had borrowed from her play, and not the other way around:

> It seems reasonable that we should have our productions brought forward in turn; instead of which Miss More has had TWO tragedies brought out, both of which were written since mine, whilst I struggled for the representation of ONE in vain. But, as there seems to be little hope of my obtaining this, or any other favour from the Winter Managers, I presume at least, that, as I do not pretend to prove—what is impossible for me to know—that Miss More ever read, or copied me, it will be admitted that I have not copied her.[25]

Cowley was, of course, jealous of More's success in staging two tragedies when her own was declined, but as she explains in her preface, she did not blame only More. Instead, she turns her anger toward the managers, Harris and Sheridan, who had rejected *Albina*: "By the conduct of the Winter Managers, I have been deprived of a reasonable prospect of several hundred pounds, and have spent years of fruitless anxiety and trouble.... My productions have been uniformly received by the Public with applause; yet I find the doors of the Winter Theatre shut against me."[26] Cowley feared that the managers, including the now-retired Garrick, who mentored and befriended More, must have used her manuscript to improve More's. Though Cowley could not prove her suspicions, her fears were not without merit. As I explained in chapter 2, Brooke also feared that Garrick had stolen ideas from the manuscript of her tragedy *Virginia* in the 1750s. Like Cowley, Brooke had given Garrick a copy of *Virginia*, and it sat in limbo until Samuel Crisp's version appeared at Drury Lane in 1754. Both Brooke and Cowley felt that their plays, which were so long in Garrick's hands, were used to augment the works of their competitors. Garrick died in 1779 and never gave an account of his role in the Cowley-More debacle.

Convinced that her work had been plagiarized, Cowley was tenacious in pursuing justice for herself in the press. Her husband, Thomas, possibly helped promote her case in his role as reviewer for the *Gazetteer*.[27] Eventually, More was compelled to respond to the aspersions cast in the papers. She wrote the following letter in her defense to the *Morning Post* on August 13, 1779:

> It is with the deepest regret I find myself compelled to take a step repugnant to my own feelings, and to the delicacy of my sex; a step as new to me as it is disagreeable; for I never, till this moment, directly or indirectly, was concerned in any paragraph in any London Newspaper. Of the low abuse bestowed on me repeatedly in the Gazetteer . . . I took no notice as it amounted to little more than I had mounted a very bad play:—To a pretty plain insinuation in a Morning Paper, that The Fatal Falsehood too much resembled a manuscript play of Mrs. Cowley's not to have been stolen from it, I forbad my friends to reply:—To frequent messages, and menaces from Mr. and Mrs. Cowley I thought proper to be silent—This has been misconstrued into fear or guilt. . . . My moral character thus grossly attacked, I am under the necessity of declaring, that I never saw, heard, or read, a single line of Mrs. Cowley's tragedy. . . . Nothing shall compel me to enter into a Newspaper altercation, nor shall I make any further reply. This much I thought due to my own character, and to that public to whom I am so largely indebted.[28]

No matter how adamant her denials, More could never prove that she had not committed plagiarism, nor could Cowley prove she had. The scandal did, however, result in both Cowley and More becoming the subjects of widespread and enduring sexist criticism.

In 1795, the musician and dramatist Charles Dibdin wrote about the incident in his *Complete History of the British Stage*, more than a decade after the actual event:

> Nothing can be more ridiculous than literary quarrels even among men, but when ladies, fearful lest their poetic offsprings should crawl through life unheeded, publicly expose themselves to the world, in order to ascertain their beauty and legitimacy, who does not wish they had occupied their time with a needle instead of a pen. The attention of the world was called, when *Fatal Falsehood* came out, to a newspaper dispute between Miss More and Mrs. Cowley, who brought out a tragedy called *Albina*. . . . Had these foolish ladies no friend to prevent their making themselves a town talk?[29]

Dibdin's analysis of the scandal not only offers a forthright example of the sexism More and Cowley faced as women playwrights, it also reveals the highly public nature of their feud. It is striking that precisely as the dispute was unfolding in the press, a young Frances Burney was told by her father and Samuel Crisp that she must not stage her own play, *The Witlings*, as discussed in chapter 3. Donkin astutely points out that More and Cowley's public feud may have been "one factor among several" in Dr. Burney and Crisp's suppression of the piece.[30]

The scandal eventually fizzled out, but it left both Cowley and More with permanent scars. Anne Stott writes that More "learned the hard way that a woman could not win in this game. If she stayed silent, she must be guilty, if she defended herself, she was indulging in unfeminine conduct."[31] More never again wrote for the London stage and stopped attending the theater altogether. When *Percy* was revived in 1788 with the celebrity actress Sarah Siddons in the role of Elwina, More did not attend. Cowley, alternatively, weathered the debacle and persevered as a playwright, but her attitude toward the theater business had fundamentally changed. Years of fighting with the duplicitous managers made her wary. She avoided writing tragedy for the next decade, distancing herself from the genre and the incident that associated her with it and steering toward the more commercially rewarding genre of comedy.

In 1780, Cowley produced her third comic play and her second full-length comedy, *The Belle's Stratagem*, at Covent Garden, a response to George Farquhar's *The Beaux' Stratagem* (1707). Either Harris held no grudge over the debacle with *Albina* or, more likely, he spotted the money-making potential of the play straight away. The well-received, five-act comedy ran for twenty-eight nights in its debut season and became part of the standard repertoire for the remainder of the century and into the next. In fact, it is one of the few eighteenth-century-era comedies that continues to be performed to this day.[32] It was followed by a dozen other original productions by Cowley over the next fourteen years (all comedies but one), placing her firmly among the top playwrights of the late century.

Though *The Belle's Stratagem* cemented Cowley's fame, the remainder of her career was not without challenges. In 1786, Cowley faced criticism for her treatment of marriage and divorce in *A School for Greybeards*. Critics objected to the dissolution of a marriage between a young woman and a much older man before consummating their union following the legal ceremony, a plotline that Cowley borrowed from Behn's Restoration comedy *The Lucky Chance* (1687). By this time, Behn was considered a morally degenerate author, and for Cowley (or any woman writer) to imitate her inevitably drew accusations of indecency. *A School for Greybeards* was viewed as offensive and was deemed unforgivable by the *Morning Chronicle* because Cowley was "a female and a parent."[33] Likewise, the *Morning Herald* criticized Cowley's *The Way as It Goes* in 1781, writing that the play "exceeds in gross ribaldry, the productions of the notorious Mrs. Behn."[34] Cowley, seeking inspiration and legitimacy from the tradition of women's comedy through Behn, as her male counterparts did when they drew on Dryden or Congreve, became increasingly frustrated by the unrelenting double standard of playwriting, and she addressed this issue in her preface to *A School for Greybeards*: "It cannot be the *Poet's* mind, which the public desire to trace, in dramatic representation; but the mind of the *characters*, and the truth of their colouring. Yet in my case it seems resolved that the point to be considered, is not whether that *dotard*, or that *pretender*, or that *coquet*, would so have given their feelings, but whether Mrs. Cowley ought so to have expressed herself."[35] Here, Cowley openly resents the lack of creative expression she was allowed as a dramatist and emphasizes that this oppression weighed most heavily on the woman playwright.

Cowley's growing frustration with gender inequality in the theater reached a peak by the late 1780s. She once again tried to write a tragedy, and she once again experienced mediocre results. *The Fate of Sparta* was performed nine times in 1788 and was never revived. John Philip Kemble, who played the lead, wrote scathingly of the play that "one would not suppose from this preface that *The Fate of Sparta* was hardly dragg'd through nine nights of empty houses."[36] Following the flop of *Sparta*, Cowley took a near four-year break from the stage before her next comedy, *A Day in Turkey*, debuted at Covent Garden on December 3, 1792. Notably, Cowley had begun writing *A Day in Turkey* amid the *Albina* debacle years earlier. She wrote at that time: "I had indeed made some progress in writing a Piece founded on Turkish manners, the Scene of which is laid in Asia, and flattered myself with success from the novelty of the attempt; but it lies, and must lie, in its present state, till I have reason to believe it will meet with a fair and candid reception from the Theatres."[37] Cowley waited for over a decade to finish *A Day in Turkey* and submit it for production at the apex of her career. The play displays Cowley's expertise as an established and skilled playwright; it is a spectacular extravaganza, featuring a sensational plot, elaborate set and costume design, and a thrilling blend of music and comedy. But underneath this glittering mirage, the play points to Cowley's disillusionment with the London theaters, with the audience's increasing demand for spectacle over wit, the sexist condemnation of critics, and the tyranny of the managers. *A Day in Turkey* encompasses a decade of Cowley's knowledge of the theater's inner workings and paints an unflattering portrait of the gender politics of the business.

Women Staging Empire

Cowley set *A Day in Turkey* against the backdrop of the Russian-Turkish War of 1787 to 1792, during which the Ottoman Empire sought, and failed, to regain land in Oczakow (modern-day Ukraine) previously lost to Russia.[38] Britain feared Russia's ascending power and prepared for the possibility that it may have to join the war. The matter was hotly debated in Parliament and in the papers, but in 1792 the conflict ended, and Britain's potential involvement became irrelevant. Cowley shrewdly capitalized on the immediacy of these events, making the recent conflict, now deflated of its immediate danger, the backdrop to her play. The prologue, possibly written by Cowley herself, explains:

> NOT from the present moment springs our play,
> Th' events which gave it birth are past away—
> Five glowing moons have chas'd night's shades from earth,
> Since the war fled which gave our Drama birth.
> "Not smiling peace o'er RUSSIA'S wide-spread land,
> Wav'd gently then, her sceptre of command.
> No! thousands rush'd at red ambition's call,
> With mad'ning rage to triumph—or to fall.
> 'Twas then our female bard from BRITAIN'S shore
> Was led by fancy to the distant roar"—
> 'Twas then she saw sweet virgins captives made,
> 'Twas then she saw the cheek of beauty fade,
> Whilst the proud soldier in ignoble chains,
> Was from his country dragg'd to hostile plains.
> Thus was her bold imagination fired
> When battle with its horrid train retired.[39]

The prologue emphasizes both Cowley's gender and her topical intervention, while carefully framing her dramatization of the conflict between Russia and the Ottoman Empire as artistically, rather than politically, motivated. Performed by the actor George Davies Harley, the prologue legitimizes a woman's writing about such affairs through the voice of a male actor who highlights the play's feminine content and describes Cowley as the "female bard."[40] In reality, Cowley's play is filled with direct and sharp political commentary and sexual jokes, and her characters are far from the helpless victims alluded to in the prologue.

Setting the play during the Russian-Turkish War also allowed Cowley to take advantage of the popularity of plays set in the East, or Oriental plays.[41] Such plays had been standard fare in the London theaters since the Restoration. Charles II was fascinated by the Ottoman Empire, and when he reopened the theaters following his return to London, the first play to be legally staged was William Davenant's Oriental drama *The Siege of Rhodes*, in 1661.[42] Oriental plays remained highly marketable throughout the eighteenth century as they allowed dramatists to capitalize on the popularity of spectacular set and costume design, while portraying the English as racially and culturally superior. An important body of recent scholarship has drawn attention to the far-reaching and insidious influence of Orientalist theater in eighteenth-century England, as well as to the complex and conflicting commentary on politics, economics, race, class, sex, and gender that exists in these plays.[43]

English women playwrights had been drawn to dramatizations of the East since the Restoration as a means to explore matters of gender inequality. Examples include Behn's *Abdelazer, or, The Moor's Revenge* (1676), Mary Pix's *Ibrahim, the Thirteenth Emperor of the Turks* (1696), and Delarivier Manley's *Almyna, or, The Arabian Vow* (1706). As Jacqueline Pearson writes, these women "found Turkey and other Islamic countries profitable for images of power relations between the sexes, for potentates, harem women, sultanas, mutes, and eunuchs."[44] By depicting "the position of women in other countries," Pearson explains, women writers opened up the possibility for "feminist debate" at home.[45] For example, Mary Wortley Montagu compared her experiences as an English woman to those of the women of Constantinople (now Istanbul) in her famous *Turkish Embassy Letters* (1763). In the theatrical context, Elizabeth Inchbald's first play, an Orientalist farce titled *The Mogul Tale*, which debuted seven years prior to *A Day in Turkey*, on July 6, 1784, contrasts the gendered experiences of English and Indian women.

Inchbald's play follows a group of three English travelers—a cobbler named Johnny, his wife Fanny, and a doctor—who accidently travel to India in a hot-air balloon. The confused travelers comically attempt to discern their location: "It is Greenland, is it not?"[46] In fact, they are in the harem of an Indian mogul, and a group of women in the harem tease the travelers by explaining that they will be put to death. In a twist, the mogul is a fair, benevolent, and rational ruler who decides to toy with the English travelers' prejudice and racism by pretending to be the tyrant they imagine him to be. The travelers, particularly the men, proceed to make fools of themselves as they pretend to be envoys from England: the doctor plays an ambassador of the king, Johnny dubs himself the pope. Disturbingly, the doctor schemes to kidnap one of the mogul's concubines, and Johnny attempts to seduce another. Fanny, Johnny's wife, is the most sensible and moral of the group of travelers, but she is continually dismissed and undermined by the two Englishmen she travels with. Her situation as a free English woman is contrasted with that of the captive harem women and found lacking. At the end of the play, the mogul gently chides the group for their chauvinism and deceitfulness: "You have imposed upon me, and attempted to defraud me, but know that I have been taught mercy and compassion for the sufferings of human nature; however differing in laws, temper and colour from myself. Yes from you Christians whose laws teach charity to all the world, have I learn'd these virtues? For your countrymen's cruelty to the poor Gentoos has shewn me tyranny in so foul a light, that I was determined henceforth to be only mild, just, and merciful."[47] Following this critique of British colonialism and English masculinity, the three travelers are allowed to leave in their balloon and return to England.

Beyond drawing connections between gender in the East and West, women playwrights also used Orientalist plays to comment on their role within the theatrical establishment itself. O'Quinn writes that "in the hands of women playwrights, representations of empire could be turned inside out to ridicule the theatrical taste which produces and consumes such fare."[48] Behn's Restoration comedy *The Emperor of the Moon* (1687), for example, is an overtly metatheatrical play. Two young women and their lovers trick their imperial-minded patriarch, a quack doctor named Baliardo, into believing he can colonize the moon. As Baliardo peers through his telescope, his daughters trick him by putting on Oriental costumes and pretending to be part of a lunar harem. Behn emphasizes the power of women in the theater by demonstrating that Baliardo's daughters can manipulate their father's gaze against an Orientalist backdrop. As the daughters exercise theatrical power, the father embodies the audience's own voyeuristic desire "to be dazzled and fooled."[49]

Cowley adopts a similar technique in *A Day in Turkey*. The play focuses on three women, Alexina, Paulina, and Lauretta, who are enslaved in a Turkish harem and who orchestrate an elaborate theatrical performance to free themselves. Alexina is a beautiful Russian bride who has been captured and imprisoned in the harem of the bassa Ibrahim. She is treated cruelly by a Turkish guard named Azim, but kindly by another named Mustapha. Alexina plans to commit suicide rather than submit to Ibrahim, but the presence of another captive, Paulina, a Russian peasant, changes her fate. Under the clever direction of the Italian captive Lauretta, Paulina pretends to be Alexina to distract Ibrahim's attention. Lauretta orchestrates the elaborate ploy and directs Paulina's performance with the assistance of Alexina and the guard Mustapha. The trick is a success, as Ibrahim falls for

Paulina and she, in turn, falls for him. Meanwhile, Alexina's husband, Count Orloff, has been captured and imprisoned by Ibrahim. After learning that his wife is still alive, Count Orloff hopes to save her. He is accompanied by his foppish French valet, A La Greque, a macaroni who is flippant, charming, and self-serving, and whose name implies the eighteenth-century interest in Greek fashion, architecture, and luxury goods.[50] He is a practical character, seeking to make the best of a bad situation and quick to forget previous loyalties. He is also the most overtly political character in the play, making continual witty allusions to the ongoing French Revolution, which are defanged by his pantomimic comedy.

In a Francophobic manner, Cowley paints A La Greque as disloyal and sexually driven. When A La Greque references the French Revolution, his calls for liberty are undercut by his insincere and submissive behavior:

> IBRAHIM. Of what country are thou?
> A LA GREQUE. Oh, Paris, Sir, Paris. I travell'd into Russia to polish the brutes a little, and to give them some ideas of the general equality of man; but my generosity has been lost;—they still continue to believe that a prince is more than a porter, and that a lord is a better gentleman than his slave. O, had they but been with me at Versailles, when I help'd to turn those things topsey turvey there!
> IBRAHIM. Did you find them equally dull in other respects?
> A LA GREQUE. Yes. Finding they would not learn liberty, I would have taught them dancing, but they seem'd as incapable of one blessing as the other; so, now I am led a dance by this gentleman (*Turning to his master*). Into your chains, in which, if I can but dance myself into your favour, I shall think it the best step I ever took.
> IBRAHIM. The freedom of thy speech does not displease me.
> A LA GREQUE. Dear Sir, I am your most obedient humble slave, ready to bow my head to your sandals, and to lick the dust from your beautiful feet.[51]

Though Cowley is obviously mocking A La Greque and his false sentiments, he is also portrayed as a court jester, speaking truth to power in a manner that borders on dangerous: "Death is an aristocrat! and I am bound, as a Frenchman, to hate him."[52]

The ongoing revolution was a divisive political issue in England, and some viewers of Cowley's play did not like to be reminded of the civil discontent that plagued France and might spread to England. William Godwin advised Inchbald to withdraw her play *The Massacre* from Covent Garden for this very reason, and Shakespeare's *Coriolanus* (c. 1605–8), which was deemed politically dangerous for its depiction of a discontented populace, was staged only seven times during the final decade of the century.[53] Following the debut of *A Day in Turkey*, the *Gazetteer and New Daily Advertiser* took issue with A La Greque and "those passages, which, by exhibiting some of the present circumstances of France to ridicule, are injurious to the cause of general liberty."[54] The *Oracle* argued that Cowley ought to edit the play: "If the Fair Author would take our advice, she would strike out every *Political Sentiment* in the Play. Why, in the name of prudence, will any Writer split an Audience into Parties, and compel dissent when all should be conciliated?"[55] The *Public Advertiser* also took issue with the play's apparent divisiveness, writing that it "possessed also a glaring error in our opinion, that of political allusions; they are equally reprehensible whether they allude to this country or any other, for on those subjects there will always be different opinions; but this being easily remedied, it is to be hoped they will be expunged before a repetition."[56] Initially, Cowley bowed to the complaints that her play was too political, removing sections of the offending dialogue for the second performance on the evening of Monday, December 5, 1791. However, after a single censored performance, she decided to replace the dialogue in full and to publish the original text in February 1792.[57]

In her strongly worded advertisement appended to the published edition of *A Day in Turkey*, Cowley denies her political intent, which she agrees would be unfeminine, and argues that the play merely reflected the needs of her characters:

> HINTS have been thrown out, and the idea industriously circulated, that the following comedy is tainted with POLITICS. I protest I know nothing about politics;—will Miss Wollstonecraft forgive me—whose book contains such a body of mind as I hardly ever met with—if I say that politics are unfeminine? I never in my life could attend to their discussion.
>
> TRUE COMEDY has always been defined to be a picture of life—a record of passing manners—a mirror to reflect to succeeding times the characters and follies of the present. How then could I, pretending to be a comic poet, bring an emigrant Frenchman before the public at this day, and not make him hint at the events which had just passed, or were then passing in his native country? . . . It is A La Greque who speaks, not I; nor can I be accountable for his sentiments.[58]

Tanya Caldwell points out that Cowley's denial of political involvement is a red herring.[59]

Here, Cowley is employing a maneuver similar to her defense of *A School for Greybeards*; she insists that her characters are not reflections of her own beliefs and stances, but rather products of creative inspiration. Cowley's denial of political commentary, her insistence of her own unwavering femininity, and her claim that her comic characters are merely meant to entertain, allows her to simultaneously distance herself from the political content of the play while also drawing attention to it. In this sense, Cowley's invocation of Mary Wollstonecraft is also particularly noteworthy. It highlights her knowledge of Wollstonecraft's work and publicly promotes her feminist ideas, while also allowing Cowley to position herself as the less radical of the two.[60] Inchbald similarly mentions Wollstonecraft in her prologue to *Every One Has His Fault* in 1793, which I will discuss in chapter 5. Cowley's interest in Wollstonecraft is further alluded to in the play when Azim and Lauretta discuss A La Greque's politics and Lauretta makes the case for women's emancipation:

> AZIM. The new French slave—Frenchmen, there is no being guarded against.—They make free every where.
>
> LAURETTA. At least they have made themselves free at home! and who knows, but, at last, the spirit they have raised may reach even to a Turkish harem, and the rights of women be declared, as well as those of men.[61]

While A La Greque's own revolutionary sentiments are mocked in the play, Lauretta employs the language of revolution to promote women's rights. The licensing copy of *A Day in Turkey* reveals that the Lord Chamberlain censored this line from performance, but Cowley reinstated it for the published edition quoted above.

In *A Day in Turkey*, Cowley invites her audience to consider not only the theater of global politics, via the Russian-Turkish conflict and the French Revolution, but also the politics of the theater itself. She asks her audience to reflect on who holds power and how that power can be subverted. Despite the negative reaction to the play's political content in the press, *A Day in Turkey* was well liked. As Frederick Link explains, by the end of the eighteenth century, "the patent theatres had been enlarged so much that intimate comedy depending on witty dialogue and facial expression could not as easily be supported, and the public was demanding ever greater portions of melodrama and spectacle."[62] Cowley took advantage of the audience's growing demand for spectacular entertainment and incorporated dances, musical numbers, and a royal procession, complete with music written by Joseph Mazzinghi, a popular English composer. She also drew on a women's tradition of Oriental comedy tracing back to Behn in order to embed gender and theatrical commentary into her play.

The Seraglio: A Woman's Playhouse

In the first act of *A Day in Turkey*, Ibrahim enters the stage during an elaborate royal procession. The stage directions read: "*A march is played. Standard bearers advance first; they are followed by female slaves, who dance down the stage to light music, and exit. The chorus singers follow; Female Slaves strewing flowers from little baskets succeed; the Bassa then appears at the top with his principal officers.*"[63] Three women of the harem, Selim, Lauretta, and Fatima, sing to welcome Ibrahim, whom they call their "prince restor'd," "Victorious hero," and "glory of our age."[64] Cowley thus establishes Ibrahim's patriarchal power within the play while simultaneously highlighting the theatrical quality of the harem—a space of singing, dancing, celebration, and sexual entertainment. Though Ibrahim appears to hold supreme authority in this space in which women are objectified for his entertainment, the women of the harem are also imbued with a certain theatrical power. Throughout the play, Cowley depicts the harem as a site that both confines women and provides them an opportunity to create, perform, and influence those around them—not unlike William Hogarth's depiction of the harem (figure 4.2). The extent to which women can extend their theatrical power, however, is complicated within the play, and particularly by its resolution.

Figure 4.2. William Hogarth after Jean Baptiste Vanmour, *The Seraglio* (1724), Harris Brisbane Dick Fund, 1917, The Metropolitan Museum of Art, New York.

All the women characters of *A Day in Turkey* participate in the theatrics of the harem in one way or another, but the clear embodiment of the woman playwright is the Italian Lauretta. Both Bolton and O'Quinn note the self-referential quality of Lauretta's character: Bolton identifies her as the "figure for the female playwright," and O'Quinn similarly describes her as the "playwright/manager" who reveals that "the realm of public affairs can be controlled through the manipulation of private desires."[65] However, the harem is far from a creative haven for Lauretta, who can perform only under the constant watch of the guards. Additionally, while the male characters of the play can filter in and out of the harem, Lauretta and the other women characters cannot leave. This nuance is critical to understanding Cowley's theatrical critique. She introduces the idea of a women-centric theatrical playing space, but it is not a theatrical utopia; rather, it is a theater divided by gender in which women have creative power but no authority—a reflection of Cowley's lived experience.

Lauretta's allegorical role as the woman playwright is made clear from the first act of the play. In an extension of gendered camaraderie, Lauretta states that her goal is to save Alexina from Ibrahim, saying, "I am interested for her, and it is for this reason I shall endeavour to make Ibrahim pursue a conduct not usual from a mighty mussulman to his slave."[66] Initially, Lauretta attempts to derail Ibrahim's pursuit of Alexina by encouraging him to try and "become the slave of your captive, if you ever mean to taste the sublime excesses of a mutual passion."[67] Ibrahim is intrigued by the concept of mutual passion and Lauretta formulates her plan for the upcoming drama in a self-consciously theatrical aside to the audience at the beginning of the second act:

> So, so! 'tis dangerous to give some people a hint, I find—I thought to have held the master-spring, and to have managed him like a puppet; but presto! he's out of sight before I knew I had lost him, and leaves his instructor groveling behind—I must seek some other field for my talents, I see. (*Considering*). Yes, I think, I think that may do—Muley, and the other four, with our little Mustapha—Yes, yes; with these half dozen, I'll weave a web of amusement to crack the sides of a dozen gloomy harems with laughter—Mercy! what a sleepy life wou'd our valiant Bassa and his damsels lead, but for my talents at invention.[68]

Lauretta reveals a dual purpose in this passage. First, she seeks to entertain the fictional characters of the harem, both men and women, clearly establishing her position as Cowley's stand-in as playwright. However, her more serious purpose is to save Alexina from sexual slavery and, through her manipulation of Ibrahim, to arrange the freedom of all the women of the harem. This feminist intention is made clear in the 1813 edition of the play, when Lauretta ends the same passage by adding, "Yes, yes, with these I'll weave a web which, whilst it fills these gloomy regions with merriment, shall preserve Alexina—and gain liberty for us all!"[69]

The star of Lauretta's drama is Paulina, the Russian peasant. Like Lauretta, she is practical and unsentimental, although she is not especially clever. When Ibrahim first appears to Paulina in the garden, believing her to be Alexina, she has no idea who he is and is unimpressed by his advances, saying, "I tell ye what, mister, you may make grand speeches about this and that; but I hate both you and your love; and if ever you teize me with it any more, I'll make you repent, that I will."[70] Ibrahim is unused to being spoken to with disdain, and he is captivated by Paulina's effort to dominate him. Lauretta, Alexina, and Mustapha, encourage Paulina to keep up this facade in order to distract Ibrahim's attention away from Alexina. Paulina, who is attracted to Ibrahim, is happy to play the part, and Lauretta directs her performance, exclaiming, "I'll teach you in half an hour all the arts of a fine lady, and you shall be able to play on your lover as you would on your harpsichord. The whole gamut of his mind shall be in your possession, and every note of it obedient to your wish."[71] Under Lauretta's direction, Paulina proves to be a good actress who enjoys the power of performance:

> IBRAHIM. You smile! Ah, did you know the value of those rosy smiles, you would not bestow upon me more than one in a thousand hours—Each is worth a diadem.
> PAULINA. I suppose you hope by all this to make me forget I am a captive, and a slave (*Pretending to cry, then turning away, laughing*).
> IBRAHIM. You can be neither—It is I who am your slave—You hold the chains of my destiny—Ha! let me catch your tears![72]

Over the course of the play, Paulina falls in love with Ibrahim, and after her true identity is revealed, Ibrahim declares his love for her. But, before the two agree to wed in the final scene, Paulina further exercises her newfound power to negotiate the release of her brother and father from bondage:

> PAULINA. It blesses my heart to see you so happy! And shall my father and brother be releas'd from slavery—Shall they witness my happiness?
> IBRAHIM. They shall partake it. Riches and honour await those so dear to thee.[73]

Paulina's performance in Lauretta's scheme is a great success. Not only is Alexina reunited with her husband, but it is implied that the other women of the harem will also be freed. However, Paulina also proves herself to be more than Lauretta's tool, as she uses her newfound power to negotiate a cross-class, companionate marriage for herself, and the liberty of her family.

As the women in *A Day in Turkey* claim theatrical agency, using the harem as their stage to leverage a performance that benefits them all, the male characters stand in for the audience and their desire to be entertained. Cowley carefully highlights the association between the audience's gaze and the male characters who peer into the harem. This construction is most obvious in the case of Ibrahim, who explicitly looks to the harem to feed his romantic *and* theatrical fantasies. Ibrahim, who has been away at war, is explicit in his desire to be dazzled, telling Lauretta to "prepare your banquets, compose your delights, let every hour teem with fresh invented joys, till I forget the toils of the sanguinary field and bathe my wounds with rosy-finger'd love."[74] Lauretta directs the drama for her own secret purposes, and Paulina performs the role of the uninterested coquette. Ibrahim, in turn, watches Paulina from a distance and revels in the theatrical nature of their romance: "Oh, fly me not—yet fly! Even the distance you throw me at gives you a thousand charms, and whilst it tortures, it bewitches me."[75] For Ibrahim, the primary pleasure in his pursuit of Paulina is a theatrical one. As Azim says in bewilderment, "Sir, she is your slave, *command* her!"[76] But Ibrahim prefers to playact the role of the Petrarchan lover, reveling in the "delicious pain" of Paulina's feigned rejection.[77] Paulina, in turn, capitalizes on Ibrahim's theatrical and romantic fantasy and leverages events for her own benefit.

A La Greque, the Harlequin-like French valet, also embodies the gaze of the audience. In the first scene of act 4, A La Greque strains to see through the harem wall, crying, "Is there no getting a peep at those jolly girls?"[78] Eventually, one of his captors points out a space where he can sometimes "get a squint at the girls."[79] The scene then immediately shifts to a musical interlude inside the garden, for which the stage directions read: "*Enter Female slaves, singing and beckoning to their companions, who enter from opposite wings all the way up. During the song others enter, dancing to the music.*"[80] On one hand, Cowley is pandering to the audience by staging spectacle that relies on the sexualization of women's bodies. However, she is also drawing attention to the gendered dynamic of the theater itself, which relies on women's bodies to titillate the male spectators. A La Greque's peep through the harem wall is manifested to the audience, as they can see all that he looks upon. In act 5, after A La Greque successfully steals into the harem, a more explicit performance of sexual fantasy takes place. An enslaved Turkish woman named Fatima and the other enslaved women set up a luxurious sofa bed, a stereotypical and highly sexualized Oriental prop, in the garden. A La Greque must hide from the palace guards, and Lauretta quickly decides to bury him under the sofa cushions, crying as she pushes him to the ground, "Lower! Lower still! rest on your hands—reach that covering—quick—quick!"[81] She then sits atop the hidden A La Greque to obscure his hiding place. A La Greque is delighted with his proximity to Lauretta's bottom, and once the coast is clear, he calls her his "precious burden," exclaiming, "Jupiter, when loaded with Europa on his back, was not half so much charmed with her as I am with you."[82] In the original myth, Jupiter abducted Europa, adding a predatory element to A La Greque's comment. The encounter fulfills his sexual and theatrical fantasy as he becomes physically enveloped in the world of the harem.

The final scene of *A Day in Turkey* sees the fruition of the women's meta-theatrical performance for freedom and the fulfillment of the male characters' sexual and romantic desires. Alexina and Orloff are reunited, and Ibrahim and Paulina agree to wed. Alexina asks Ibrahim to forgive the cruel Azim, and Ibrahim, touched by her kindness, suddenly—even absurdly—converts to Christianity:

> ALEXINA. . . . Let Azim have frank forgiveness.
> IBRAHIM. Charming magnanimity! if it flows from your CHRISTIAN DOCTRINES such doctrines must be RIGHT, and I will closely study them.[83]

Ibrahim's spontaneous conversion panders to the audience's expectations of English superiority over Eastern heathenism; however, it is also clearly ridiculous and the sincerity of the conversion is questionable. In a further invocation of the audience through Ibrahim, Alexina next steps forward to address the spectators directly: "And may our errors have frank forgiveness too! Bestow on us your favour, and make the DAY IN TURKEY one of the happiest of this happy season!"[84] For Mellor, the play's somewhat hackneyed resolution "reveal[s] Cowley's conservative feminism in its clearest form," as "female Christian virtue is the power that resolves the conflicts in the play."[85] However, I suggest that a deep flaw disrupts the shiny surface of Christian marital bliss described by Mellor at the end of the play.

While it is suggested that Ibrahim will free his slaves following his conversion and marriage to Paulina, at the time of the play's conclusion this has not been explicitly declared or enacted. The failure to achieve liberation harkens to an earlier line in the play, when Azim reminds the audience, in one of the few direct critiques of England, that "the christians in one of the northern islands have established a slave trade, and proved by act of parliament that freedom is no blessing at all."[86] Here, Cowley is referring to William Wilberforce's failed motion in Parliament on April 19, 1791, to abolish slavery.[87] Lauretta, the orchestrator of this play's metatheatrical drama, remains in captivity. After imprisoning the cruel Azim in the same cell in which he trapped Alexina, Lauretta is not heard from again. In case the audience has missed this lack of resolution, Cowley reminds them of it in the epilogue to the play:

> Escap'd from Turkey, and from prison free,
> Yet still a SLAVE you shall behold in me;
> An *English* slave—slave to your ev'ry pleasure,
> Seeking your plaudits as her richest treasure.[88]

In the epilogue, delivered by the actress Elizabeth Pope, who played Alexina, Cowley compares her own identity as a woman playwright to that of the harem slave, further emphasizing the self-referential nature of her theatrical criticism. While the framing of the playwright as a public servant was not unusual, Cowley pushes this notion to the extreme by invoking the slave trade. She reminds the audience that her creative freedom is dependent on their whim and that of the theatrical establishment.

While Cowley's criticism of gender inequality in the theater is veiled by allusion and symbolism in *A Day in Turkey*, a few years later, she stated her position bluntly. In the preface to her next and final play, *The Town Before You* (first performed in 1794 and published in 1795), Cowley announced her retirement from playwriting. She directly identifies the audience's voracious demand for spectacle and physical comedy over witty dialogue and complex character as the source of her frustration, indicating that she felt some distress, or at least ambivalence, about the spectacle that she had staged in *A Day in Turkey*:

> The patient developement [*sic*] of character, the repeated touches which colour it up to Nature, and swell it into identity and existence (and which gave celebrity to CONGREVE), we have now no relish for. The combinations of interest, the strokes which are meant to reach the heart, we are equally incapable of tasting. LAUGH! LAUGH! LAUGH! is the demand....
>
> Let Sadler's Wells and the Circus empty themselves of their performers to furnish our Stage; the expence to Managers will be less, and their business will be carried on better. The UNDERSTANDING, DISCERNMENT, and EDUCATION, which distinguish our modern actors, are useless to them;—strong muscles are in greater repute, and grimace has more powerful attraction.[89]

In this passage, Cowley not only compares herself with the canonical and celebrated playwright William Congreve, who was famous for his wit and comedies of manners, but also is openly critical of the contemporary audience and managers who no longer have a taste for such comedy. She invokes Sadler's Wells Theatre, famous for its impressive entertainments including large water features, and the Royal Circus, which featured animal acts and pantomimes, as examples of new theatrical trends, and she criticizes the managers for pandering to these modes. As the century progressed, Cowley no longer saw a place for herself in the changing theater scene.

Following her retirement from the theater, Cowley left London and returned to her hometown of Tiverton. Her husband had died overseas in 1797, and her only surviving daughter, Frances, lived in Calcutta, while her son, Thomas, lived in Portugal. Cowley's sister Mary had taken over the family bookshop in Tiverton after their father's death, and Cowley decided to return home.[90] These final years of Cowley's life appear to have been happy ones. She was an engaged member of her community, and her biographer, Mary De la Mahotière, writes that she continued to be "concern[ed] with the injustices which beset women," evidenced by her organization of a women's group that met each Monday and raised funds for struggling married women.[91] She also worked on editing her plays for *The Works of Mrs. Cowley*, excising their more daring aspects—including her original gutsy prefaces that railed against the theatrical establishment—in order to make the collection more palatable. Sadly, Cowley's edits muted the fierce feminism that had defined her playwriting career, as she considered her reputation for posterity. After her death in 1809, *The Works of Mrs. Cowley* was published by George Wilkie and John Robinson in a testament to the ongoing marketability of her plays.

Though Cowley had one of the most remarkable careers of any eighteenth-century woman playwright, tracing her struggles with *Albina* in the 1770s through her theatrical commentary in *A Day in Turkey* reveals a playwright beleaguered by the industry's gendered limitations. By 1795, when Cowley published her preface to *The Town*, she no longer saw stage comedy as an effective outlet for her creativity, nor did she view it as a safe mode for a woman writer, as her earlier preface to *A School for Greybeards* reveals. While women throughout the century had managed to leverage comedy as the most effective means of balancing creative and professional reward, shifting theatrical trends were beginning to upend that harmony. As demonstrated by Burney's decision not to stage *The Witlings* because of the Daddies' fear of infamy, and Cowley's admonition of Wollstonecraft in *A School for Greybeards*, the immense social pressure to maintain respectability was often at odds with the feminist impulses of women's comic playwriting in the late part of the century. No woman playwright made a greater effort to balance her professional success with personal virtue than Elizabeth Inchbald, whose remarkable comedy career and careful treatment of feminism will be discussed in the next chapter.

5

Sentimental Comedy and Feminism
Elizabeth Inchbald

On the evening of April 19, 1797, the audience at Drury Lane was eagerly anticipating the debut of Frederic Reynolds's *The Will* when a heated confrontation broke out between Elizabeth Inchbald (née Simpson; 1753–1821), the foremost woman playwright of London, and Mary Wollstonecraft (1759–97), the well-known advocate for women's rights and author of *A Vindication of the Rights of Woman* (1792).[1] A week before the confrontation, Inchbald had learned of Wollstonecraft's sudden marriage to her friend and colleague William Godwin. Affronted, Inchbald wrote a salty note to Godwin and cancelled their arrangement to attend the play together with a group of friends: "I most sincerely wish you and Mrs Godwin joy— But, assured that your joyfulness would obliterate from your memory every trifling engagement, I have entreated another person to supply your place and perform your office in securing a Box on Reynold's [sic] night. If I have done wrong—when you next marry I will act differently."[2] The new Mrs. Godwin, hereafter referred to as Wollstonecraft, found Inchbald's behavior "very rude," but enlisted their mutual friend Amelia Alderson to calm Inchbald and "set the matter right."[3] The theatrical visit went ahead, but tensions were high, and on arrival, Inchbald and Wollstonecraft fought. Godwin later characterized Inchbald's behavior as "shuffling"—possibly she refused to sit next to Wollstonecraft—and her words as "base, cruel & . . . insulting."[4] The two women never spoke again.[5]

Biographers and critics have long attributed Inchbald and Wollstonecraft's feud to their supposed competing romantic affection for Godwin and Inchbald's discomfort on learning of Wollstonecraft's sexual history, thus dismissing the quarrel as unimportant. When Godwin and Wollstonecraft married in 1797, they inadvertently revealed that Wollstonecraft was not already married to the American diplomat Gilbert Imlay as she had claimed, and that her daughter, Fanny, was illegitimate. Consequently, many people sought to distance themselves from the new couple, but

Inchbald's reaction was the most public. Decades later, in 1836, Mary Shelley, Godwin and Wollstonecraft's daughter, posited that Inchbald must have been in love with Godwin and wrote that Inchbald "had reason to ... shed tears when he announced his marriage."[6] C. Kegan Paul printed Shelley's reflection in his 1876 biography of Godwin, and S. R. Littlewood, in his 1921 biography of Inchbald, advanced the broken-heart theory further, proposing that Inchbald's ire at Wollstonecraft was sparked by "wounded vanity."[7] This dubious narrative of events has continued to influence modern criticism. Katherine S. Green describes Inchbald and Godwin as "intimate friends, if not lovers," and Ildiko Csengei argues that Inchbald rejected Wollstonecraft "out of social prejudice—or possibly even jealousy."[8] However, Inchbald and Godwin's surviving correspondence reveals no passionate declarations of love; instead, it is largely devoted to discussion of manuscripts and other literary matters.[9]

Regrettably, reducing Inchbald and Wollstonecraft's dispute to a love triangle obfuscates the significant creative, professional, and personal differences between two of the most important women writers of the late eighteenth century, and it has served as a denotation of the end of Inchbald's interest in progressive politics. This chapter uses the feud between Inchbald and Wollstonecraft (figures 5.1 and 5.2) as a starting point to explore the status of the professional woman playwright at the end of the eighteenth century, and the ways in which Inchbald used sentimental comedy to promote her own progressive ideologies following her break with Godwin and Wollstonecraft. I focus specifically on Inchbald's feminist politics and explore how she used sentimental tropes in her novels and plays to advocate for women. Wollstonecraft objected to Inchbald's reliance on sentimental women characters as antithetical to feminist progress, however, in scathing reviews of Inchbald's two novels, *A Simple Story* (1791) and *Nature and Art* (1796). While Inchbald never wrote a public rebuttal to Wollstonecraft's criticism, I argue that her play *Lovers' Vows* (1798), an adaptation of the German playwright August von Kotzebue's *Das Kind der Liebe* (1790), produced the year after Wollstonecraft's death, is a defense against such criticism and an articulation of Inchbald's own feminist strategies that relied on sentiment as a key technique to advocate for women.[10]

Inchbald's feminism has been treated ambiguously in modern scholarship. She is not easily grouped with outspoken feminists like Wollstonecraft who sought an overthrow of patriarchal social structure, nor with more conservative women like Hannah More who defended women's education. Annibel Jenkins, Inchbald's most recent biographer, suggests that Inchbald stands among the feminist writers of the period, but argues that she was more moderate in her thinking than others, writing, "[Inchbald] did not

Figure 5.1. Wooding after John Russel, *Mrs. Inchbald* (1788), © National Portrait Gallery, London.

promote feminism as much as [Anna Laetitia] Barbauld or Catherine Macaulay."[11] Alternatively, Misty Anderson points out that while Inchbald indicates support for women's rights in her plays, she cannot be defined as a feminist by modern standards: "[Inchbald's] politics are hardly feminist, but her plays express her passionate concern for the legal status of women."[12] While it is true that Inchbald was reticent to promote ideologies that might garner public condemnation, including calls for women's rights, considering Inchbald within the body of historical feminists helps to illuminate a fundamental tenet of her identity as a playwright. In focusing on Inchbald's encounters with Wollstonecraft, who is often referred to as the mother of modern liberal feminism, this chapter draws needed attention to the

Figure 5.2. James Heath after John Opie, *Mary Wollstonecraft Godwin* (c. 1797), © National Portrait Gallery, London.

feminist underpinnings of Inchbald's late-century sentimental comedy. *Lovers' Vows* represents Inchbald's vexed efforts to blend the feminist tradition of women's comedy—with its focus on women characters, their interests, and their success—with the generic conventions of a popular genre that relied on benevolent patriarchs and subservient daughters.

From Farmhouse to Playhouse

To understand how Inchbald's professional identity as a playwright intersected with her interest in reform politics and feminism, it is vital to consider the evolution of her theatrical career.[13] She was born to the Simpson family in Stanningfield, Suffolk, in 1753, and her childhood was one of hard-working farm life. Her two brothers were sent to school, while she and her five sisters were taught at home. Though John Simpson, the family patriarch, died in 1761, his resourceful wife and children managed to preserve the farm. The remaining family members, devout Roman Catholics, were also enthusiasts of the local theater, and they attended performances by the Norwich Company, which Inchbald's older brother, George, joined in 1770. As a teenager, Elizabeth also dreamed of a life on the stage. After being declined a post by the Norwich manager Richard Griffith, she ran away from home on April 11, 1772, to pursue becoming an actor in London. Remarkably, without training or experience—and with the additional barrier of a stutter—she succeeded. Only a few months after leaving home, Elizabeth married a traveling actor, Joseph Inchbald, whom she had met on a visit to London the previous year. The couple married in a Catholic ceremony on June 9, 1772, and in a Protestant ceremony the following day. Joseph was nearly twenty years older than his teenaged wife, and he had two children from previous relationships. Despite these drawbacks, the marriage did offer Elizabeth access to her first acting roles, alongside Joseph, who was employed for the summer season in Bristol; she made her debut at the end of the season on September 4, 1772, as Cordelia in Shakespeare's *King Lear* (c. 1606).

That fall, the new couple joined actor-manager West Digges's company and spent the next four years performing in theaters across Scotland.[14] According to Inchbald's diaries, these years were grueling and her marriage often unhappy. Joseph was a heavy drinker and resented that his wife was paid separately. However, he also helped Inchbald to overcome her stutter and trained her in acting as they traveled, often by foot, across the unforgiving Scottish countryside. In June 1776, the Inchbalds were abruptly forced to leave the company after Joseph fought with the audience in Edinburgh for unclear reasons. They briefly moved to Paris, where Inchbald studied French and Joseph studied painting, but they returned to London after one month, with few remaining funds. Over the following years, the couple performed in the provincial theater circuit with various companies, including Joseph Younger's company in Liverpool and then Tate Wilkinson's York Company, until, in 1779, Joseph died suddenly.[15] The newly widowed Inchbald, only twenty-five, decided to move permanently to London, where she had connections to the theatrical community and was able to secure roles at Covent Garden, under the management of Thomas Harris, during the winter season, and at the Haymarket, under the management of George Colman the Elder, during the summers (see figure 5.3). She chose not to remarry, but instead to live an independent life as an actress and, eventually, a playwright.

Figure 5.3. C. Sherwin after H. Ramberg, *Mrs. Inchbald in the Character of Lady Abbess* (1785), © The Trustees of the British Museum.

Following in Catherine Clive's footsteps, Inchbald identified farce as the best genre to break into the profession of playwriting. She leveraged her insider status as a London actress to get her first play produced at the Haymarket on July 6, 1784, a two-act farce titled *The Mogul Tale* (which I describe in chapter 4). The farce was well received, running for ten performances in its first season and revived for many years after. Over the next two decades, Inchbald wrote another twenty plays, many of which were adaptations from French and German works, that both challenged and delighted her audiences. Unlike Clive, Inchbald did not write parts for herself to further her career as an actress. Instead, she quickly retired from the stage once she was able to support herself entirely by her writing. Alongside Hannah Cowley, Inchbald achieved unprecedented commercial success as a playwright and "dominate[d] comedy" in London in the final part of the century.[16] Inchbald primarily wrote comedies, both mainpieces and afterpieces, although she also wrote two tragedies that were never performed and only posthumously published: *The Massacre*, which was set to be printed in 1792 but was suppressed because it dealt explicitly with *la Terreur* in France, and *The Case of Conscience*, written in 1800.[17]

Inchbald was a shrewd negotiator and manager of her own financial success. Anderson deems her theatrical career "the most commercially successful . . . of any woman dramatist in the late eighteenth century," and Milhous and Hume calculate her benefit earnings as well above average.[18] In addition to maintaining an unvarnished reputation and writing plays in the most popular genre of the era, Inchbald furthered her career by taking control of her plays in print. She consistently printed her plays after their debuts in the theaters, mostly selling the copyrights to the publisher G. G. and J. Robinson for a profit additional to the earnings from her benefit nights. Jane Wessel lays out Inchbald's numerous objectives in printing her plays in this way.[19] First, it ensured that Inchbald's original play was available to theaters across the country, thus preventing the performance of poor-quality knock-off productions. In addition to protecting her "authorial reputation," by printing her plays Inchbald ensured that her works could be performed by other theaters, limiting the control that her own powerful managers—Thomas Harris at Covent Garden and George Colman at the Haymarket—had over productions of her works.[20]

As I have shown in previous chapters, women were often criticized as unfeminine when they wrote stage comedy, as in Hannah Cowley's and Frances Burney's cases, and Inchbald was not immune to such sexism. Following the debut of her first full-length comedy, *I'll Tell You What* (1785), one critic disparaged the play on the basis of Inchbald's gender: "We also confess ourselves to have been displeased with the highflown and absurd compliments which have been paid, in this case, to the authoress. . . . Her silly admirers boldly place her upon a level with Sheridan."[21] Highly aware of the scrutiny and sexism she faced as a woman playwright, Inchbald maintained a polished personal and professional image throughout her career in order to counter such detractions related to her sex and gender identity. Though she adopted certain risks in writing comedy, Inchbald was influenced by the theatrical climate at the end of the eighteenth century—namely, the voracious demand for comedy over tragedy and the generic shift toward what Jean Marsden describes as a transformation of the theater into a "world of feeling."[22] More deeply emotional theatrics became popular and precipitated the shift toward the melodramatic conventions of the nineteenth-century stage.[23] Allardyce Nicoll correspondingly summarizes Inchbald's playwriting as a "more advanced style of sentimental humanitarian drama," and, more recently, Wendy Nielsen has drawn a connection between Inchbald's dramatic oeuvre and theatrical trends in continental Europe, including the *Sturm und Drang* (storm and stress) movement in Germany and *genre sérieux* in France, forms that heavily emphasized deep emotion.[24]

Although she drew on popular theatrical trends, Inchbald's comedies can hardly be called formulaic. Indeed, Jane Moody argues that Inchbald "conducted radical experiments into the limits of sentimental comedy."[25] As Daniel O'Quinn describes, Inchbald expertly "navigat[ed] factional waters while remaining resolutely topical."[26] Her late-century comedy pushed the boundaries while translating topical public concerns—the growing British Empire, the abolition movement, the regency crises, and the French Revolution—into "comic events that diffused some of the anxieties of fin de siècle England."[27] Alongside tearful heroines, male gallants, and family reconciliations, Inchbald's plays contain interrogations of colonialism, despotism, slavery, and unhappy marriages. For example, *Such Things Are* (1788) features a benevolent sentimental hero, Haswell, based on the real-life prison reformer John Howard; *Every One Has His Fault* (1793) portrays a virtuous lower class juxtaposed against a corrupt nobility; and *Wise Man of the East* (1799) contains a scene of suicide brought on by an abusive relationship. Thus, Inchbald's sentimental comedies provided the playwright with the optimal commercial success and a fair degree of subversive expression.

Inchbald as Literary Radical

While Inchbald was a meticulous administrator of her professional success, her dramatic work was also deeply influenced by her interest in radical politics. By the early 1790s, she had established a large literary network in London among theater creators, artists, and writers, many of whom were grappling with the political climate of the French Revolution. During this period, Inchbald became associated with leading English radicals who supported the Revolution, including Thomas Holcroft, a playwriting colleague; George Robinson, her publisher; and William Godwin, the political philosopher.[28] This particular group of "literary Jacobins," as Gary Kelley dubs them, were English intellectuals and writers who sympathized with the values that instigated the Revolution and, in their works, called for the widespread reform of government and society in order to expand and protect individual liberties.[29] Gary Kelly characterizes the ideology of Inchbald's circle thus: "They opposed tyranny and oppression, be it domestic, national or international, spiritual or temporal; they were against all distinctions between men which were not based on moral qualities, or virtue; and they were utterly opposed to persecution of individuals, communities, or nations for their beliefs on any subject."[30] For the women in the group—Charlotte Smith, Mary Robinson, and Inchbald herself—the reform movement ushered in an exciting opportunity to interrogate social and legal norms that had oppressed English women for centuries. Inchbald's correspondence and journals of 1793 reveal the significance of her growing association with the movement in the early 1790s. Both Godwin and Holcroft regularly visited Inchbald at her home, where they would discuss current events, politics, and literature; on August 24, 1793, she writes that "Mr. Godwin &c called," and on September 26 she "walkd with Mr. Holcroft."[31] Godwin had emerged as a leading voice in British reform politics after publishing *An Enquiry concerning Political Justice* in 1793, and Inchbald's diary from the same year reveals her developing relationship with him. The two established the practice of reading and editing each other's writing. Inchbald read Godwin's *Political Justice* and edited a manuscript of his novel *Caleb Williams* (1794), writing, "Your first volume is far inferior to the two last. Your second is sublimely horrible—captivatingly frightful."[32] In turn, she allowed Godwin to read her manuscripts, including drafts of both of her novels, and trusted his opinion on literary matters.

Godwin encouraged Inchbald's interest in novel writing. Not only did he edit drafts of both *A Simple Story* and *Nature and Art*, but he also generally encouraged her to pursue novel writing over playwriting, saying, "It seems to me that the drama puts shackles upon you, and that the compression it requires prevents your genius from expanding itself."[33] Inchbald would later agree with Godwin's assertion that the novel provided her more creative freedom than the stage, writing in 1807, "The Novelist is a free agent. He lives in a land of liberty, whilst The Dramatic Writer exists but under a despotic government.—Passing over the subjection in which an author of plays is held by the Lord Chamberlain's office, and the degree of dependence which he has on his actors—he is the very slave of the audience."[34] Inchbald's words echo Cowley's similar complaints about the state of theatrical censorship in 1786, when she wrote that she was "encompassed with chains when I write, which check me in my happiest flights, and force me continually to reflect, not, whether this is *just*? But, whether this is *safe*?"[35] Both of Inchbald's novels contain overt political commentary, including criticism of patriarchal oppression, class prejudice, and abuse of power in the church.

While Inchbald felt that the novel allowed her more freedom than playwriting to express political and social dissent, it would be a mistake to view her theatrical work as unaffected by her participation in the reform movement. O'Quinn, Anne K. Mellor, and Amy Garnai have made significant contributions to uncovering the radical politics in Inchbald's plays.[36] Mellor observes that "implicit in Inchbald's plays is the argument that Britain is not the land of liberty that it claims to be, that its wives are prisoners, its subjects the victims of an oppressive class system that sends many honest workers to debtor's prison, and its ruling classes the slaves of dissipation and folly."[37] Indeed, Inchbald's plays were scrutinized by the press for any note of political allusion. After the debut of *Every One Has His Fault*, a review in the *True Briton* deemed the play "highly objectionable" for its exposure of poverty in London, and there was even a politically motivated riot in the Portsmouth Theatre in February 1795 when a group of military officers disrupted a performance of the play because it was perceived to be unpatriotic.[38] Inchbald responded by denying that she had a political agenda in her play, writing, "Had I been so unfortunate in my principles, or blind to my own interest, as to have written anything of the nature of which I am accused, I most certainly should not have presented it for reception to the manager of Covent Garden theatre."[39] The controversy did not appear to have a detrimental effect on the popularity of *Every One Has His Fault* and may even have stirred interest in it, as the debut run was extended to an impressive thirty-one nights.

Inchbald's pragmatic choice to obfuscate and even deny the political and social underpinnings in her plays proved an effective strategy for her professional success, but her caution has also resulted in a muddying of her political orientation by later critics.[40] The biographer James Boaden wrote in his *Memoirs of Mrs. Inchbald* (1833) that her political writings were a short-lived product of the revolutionary decade and "happily perished in the furious season that gave birth to them."[41] Likewise, S. R. Littlewood wrote in his 1921 biography that Inchbald "did not go to anything like the lengths [Godwin] demanded over the various causes in which . . . he was so courageous a pioneer."[42] Even Jenkins writes that "Mrs. Inchbald had a wide knowledge of the political scene," but "she [was] never outspoken about the government nor [did] she discuss the views of her friends who were involved."[43] Such assessments misguidedly attempt to save Inchbald from the impropriety of politics, painting her as a temporary political satellite merely orbiting more significant political figures like Godwin and Holcroft. Yet, Kelly has shown that both men actually went on to "imitate particular aspects" of *her* novels when they realized that "a novel of ideas, to be effective, had to be effective artistically, as well as philosophically."[44] Assessing

Inchbald as moderate or politically ambivalent fails to consider the significance of her plays and the nuances of her disagreement with Mary Wollstonecraft.

Enter Wollstonecraft

It was through her relationship with Godwin that Inchbald was first introduced to Wollstonecraft in 1796. The two should have been natural allies and even friends, as they shared much in common. They were roughly the same age, they published in the same period, and they were part of the same social networks. Like Inchbald, at eighteen, Wollstonecraft made the unorthodox decision to leave home and make her own way in the world. She worked variously as a lady's maid, school mistress, and governess, and traveled across Ireland, Wales, the provinces, and, later, France and Scandinavia. In 1787 she published her first book, a conduct manual advocating for women's education titled *Thoughts on the Education of Daughters*, followed by several other works, including a novel, *Mary: A Fiction* (1788).[45] In 1790, Wollstonecraft was the first writer to respond to Edmund Burke's provocative *Reflections on the Revolution in France* (1790), with her own *Vindication of the Rights of Men* (1790). When Wollstonecraft published *Rights of Woman* two years later—calling for "a revolution in female manners"—her name became closely associated with women's rights and the reform of gender norms.[46] *Rights of Woman* was quickly republished, and in the first five years after its initial publication it sold between 1,500 and 3,000 copies.[47] It was also controversial, and Wollstonecraft was subjected to numerous gendered attacks. In 1792, she was viciously satirized in Thomas Taylor's *A Vindication of the Rights of Brutes*, which mockingly compared women's rights to animal rights.

There is evidence that Inchbald had been drawn to Wollstonecraft's call for gender equality in *Rights of Woman* long before the two were introduced. When *Every One Has His Fault* debuted at Covent Garden on January 29, 1793, it was introduced with a prologue that promoted Wollstonecraft's feminist text:

> *The Rights of Women*, says a female pen,
> Are, to do every thing as well as Men.
> To think, to argue, to decide, to write,
> To talk, undoubtedly—perhaps, to fight.
> (For Females march to war, like brave Commanders
> Not in old Authors only—but in Flanders.)[48]

Though the prologue was written by the Reverend Robert Nares, not Inchbald, Green argues that Inchbald would have been consulted and may even have "participated in the process" of creation.[49] The reference to *Rights of Woman* in Inchbald's play emphasizes the way the two women were publicly linked by their shared interests. It also reveals that Inchbald had no qualms about being compared to the author of *Rights of Woman*, at least in the early part of the decade, and perhaps even saw the association as a beneficial marketing opportunity, as Cowley did when referencing Wollstonecraft in her preface to *A Day in Turkey* in 1791, which I discussed in chapter 4.[50]

By the time Inchbald and Wollstonecraft's worlds collided in 1796, they had built quite different writing careers and professional identities, the distinctions of which would come to divide them. The first recorded meeting between Inchbald and Wollstonecraft took place at a dinner party on April 22, 1796. The two women did not warm to each other. In letters to Godwin over the following months, Wollstonecraft refers to Inchbald as "Mrs. Perfection" and expresses irritation over the time Godwin spent with her.[51] However, over time, Wollstonecraft's icy references to Inchbald began to thaw. On September 4, 1796, Wollstonecraft writes fondly about a walk she took with Inchbald, writing to Godwin: "I have spent a pleasant day, *perhaps*, the pleasanter, for walking with you first, with only the family, and Mrs. Inch—We had less wit and more cordiality—and if I do not admire her more I love her better—She is a charming woman!"[52] In another letter sent to Godwin on November 18, 1796, Wollstonecraft asks him to bring her a copy of Inchbald's new play to read, and on February 3, 1797, she writes that she tried to call on Inchbald, but Inchbald was not home. These references suggest the possibility that a relationship was developing between Inchbald and Wollstonecraft independent of their shared relationship with Godwin. However, Wollstonecraft and Godwin's marriage on March 29, 1797, terminated the possibility of friendship between the two women.

The clandestine marriage, rushed when the couple discovered Mary was pregnant, had significant social repercussions. It revealed that Wollstonecraft had been lying about being married to Imlay, whose last name she had adopted to avoid the social stigma of being an unmarried mother. After Wollstonecraft and Godwin's marriage became public, two weeks after the actual event, many of Godwin and Wollstonecraft's friends—notably Inchbald, the actress Sarah Siddons, and the retired actress Frances Twiss (Siddons's sister)—distanced themselves from the couple.[53] The fact that three actresses (though Inchbald and Twiss were retired from acting by this time) were quick to make their disapproval known points to the particular scrutiny women theater professionals faced at the time. As Janet Todd writes, "Theatrical people could not afford tainted acquaintances," and this was especially true for women like Siddons, Twiss, and Inchbald, who carefully balanced their highly publicized careers with virtuous reputations.[54] Inchbald's social rejection of Wollstonecraft was first and foremost an act of preservation. Ben Robertson observes that Inchbald "kept careful watch over her reputation, in personal terms as a woman and in professional terms as an actor and writer," and Anna Lott agrees that Inchbald's immediate efforts to distance herself from the couple "demonstrate the precarious nature of her own reputation as a public, professional woman."[55] Inchbald's status as a single woman and her closeness to Godwin—the two were often seen in public together—became a major liability following his marriage to Wollstonecraft and the revelation of the latter's sexual history.

Exacerbating matters, Godwin was infamous for his call to abolish marriage after writing in *Political Justice*, "Marriage is law, and the worst of all laws."[56] As Harriet Guest observes, Godwin and Wollstonecraft's marriage was "particularly alarming to fellow radical intellectuals" because it put their ideas into practice, with implications for the larger group.[57] As a woman and a playwright, Inchbald had to be careful about the extent to which she was perceived to challenge conventional morality. While fellow playwright Thomas Holcroft stood by Godwin and Wollstonecraft following their marriage, he was in a far less precarious position than Inchbald, whose professional success relied on her personal reputation as a woman. Godwin's abandoned views on marriage help explain Inchbald's rude treatment of Wollstonecraft at the theater on April 19, 1797. It was the first time Inchbald had been seen with Godwin or Wollstonecraft since learning of the marriage, and the encounter was taking place in a crowded theater, the space most associated with Inchbald's professional identity. Godwin may have thought that the public nature of the meeting would encourage Inchbald to behave discreetly. But it had the opposite effect, as Inchbald was quick to make her feelings clear to observers with more decisiveness than may have occurred had the meeting been in private.

Any hope of reconciliation between the two women was forever lost when, only five months later, on September 10, 1797, Wollstonecraft died from complications following the birth of her and Godwin's daughter, Mary. Mere hours after Wollstonecraft's death, Godwin wrote a note to Inchbald and revisited their dispute: "My wife died at eight this morning. I always thought you used her ill, but I forgive you. You told me you did not know her."[58] Inchbald responded later that day, offering her condolences, but defending herself: "I did not *know* her—I never wished to know her—as I avoid every female acquaintance who has no husband, I avoided her—against my desire you made us acquainted—with what justice I shunned her, your present note evinces, for she judged me harshly."[59] While not a particularly compassionate note, Inchbald's letter offers two illuminating defenses for her rejection of Wollstonecraft. First, that as a woman playwright, she was especially vulnerable to attacks on her reputation and, therefore, cautious of associating with women who were perceived to be sexually dubious. She reiterates this defense more strongly in a subsequent letter to Godwin on September 14, 1797, writing, "As the short and very slight acquaintance I had with Mrs Godwin, and into which I was reluctantly impelled by you, has been productive of petty suspicious detractions, and revilings (from which my Character has been till now preserved) surely I cannot sufficiently applaud my own penetration in apprehending, and my own firmness in Resisting a Longer and more familiar acquaintance."[60] While these statements are painfully blunt, Inchbald's comments reveal that it was not Wollstonecraft's reputation alone that caused her anxiety, but Godwin's attempts to further develop the association between them. Perhaps if Godwin had allowed his friend and confidant to distance herself from the initial scandal of the marriage, she may have felt able to extend her friendship at a later time. Inchbald's second point of defense against Godwin's charge that she treated Wollstonecraft badly is that Wollstonecraft, not she, threw the first punch and "judged [her] harshly."[61] Here, Inchbald is likely referring to two negative reviews of her novels that Wollstonecraft had published in the *Analytical Review* in 1791 and 1796.[62]

Wollstonecraft's Reviews of Inchbald's Novels

Both of Inchbald's novels were generally well received by the public and critics alike, but Wollstonecraft disliked aspects of both works, and her feminist critiques reveal a philosophical discord with Inchbald. Inchbald's first novel, *A Simple Story*, reached its second edition only a few months after its initial publication in early 1791 and garnered praise from many reviewers. The novel follows the romantic relationship between Dorriforth, a Catholic priest, and Miss Milner, his ward. The two marry when Dorriforth takes up his inheritance as Lord Elmwood, but they later separate after Lady Elmwood has an affair. Lord Elmwood shuns his wife and daughter, Matilda, who is left exposed to the predatory behavior of another local lord following her mother's death. The plot is resolved by a reunion between father and daughter through his restored benevolence as patriarch and her voluntary subservience as his child. The *Gentleman's Magazine* complimented Inchbald's creativity, writing, "We do not recollect an instance of invention so happily calculated."[63] Similarly, the *Lady's Magazine* expressed total admiration for the novel, particularly its emotional authenticity: "She traces the working of a passion with justice and minuteness, places it in every *setting*, if we may use the expression, and exhibits its luster and its dimness, its brilliancy and its specks, precisely as we may observe in real life."[64] Wollstonecraft, in contrast, was highly critical of the novel's sentimental tropes.

Wollstonecraft's critique, published in the *Analytical Review* in May 1791, stands apart from others both because of its overtly feminist critique of the novel and because of its personal criticism of Inchbald, who by this time was a highly respected and admired playwright. Wollstonecraft begins by noting that *A Simple Story* has a "useful moral in view, namely, to show the advantage of a good education" for women, but argues that the novel never fully realizes its goal: "[Matilda] should have possessed greater dignity of mind. Educated in adversity she should have learned (to prove that a cultivated mind is a real advantage) how to bear, nay, rise above her misfortunes, instead of suffering her health to be undermined by the trials of her patience, which ought to have strengthened her understanding."[65] For Wollstonecraft, Matilda is guided too strongly by sentiment, rather than reason. This emphasis is problematic for Wollstonecraft because Matilda is better educated than "the vain, giddy" Miss Milner but behaves similarly.[66] The contrast between the two characters, Wollstonecraft argues, should be more obvious. Wollstonecraft then turns her criticism directly on Inchbald, accusing her of writing women characters that promote sexist impressions of women: "Why do all female writers, even when they display their abilities, always give a sanction to the libertine reveries of men? Why do they poison the minds of their own sex, by strengthening a male prejudice that makes women systematically weak? We allude to the absurd fashion that prevails of making the heroine of a novel boast of a delicate constitution; and the still more ridiculous and deleterious custom of spinning the most picturesque scenes out of fevers, swoons, and tears."[67] Wollstonecraft is particularly disturbed by the heightened emotion of women in *A Simple Story*. In the novel, such characters stifle or break into tears more than fifty times, while men are described in the same condition only twenty times. For Wollstonecraft, this gendered disparity of sentimental display promoted the idea of women's weakness—an egregious portrayal when made by a woman writer.

Wollstonecraft was seriously concerned about the influence that sentimental characters had on women readers. In *Rights of Woman*, published less than a year after her review of *A Simple Story*, Wollstonecraft argues that women, when deprived of formal education, "naturally imbibe the opinions expressed in the only kind of reading that can interest an innocent frivolous mind."[68] She further argues that unchecked sentiment is a feature of "feminine weakness" and a tool of patriarchal oppression: "Women subjected by ignorance to their sensations, and only taught to look for happiness in love, refine on sensual feelings, and adopt metaphysical notions respecting that passion, which lead them shamefully to neglect the duties of life."[69] This is not to say that Wollstonecraft was fundamentally anti-sentimental. Critics have shown that her approach to this issue was complicated.[70] Rather, she drew a distinction between the ability to sympathize within reason and what she perceived as artificial displays of sentiment. For Wollstonecraft, the portrayal of women with "false sentiments and over-stretched Feelings" was not merely a product of poor writing but an attack on women's equal ability to exercise rational thought, a theme Wollstonecraft explored in her own novels, *Mary: A Fiction* and *Maria: or, The Wrongs of Women*, both of which are critical of sentimental tropes and feature heroines who seek fulfillment beyond marriage.[71]

It is worth noting that other women writers of feminist inclination did not share Wollstonecraft's disdain of sentimentalism in *A Simple Story*. The novel appeared in volume 28 of Anna Laetitia Barbauld's *The British Novelists* (1810), in which Barbauld praises Inchbald's "strokes of pathos."[72] Around 1816, the playwright Joanna Baillie borrowed a copy of Barbauld's edition of *A Simple Story* and deemed Inchbald's writing "original, well-imagined & skillfull."[73] At Inchbald's request, Baillie delayed reading Barbauld's exultant preface of the novel until she had "read thro' the book."[74]

Wollstonecraft took a slightly more positive view of Inchbald's second novel, *Nature and Art*, published in May 1796, deeming it to be "more philosophical."[75] *Nature and Art* follows two brothers, William and Henry, who fall out when William advances in London society and Henry does not. Their two sons, also named William and Henry, are models of their fathers: William is socially successful but morally bankrupt, while Henry, raised away from English society in a remote area of Africa, has a kind and generous spirit. As in *A Simple Story*, two women become the focus of sentiment in the novel. Rebecca is a righteous woman who sacrifices her reputation, but not her virtue, to protect an illegitimate child, while Hannah is seduced by young William and suffers as a social outcast after becoming pregnant. Initially, Wollstonecraft praised the novel for its intellectual quality, but she also adds bitingly that it does not have enough "lively interest to keep the attention awake."[76] As in her criticism of Matilda in *A Simple Story*, Wollstonecraft takes issue with the fact that Rebecca is an educated woman who martyrs herself to feminine virtue: "The making a young modest woman, with some powers of mind, acknowledge herself the mother of a child that she humanely fostered, in the presence of the man she loved, is also highly improbable, not to say unnatural."[77] She is similarly critical of the sensational progress of Hannah's character. In the latter half of the novel, Hannah is forced to turn to sex work and theft as her only means of survival. In a melodramatic turn of events, Hannah is then arrested and sentenced to death by young William, now a magistrate, who no longer recognizes the woman he seduced years earlier. Inchbald's sympathetic treatment of Hannah, a woman who has sexual relationships outside of marriage, was controversial for the time. Possibly in response to accusations of impropriety, Inchbald later excised a number of passages related to Hannah and William's illegitimate child in the second edition of the novel released in 1797.[78] Wollstonecraft, whose posthumously published novel *The Wrongs of Woman* took a similarly sympathetic approach to the character of a sex worker, was concerned not with Inchbald's portrayal of Hannah's sexual behavior, but rather with the melodramatic occurrences of her plotline: "The story of Hannah Primrose we found particularly affecting: the catastrophe giving point to a benevolent system of morality. The transitions, however, from one period of the history to another, are too abrupt; for the incidents, not being shaded into each other, sometimes appear improbable. This we think the principal defect of the work as a whole."[79] Though Wollstonecraft approves of *Nature and Art* more than *A Simple Story*, she remains frustrated that women are portrayed in sensational circumstances and lack agency.

When Wollstonecraft published her review of *A Simple Story* in May 1791, Inchbald would not have known who wrote it. Articles for the *Analytical Review* were published under the authors' initials only, and Wollstonecraft published this review under the initial "M."[80] This anonymity explains why Inchbald had no qualms about allowing a reference to Wollstonecraft to appear in the prologue to *Every One Has His Fault* in 1793. However, by the time that Inchbald and Wollstonecraft were introduced in April 1796, Inchbald likely would have known that "M," who had recently published a lukewarm review of *Nature and Art*, and a scorching review of *A Simple Story* years earlier, stood for Mary Wollstonecraft. Not only was Wollstonecraft now a famous feminist author with a distinct critical voice, she and Inchbald were also part of the same social circle. Todd argues that when Inchbald met Wollstonecraft, she "probably remembered the mocking review of [*A Simple Story*] as insipid and pandering to male prejudice ... and she could not have relished the recent review of her new work, *Nature and Art*, which damned her with faint praise."[81] Lott concurs, writing that Wollstonecraft's reviews contributed to "Inchbald's dislike for her."[82] Of course, Inchbald was not the only sentimental novelist that Wollstonecraft strongly critiqued in the *Analytical Review*: she deemed Charlotte Lennox's women in *Euphemia* "very affected" and "*ridiculously* squeamish," and criticized the "preposterous sentiments" of Charlotte Smith's *Emmeline, the Orphan of the Castle*.[83] Wollstonecraft's criticism of Inchbald, however, was especially severe, and Inchbald, who foregrounded women and their experiences in her novels, was likely deeply offended by the charges laid against her. Regrettably, Wollstonecraft's premature death in 1797 eliminated any possibility of further debate between the two women or the chance for Inchbald to defend her characters and sentimental strategies.

Lovers' Vows: *Sentimental Comedy and Feminism*

For Inchbald, whose theatrical oeuvre was made up of sentimental comedies, displays of emotion were a necessary tool of her professional success. She wrote that playwrights must appeal to the audience's "habits, passions, and prejudices, as the only means to gain this sudden conquest of their minds and hearts."[84] Though Inchbald never confronted Wollstonecraft about the criticism of her novels, her next play, which followed Wollstonecraft's death, offers a striking reclamation of an unwed mother and a positive depiction of women's sexuality. I suggest that Inchbald's *Lovers' Vows*, an adaptation of Kotzebue's *Das Kind der Liebe*, can be read as a response to Wollstonecraft's criticism of her novels, a rebuttal to Godwin's accusations that she mistreated Wollstonecraft out of bigotry, and a model of her own feminist strategies, grounded in the affective bonds of sentiment. *Lovers' Vows*, first performed at Covent Garden on October 11, 1798, was one of Inchbald's most successful plays. It ran for forty-two consecutive nights in its first season, well above Inchbald's average debut, and was positively reviewed by critics. The *London Chronicle* deemed the play "unquestionably the most interesting and best Performance the stage has for many years witnessed," though the reviewer also expresses some discomfort over the depiction of "pardon[ing]" an unwed mother."[85]

The plot of *Lovers' Vows* follows Agatha Friburg, who was seduced and became pregnant in her youth by a local baron. Abandoned by the Baron and his family, Agatha raises her son Frederick with the help of a kind local chaplain. However, after the chaplain's death, Agatha is rejected by the community, and the play opens with her suffering from starvation and illness. The local landlord of a nearby inn will not help her, and her death seems imminent when her son unexpectedly arrives, returned from the military to retrieve his certificate of birth. Consequently, Agatha is forced to reveal the truth that he is the illegitimate son of Baron Wildenhaim. Horrified by his mother's suffering but penniless himself, Fredrick begs on the streets for money to help her. In a twist of fate, he comes across the Baron, recently returned from Alsace with his only daughter after the death of his noble wife. When the Baron offers only a nominal sum to help, Frederick tries to rob him at knifepoint. The Baron quickly arrests Fredrick and sentences him to death. Only then does Frederick realize that he almost killed his own father. The subplot of *Lovers' Vows* focuses on the Baron's young daughter Amelia who is being courted by Count Cassel, a rich but superficial nobleman. Amelia is actually in love with her tutor and chaplain, Anhalt. Anhalt explains to Amelia that a marriage between them is impossible due to her noble birth. Later, once Frederick's true relation to the Baron is revealed, Anhalt encourages the Baron to marry Agatha and make his son legitimate. The Baron agrees, and, grateful for Anhalt's good counsel, he consents to the marriage between Anhalt and Amelia.

Adapting Kotzebue's *Das Kind der Liebe*, rather than writing an original play, offered Inchbald a chance to explore controversial themes while distancing herself from them personally. While English adaptations of Kotzebue's plays were popular and likely to succeed commercially—between 1796 and 1802, twenty of his plays were translated from German and staged in England—they were also known for their risqué content.[86] For example, when Richard Brinsley Sheridan's *The Stranger* (1798), another Kotzebue adaptation, achieved great commercial success, the *Anti-Jacobin Review* wrote, scathingly, "Kotzebue's Stranger holds out falsehood and promotes immorality."[87] Interestingly, the review places blame primarily on the original playwright, Kotzebue, rather than the adaptor, Sheridan. Similarly, adaptation provided Inchbald with, as Moody describes, a "strategic form of theatrical disguise," allowing her to obscure her own personal and political views behind those of the original author.[88] John Loftis argues that Inchbald was likely particularly drawn to Kotzebue's plays because they offered her a chance to portray "social and even sexual themes that English conservatism had kept off the stage for generations."[89] In the preface to *Lovers' Vows*, Inchbald excuses her own authorial interventions as mere stylistic improvements, writing, "It would appear like affectation to offer an apology for any scenes or passages omitted or added, in this play, different from the original: its reception has given me confidence to suppose what I have done is right; for Kotzebue's 'Child of Love' in Germany, was never more attractive than 'Lovers' Vows' has been in England."[90] According to her own preface, Inchbald was given a rough, literal translation of the original play that necessitated many alterations and allowed her to transform the work to suit her own taste and style. While Christoph Bode criticizes Inchbald's adaptation as a "de-politicized" version of Kotzebue's original, her changes, in fact, were not purely reductive.[91] Inchbald does dismantle some of Kotzebue's political commentary, including references to Revolutionary France (likely cut to ensure her play would pass English censorship laws), but she also expands the play's treatment of women's sexuality and its criticism of gender inequality, as I will discuss below.[92] In a testament to the disruptive treatment of gender and sexuality in the play, Jane Austen later incorporated a scene featuring *Lovers' Vows* in her novel *Mansfield Park* (1814), when the Bertram family attempts to stage Inchbald's play, to the horror of the family patriarch and embarrassment of the heroine, Fanny.[93]

As in her novels, in *Lovers' Vows* Inchbald once again places two sentimental characters, Agatha and Amelia, at the center of the story—with one new twist. In her novels, the sexually compromised women, Miss Milner (later Lady Elmwood) and Hannah Primrose, die—a conventional resolution for fallen women in sentimental novels that functions to affirm Christian morality and unburden the plot of an inconvenient character. *Lovers' Vows* offers a striking alternative to this convention when Agatha, an unwed mother, does not die and throughout the course of the play is absolved of guilt and reintegrated back into the community. Amelia, on the other hand, is a young woman filled with desire for a man who is of a lower class, and she successfully negotiates her marriage to him. *Lovers' Vows* manages these unconventional narratives by relying on heightened displays of emotion, rather than action, to maintain narrative suspense. The play contains some moments of action—for example, when the landlord throws Agatha out onto the street, or when Frederick attempts to stab the Baron—but for the most part, the play foregrounds the emotional bonds between mother and son, father and daughter, husband and wife.

In adapting the role of Amelia, Inchbald made some of her most significant deviations from Kotzebue's *Das Kind der Liebe*. Kotzebue's character is a simple ingenue, but Inchbald transforms Amelia into a complex character infused with wit, sexual desire, and strength. Inchbald defends her alterations in her preface to the play: "The part of Amelia has been a very particular object of my solicitude and alteration: the same situations which the author gave her remain, but almost all the dialogue of the character I have changed."[94] Though she insists that her alterations merely make Amelia more suited to English taste, in actuality, Inchbald's changes do more. Inchbald rejects Kotzebue's depiction of Amelia's sexual desire as naïve and instead imbibes her with a confident understanding of her own desire and the will to pursue its fulfillment. Because of his own unhappy marriage, the Baron is insistent that his daughter Amelia marry someone with whom she is romantically compatible. He hopes that this will be Count Cassel:

> BARON. Amelia, you know you have a father who loves you, and I believe you know you have a suitor who is come to ask permission to love you. Tell me candidly how you like Count Cassel?
> AMELIA. Very well.
> BARON. Do not you blush when I talk of him?

AMELIA. No.

BARON. No. [*Aside*] I am sorry for that. [*To her*] Have you dreamt of him?

AMELIA. No. . . .

BARON. But do you not feel a little fluttered when he is talked of?

AMELIA. [*Shaking her head*] No.

BARON. Don't you wish sometimes to speak to him, and have not the courage to begin?

AMELIA. No.

BARON. Do not you wish to take his part when his companions laugh at him?

AMELIA. No, I love to laugh at him myself.[95]

Instead, Amelia loves Anhalt, and not the rich count that her father has chosen for her. The Baron assumes that Amelia does not understand love, and in act 3, scene 2, he enlists Anhalt to try and discover if Amelia is in love with the count. Amelia is quick to turn the interrogation on Anhalt and express her desire for him:

AMELIA. What is the subject?

ANHALT. Love.

AMELIA. (*Going up to him*) Come, then, teach it me. Teach it me as you taught me geography, languages and other important things.

ANHALT. (*Turning from her*) Pshaw!

AMELIA. Ah! You won't. You know you have already taught me that, and you won't begin again.[96]

The eighteenth-century translator Anne Plumptre, who published the first complete English translation of *Das Kind der Liebe*, was so horrified by Inchbald's amorous portrayal of Amelia that she wrote, "Amelia in *Lovers' Vows*, so far from being the artless innocent Child of Nature, drawn by Kotzebue, appears a forward Country Hoyden, who deviates in many Instances from the established Usages of Society, and the Decorums of her Sex, in a manner wholly unwarranted by the Original."[97] Paula Byrne confirms that Inchbald's depiction of Amelia was salacious for the period, writing that Inchbald takes "a huge leap in notions of female propriety" by "tak[ing] up the cause of a woman's right to court."[98] By emphasizing Amelia's desire for Anhalt and her practical efforts to achieve his love, Inchbald shows women's desire to be both natural and morally good. Thus, Inchbald counters the fallen woman trope in Agatha's plotline with a positive display of sexual desire in Amelia's.

Though Agatha's narrative is one of improper sexual activity outside of marriage, Inchbald is careful not to suggest that her sexual desire is unnatural. When Agatha first reveals to her son, Frederick, that he is the illegitimate son of Baron Wildenhaim in the first scene of the play, she is explicit that she was not forced by the Baron, but motivated by desire and promises of love: "He was a handsome young man—in my eyes a prodigy, for he talked of love, and promised me marriage. He was the first man who had ever spoken to me on such a subject. . . . I was intoxicated by the fervent caresses of a young, inexperienced, capricious man, and did not recover from the delirium till it was too late."[99] Frederick expresses sympathy toward his mother and orients blame on the Baron's broken promises, not Agatha's sexual transgression, exclaiming, "He is a villain!"[100] After the Baron and Frederick are reunited, the Baron proposes that his son become his rightful heir, but Frederick refuses to be separated legally from his mother: "My fate, whatever it may be, shall never part me from her. This is my firm resolution, upon which I call Heaven to witness! My Lord, it must be Frederick of Wildenhaim, and Agatha of Wildenhaim—or Agatha Friburg, and Frederick Friburg."[101] Because of his love for his mother, Frederick insists that her legal identity be restored through marriage.

After the Baron agrees to marry Agatha, Anhalt further insists that the marriage be attended by the entire community, reinstating Agatha's social standing:

> BARON. Where is she?
> ANHALT. In the castle—in my apartments here—I conducted her through the garden, to avoid curiosity.
> BARON. Well, then, this is the wedding-day. This very evening you shall give us your blessing.
> ANHALT. Not so soon, not so private. The whole village was witness of Agatha's shame—the whole village must be witness of Agatha's re-established honour. Do you consent to this?
> BARON. I do.[102]

Though the play ends with a conventional marriage plotline, Anhalt's insistence that the marriage be treated as an act of community reconciliation and public redemption for Agatha adds a radical quality to the resolution. Here, Inchbald pushes the generic bounds of sentimental comedy, proposing that the reintegration of sexually compromised women and illegitimate children into society is both possible and admirable.

In 1808, Inchbald wrote a new set of remarks for *Lovers' Vows* for a series of plays titled *The British Theatre*.[103] Her preface reiterates her call for compassion to be directed toward unmarried mothers and their children:

> The grand moral of this play is to set forth the miserable consequences which arise from the neglect, and to enforce the watchful care, of illegitimate offspring; and, surely, as the pulpit has not had eloquence to eradicate the crimes of seduction, the stage may be allowed an humble endeavour to prevent its most fatal effects. But there are some pious declaimers against theatrical exhibitions; so zealous to do good, they grudge the poor dramatist his share in the virtuous concern.... Those critics arraign its catastrophe, and say—"the wicked should be punished"—they forget there is a punishment called *conscience*, which, though it seldom troubles the defamer's peace, may weigh heavy on the fallen female and her libertine seducer.[104]

Inchbald argues that it is not society's place to punish women for their perceived sexual wrongdoings, but, rather, it should care for the vulnerable and leave judgement to the individual's conscience. The frontispiece appended to the play (see figure 5.4) emphasizes Inchbald's message that

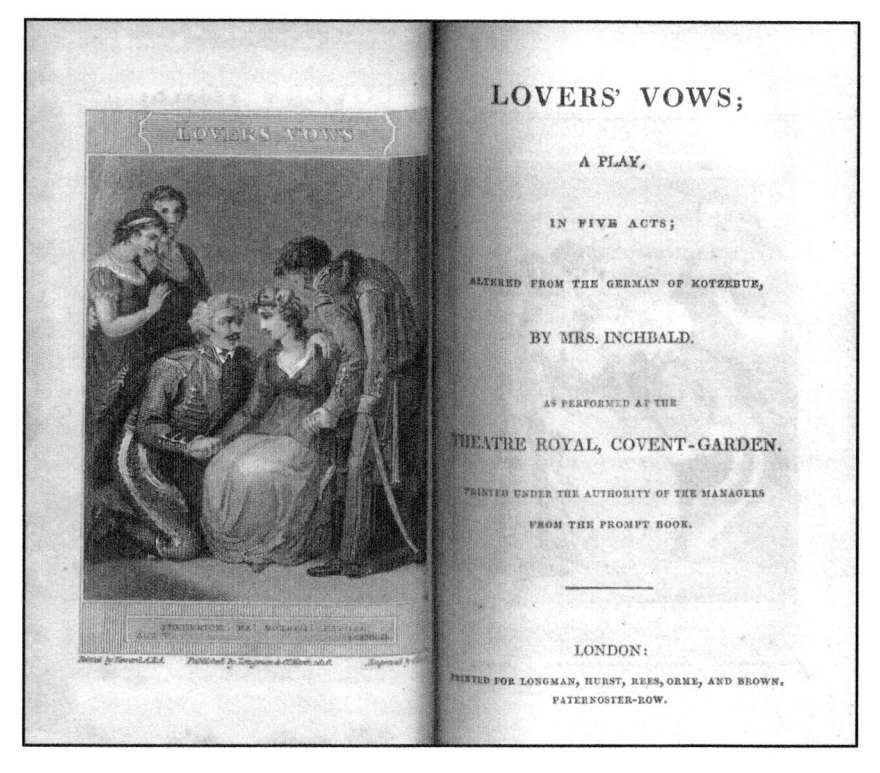

Figure 5.4. Frontispiece of *Lovers' Vows*, in *The British Theatre*, vol. 23 (London: Longman, Hurst, Rees, and Orme, 1808), The British Library.

sentiment is key to reconciliation and to alleviating women's suffering. Agatha is seated at the center of the scene, with the Baron kneeling beside her and holding her hand. Frederick stands over his mother, gripping her other hand. In the background, Anhalt stands with his arm around Amelia as she rests her hand on his chest. The caption beneath the frontispiece is a line of Frederick's from act 5: "Ha! Mother! Father."[105] Frederick's exclamation emphasizes the highly affective nature of the scene and the play and tethers this emotional outburst to the family's restoration.

So unusual was Inchbald's sympathetic treatment of a fallen woman in *Lovers' Vows* that her friend, the actress Mary Wells, believed that Inchbald must have based the character of Agatha on her. In her memoirs, Wells writes, "In [Inchbald's] play of *Lovers' Vows* she alludes to my children, where Frederick says to his mother, 'Cursed be that child who could find his mother guilty, though all the world should call her so.'"[106] While there is no clear evidence that Inchbald did base the character of Agatha specifically on Wells, her sympathetic portrayal of a woman's sexual activity outside of marriage may very well have been informed by this relationship and others. Inchbald's sister Debby, for instance, was a sex worker in London, and though Inchbald was estranged from her, she supported her financially until her death in 1794 and later expressed regret for rejecting her.[107] Consistent with her treatment of Wollstonecraft, Inchbald distanced herself from women she cared about when their reputations threatened her livelihood. This behavior is not necessarily evidence of Inchbald's bigotry, but rather her pragmatic response to society's strictures on women's sexuality. Inchbald's literary and theatrical works, in turn, reveal a fierce advocacy for women.

By the end of the eighteenth century, Inchbald had accumulated widespread acclaim in a profession that was dominated by men. Her two novels remained in high regard, and nearly all of her plays were published, many in multiple editions for publishers in England, Ireland, and America. Most of the plays had successful runs of ten or more performances, and some were revived for decades. Following the completion of her final play, *To Marry or Not to Marry* (1805), Inchbald was commissioned by the publisher Thomas Norton Longman and his partners to write introductory remarks to 125 plays for *The British Theatre* series. The collection was initially released serially over a span of two years before being published in a twenty-five-volume edition in 1808. Inchbald's remarks denote the most substantial theatrical criticism—widely considered a masculine genre requiring a classical education—ever to be written by a woman, and the commercial success of the collection confirmed her reputation as England's pre-eminent woman dramatist and judge of theatrical taste.[108] As Lisa Freeman explains, the remarks are particularly notable for their focus on stagecraft and theatrical production, further revealing Inchbald's mastery of the playhouse and live performance.[109]

Five of Inchbald's own plays appear in the twenty-third volume of the collection, making her one of the most represented playwrights in the series, behind only Shakespeare and George Colman the Younger—eight of whose plays appear—and tied with Richard Cumberland. In a testament to Inchbald's uncontested standing as England's top woman playwright, besides her five plays, only six other plays by three other women appear in the collection: three by Susanna Centlivre, two by Hannah Cowley, and one by Joanna Baillie. Inchbald's comments on the plays of these women are generally positive; she makes a point of praising Centlivre's contributions to the profession and deems Baillie's *De Monfort* "a work of genius."[110]

The commercial success of the *The British Theatre* instigated the jealousy of a rival playwright, George Colman the Younger, who wrote a letter to Inchbald's publisher that mocked her unlearned and unfeminine venture into the masculine tradition of literary criticism. In the letter, he takes issue with Inchbald's perceived ingratitude toward his father, George Colman the Elder, and rejects her analysis—largely complimentary—of his own plays. Inchbald, warned of Colman's displeasure from her publisher, carefully prepared a written response over a period of weeks.[111] She did not respond to his insulting attack with matching vitriol; instead, she adopted a sarcastic tone, apologizing for the mere "cursory remarks of a female" and thereby mocking Colman's arrogance, sexism, and temper.[112] Both letters were published in *The British Theatre* alongside Colman's play *The Heir at Law* (1797), with Inchbald bitingly noting that "*taste* seems wanting" in his play."[113]

In the final decade of her life, Inchbald continued to be an engaged member of London's literary community and a trusted advocate and role model for professional women writers, especially those with a feminist bent. She wrote a number of essays on literary matters for the periodical *The Artist*, stating in one that the novelists Maria Edgeworth and Anne Radcliffe could not be equaled.[114] She befriended Edgeworth personally, and in 1814 she read and edited a manuscript copy of the young novelist's *Patronage*, providing detailed criticism of the novel and sending corrections to the publisher.[115] Inchbald remained close friends with Amelia Alderson, through whom she was introduced to the French author, political theorist, and Napoleon critic Anne Louise Germaine de Staël in 1813.

By 1800, London was the largest city in the world, and the population continued to grow exponentially over the coming decades.[116] New "illegitimate" theater venues appeared throughout the city to meet the demand of this growing and diverse public.[117] The patent theaters legally monopolized spoken drama, and the so-called minor theaters, including the Lyceum, the Royal Circus, Astley's Royal Amphitheatre, and Sadler's Wells, specialized in providing music, melodrama, spectacle, pantomime, and even animal entertainments. As these new venues became more popular, Parliament, the press, and the public anxiously discussed the state of the theater and the apparent decline of the previous century's key genres, tragedy and comedy. For women, the new abundance of genres and venues eroded a system, however flawed, within which they had carved space for themselves. But the new century also created fresh opportunities for women.

In the face of major change, women playwrights did not disappear from the London theater, as has sometimes been suggested by theater historians; instead, as Katherine Newey argues, they thrived in new and varied ways, seizing the chance to test new genres and modes of performance.[118] At least ninety women playwrights were active in the theaters between the late 1770s and the 1830s, including many notable examples of women who flourished in the first decades of the nineteenth century.[119] The actress Marie Thérèse du Camp, wife of Charles Kemble and mother of Fanny Kemble, followed in Clive's footsteps by writing comedies for her and her husband's benefit performances through 1815; the prolific Jane M. Scott wrote more than fifty theatrical entertainments for her and her father's Sans Pareil Theatre, founded in 1806 (later renamed the Adelphi); and, though she struggled to have her plays produced, Joanna Baillie was widely considered to be England's greatest living playwright. Building on the gains made in the late eighteenth century, the next century saw a new era of experimentation, adaptation, and survival for women playwrights.

Conclusion

Feminist Comedy 250 Years Later

At the 2013 Edinburgh Fringe Festival, the English comedy writer and performer Phoebe Waller-Bridge staged a ten-minute, one-woman comedy act titled *Fleabag* about a disenchanted bisexual woman in her early thirties living and working in London. The performance was an unexpected hit, receiving a Fringe First Award and later forming the basis of a highly celebrated BBC series of the same name, which launched Waller-Bridge into comedy stardom. Her writing and performance in the series garnered a BAFTA, three Emmy Awards, and two Golden Globe Awards. Though transformed from stage to screen, the theatrical origins of *Fleabag* remain present in the television series, as the protagonist, known only as Fleabag, regularly breaks the fourth wall and comments directly to the audience. In season 2, episode 2, for example, Fleabag's therapist asks why her father has insisted she seek help, and she responds drolly, "Um, I think because my mother died and he can't talk about it, and my sister and I didn't speak for a year because she thinks I slept with her husband, and because I spent most of my adult life using sex to deflect from the screaming void inside my empty heart."[1] In a moment reminiscent of eighteenth-century direct address in prologues, epilogues, and asides, Waller-Bridge then turns directly to the camera, as depicted in figure C.1, and, grinning broadly, exclaims, "I'm good at this!"[2] Waller-Bridge's sarcastic, metatheatrical style helps build her character's connection with the audience, inviting women in particular to laugh with her about the familiar realities of being a twenty-first-century woman navigating sex, death, and family.

Fleabag is a self-declared feminist, but not a flawless one. She muses awkwardly at a Quaker meeting in season 2, episode 4, "I sometimes worry that I wouldn't be such a feminist if I had bigger tits."[3] Feminist imperfection, as I have explored in the various case studies of this book, is a common feature of feminist humor. In fact, many of the comic techniques that Waller-Bridge deploys in *Fleabag* derive from trends in eighteenth-century women's comedies that can be found in the works of the women writers explored in the previous chapters. Like Frances Burney, Waller-Bridge centers working women's experiences and relationships with one another.

Figure C.1. Phoebe Waller-Bridge in *Fleabag*, screen grab, BBC Three, 2019.

Like Frances Brooke, she mocks men—from her sister's patronizing husband to her own various sexual partners—for their patriarchal and misogynist attitudes and actions. Like Elizabeth Inchbald, she creates female characters motivated by sexual desire who push the boundaries of socially acceptable sexual behavior for women. Like Hannah Cowley, she writes women characters who are intelligent, theatrical, and manipulative. Like Catherine Clive, her protagonist is semi-autobiographical and relies on self-deprecating humor to connect with her audience. In an appearance on *Saturday Night Live* in 2019, Waller-Bridge joked that "people often assume that I am like the character, Fleabag, simply because I wrote it—sexually depraved, foulmouthed, and dangerous—and I always have to say to them, yes, you're absolutely right."[4]

Notably, *Fleabag* is not the only feminist comedy series to share in these techniques and garner widespread popularity in recent years. Issa Rae's award-winning HBO series *Insecure* (2016–21), inspired by Rae's comedy web series *Awkward Black Girl* (2011–12), is based on the creator's experiences as a young, Black American woman living in Los Angeles. The protagonist Issa (played by Rae) and various friends navigate the intersecting barriers of sexism and racism in their daily lives. The season 2 premiere of *Insecure* deals with the issue of wage discrepancy between men and women, when Molly learns that her white, male co-worker earns significantly more money than she does.[5] Later that night, Molly vents to her girlfriends Issa, Kelli (Natasha Rothwell), and Tiffany (Amanda Seales): "I can't just roll up to the partners and be like, 'Hey guys, so I accidently noticed that you pay this white man more than me.'"[6] Her friends respond with immediate understanding and sympathy. "That's why I make sure my white clients get less on

CONCLUSION

Figure C.2. Issa Rae, Yvonne Orji, Amanda Seales, and Natasha Rothwell in *Insecure,* screen grab, HBO, 2017.

their tax returns," quips Kelli; "It's reparations."[7] This scene, depicted in figure C.2, not only tackles a major issue of feminist concern, the gender pay gap, but also illuminates the nuanced experiences of Black women not regularly displayed on television, and certainly not represented on eighteenth-century English stages. It was not until the nineteenth century that Black women writers and performers were allowed to access English stages, and they continue to face the intersecting barriers of sexism and racism—something that Rae highlights through her intersectional feminist humor.

Similarly, the comic duo Ilana Glazer and Abbi Jacobson created *Broad City* (2014–19), based on their own lives as Jewish American millennial women living in New York. The series depicts Ilana and Abbi on various feminist adventures, from campaigning for Hillary Clinton to volunteering at an abortion clinic, while regularly acknowledging their Jewish identities. In the finale of season 3, Abbi gets her period while on board a plane to visit Israel on a heritage trip, but she forgot to pack a tampon in her carry-on luggage. Ilana suggests that she "woman up" and use some toilet paper from the bathroom instead.[8] Abbi explains to Ilana that the situation is more urgent, in a series of graphic similes that hold insider humor for those who menstruate:

> ABBI. Dude, it's the first day.
> ILANA. Oof, first day. That's like putting your spoon into a molten lava cake.
> ABBI. It's like the first bite of a jelly doughnut.

Figure C.3. Ilana Glazer and Abbi Jacobson in *Broad City*, screen grab, HBO, 2016.

> ILANA. It's like a side of chutney.
> ABBI. It's like fruit on the bottom.
> ILANA. That's you right now.[9]

After asking nearly all the other travelers on the plane if they have a tampon, without success, Ilana eventually rolls up a pita and offers it to a horrified Abbi, as a young Hasidic boy walks by (see figure C.3). Translating her experience into one of women's right to menstrual health and hygiene, Abbi declares, "Every woman should have access to tampons, all different sizes."[10]

As the previous examples demonstrate, much has changed socially, culturally, and politically for women since the eighteenth century, particularly with regard to the diversity of women permitted to access the stage and the range of topics they can discuss. Still, reverberations of eighteenth-century women's comedy can be seen in the modern feminist comedy of today. The first generation of women to make careers writing comedy for mass public delivery had to navigate an industry without precedent for women's participation. In the introduction, I described how these early women playwrights turned to stage comedy as a lucrative professional opportunity and to raise awareness of gender inequality and patriarchal oppression. They cemented a distinct comic tradition that relied on women's grit, resilience, and ambition, the overt resistance of gender inequality, and the creation of comedy that centralized women and their concerns.

The survival of women's comedy in the second half of the mid-eighteenth century and beyond owes a great debt to Clive, who, I argued in chapter 1, played a crucial role in instigating a renaissance of women playwrights of comedy. Through her four comic afterpieces, Clive successfully reclaimed space for herself and other women by demonstrating that women's comedy remained entertaining and marketable. Brooke's comic operas, *Rosina* and *Marian*, staged in 1782 and 1788, proved the marketability of women's comedies, as both became smash hits and *Rosina* in particular was staged consistently for over a century. Throughout their careers, both Clive and Brooke faced serious gender discrimination from within the theater industry, but my study of Burney's comic playwriting in chapter 3 reminds us that women also faced major social barriers in writing comedy as well, largely stemming from the genre's association with masculinity. Cowley also faced accusations of unfeminine behavior throughout her comedy career, and she fought back through her prefaces, letters to the press, and biting satirical plays. Inchbald, the most celebrated woman dramatist of the late eighteenth century, adopted a different strategy and devoted much of her career to crafting a reputation of feminine decorum, going so far as to shun women whom she felt threatened her standing. Using that status, Inchbald leveraged the popular genre of sentimental comedy to make biting critiques of her society's anti-woman beliefs and successfully established a reputation as London's foremost comic playwright.

Two hundred years after Inchbald's death in 1821, the comic stage continues to be a powerful platform for feminist content and activism. Ali Wong, one of the best-known woman stand-up comedians today, became famous when she performed a Netflix special, *Baby Cobra* (2016), while seven and a half months pregnant (see figure C.4). In her set, Wong juxtaposes her pregnant body with brash, lewd, and obscenity-laced jokes that conflict humorously with the gendered expectations that mothers are nurturing, happy, and fulfilled, and that Asian women are submissive and reserved. She also confronts the fact that male comedians with children are rewarded by the industry, while women are punished:

> It's very rare and unusual to see a female comic perform pregnant, because female comics don't get pregnant. Just try to think of one. I dare you. There's none of them. Once they do get pregnant, they generally disappear. That's not the case with male comics. Once they have a baby, they'll get up on stage a week afterwards and they'll be like, "Guys, I just had this fucking baby. That baby's a little piece of shit. It's so annoying and boring." And all these other shitty dads in the audience are, like, "That's hilarious. I identify." And their fame just swells because they become this relatable family funny man all of a sudden. Meanwhile, the mom is at home, chapping her nipples, feeding the fucking baby, and wearing a frozen diaper 'cause her pussy needs to heal from the baby's head shredding it up. She's busy.[11]

Figure C.4. Ali Wong in *Hard Knock Wife*, screen grab, Netflix, 2018.

Wong explains that it is unprecedented for women to perform stand-up while pregnant. In the 1960s, Joan Rivers was forbidden by producers from mentioning her obvious pregnancy on *The Ed Sullivan Show*.[12] Wong choosing to perform while pregnant is an act of feminist resistance to this sexist industry standard. In 2018, in her second Netflix special, *Hard Knock Wife*, she again performed visibly pregnant. Once more, she shares an unapologetically blunt perspective on domestic life, telling audiences, "I tried being a stay-at-home mom, for eight weeks. I like the stay-at-home part. Not too crazy about the mom aspect. That shit is relentless."[13] Wong's choice to do two tours and shoot specials while pregnant has paved the way for other women comics to do the same; in 2019, Amy Schumer filmed her Netflix special *Growing* during her second trimester.

While eighteenth-century women playwrights had to be extremely cautious about the topics they publicly explored, especially topics related to their bodies and sexuality, feminist comedy today directly addresses women's experiences that are considered indelicate or private. In her stand-up routines and TV show *One Mississippi* (2015–17), Tig Notaro explores her battle with breast cancer. Days after being diagnosed in 2012, Notaro performed a set in Los Angeles where she shared her news. "Good evening. Hello," Tig welcomed the audience in her famous deadpan voice, "I have cancer. How are you?"[14] Continuing, Tig mused, "It's weird because with humor the equation is tragedy plus time equals comedy. I am just at tragedy right now."[15] Notaro's deeply personal and confessional comedy resonated with audiences and launched her comedy career to new heights. She went on to headline shows, starred in an HBO special, and in 2015, released a documentary about fighting cancer and her efforts to become pregnant with her fiancée. Notaro is not the only queer feminist comedian weaving into her routines gendered subject matter previously considered taboo. Nonbinary comedian Hannah Gadsby's groundbreaking stand-up special *Nanette*, discussed briefly in chapter 4, made waves in 2018 for the comedian's deeply intimate discussion of surviving gender and sexual violence.

Notably, in response to one of the most pressing and politicized issues facing women today, the rollback of reproductive rights around the globe, many feminists are turning to comedy to push back. Sarah Silverman, a household name in contemporary comedy, regularly uses her popular podcast to confront the issue of reproductive healthcare access and the criminalization of women's and gender-diverse people's bodies.[16] She is not alone. Following the 2022 overturning of *Roe v. Wade*, Alison Leiby toured her one-woman comedy show *Oh God, a Show about Abortion*, in which she discusses her own abortion experience with lighthearted banter: "Yoga pants? Just call them abortion pants."[17] Similarly, the critically acclaimed musical *The Appointment*, first staged in New York in 2019 and produced again in 2023 in the post-*Roe* era, features dancing fetuses performing outrageous chorus numbers as the main character, Louise, is shepherded through the absurd bureaucratic complexities of getting an abortion.[18] Both *A Show about Abortion* and *The Appointment* resist the politicized trauma narratives about abortion and normalize the procedure through relatable humor. All the while, the performances are fueled by an unapologetic demand for bodily autonomy and agency.

In the final pages of this book, by no means do I claim to have fully represented the rich, vibrant, and diverse landscape of feminist comedy and the topics that drive it in our current moment, but by drawing on a handful of examples, I hope to have shown that there are noteworthy connections between feminist comedies of the past and the present day. Modern feminist comedians, like those of the eighteenth century, create comedy that is innovative, bold, relatable, and powerful, and that consistently advances women's liberation from patriarchy. At the heart of *Feminist Comedy* is a desire to raise awareness of a lineage of women writing stage comedy and to reclaim comedy as a key genre of feminist discourse and distribution since the eighteenth century that is worthy of scholarly scrutiny. Further stores of feminist knowledge, creativity, and practice are waiting to be recovered in the vast archive of women's comedy.

Appendix

Women's Plays Staged in London's Patent Theaters, 1750–1800

Table A.1 provides a foundation for further research on the renaissance of women's comedy in the second half of the eighteenth century. Categorizing eighteenth-century comedy is a tricky venture, as comedic genres and forms varied widely at this time. Here, "mainpiece" refers to a full-length play and "afterpiece" refers to a shorter piece—including burlesque, farce, pantomime, interludes, or musical and dance numbers—performed after the mainpiece and meant to provide lighthearted, often humorous, entertainment. Comic opera, or musical comedy, is a particularly nebulous category that involves plays of varied lengths that feature prominent musical numbers. For example, I have chosen to identify Cowley's *A Day in Turkey* as a comic mainpiece. Still, with its significant musical and dance numbers, it could also be categorized as a comic opera.

TABLE A.1. WOMEN'S PLAYS STAGED IN LONDON'S PATENT THEATERS, 1750–1800

Debut	Play	Playwright	Genre/Form	Venue
March 15, 1750	*The Rehearsal; or, Bayes in Petticoats*	Catherine Clive	Comic afterpiece	Drury Lane
March 17, 1752	*The Oracle*	Susannah Cibber	Comic afterpiece	Covent Garden
March 23, 1754	*The London 'Prentice*	Attributed to Catherine Clive	Comic afterpiece	Drury Lane
March 20, 1760	*Every Woman in Her Humour*	Catherine Clive	Comic afterpiece	Drury Lane
March 20, 1761	*The Island of Slaves*	Attributed to Catherine Clive	Comic afterpiece	Drury Lane
February 3, 1763	*The Discovery*	Frances Sheridan	Comic mainpiece	Drury Lane

(continued)

TABLE A.1. (*continued*)

Debut	Play	Playwright	Genre/Form	Venue
March 21, 1763	*The Sketch of a Fine Lady's Return from a Rout*	Catherine Clive	Comic afterpiece	Drury Lane
December 10, 1763	*The Dupe*	Frances Sheridan	Comic mainpiece	Drury Lane
January 24, 1765	*The Platonic Wife*	Elizabeth Griffith	Comic mainpiece	Drury Lane
March 18, 1765	*The Faithful Irish Woman*	Catherine Clive	Comic afterpiece	Drury Lane
January 9, 1766	*The Double Mistake*	Elizabeth Griffith	Comic mainpiece	Covent Garden
April 21, 1767	*The Young Couple*	Jane Pope	Comic afterpiece	Drury Lane
February 4, 1769	*The School for Rakes*	Elizabeth Griffith	Comic mainpiece	Drury Lane
February 18, 1769	*The Sister*	Charlotte Lennox	Comic mainpiece	Covent Garden
April 27, 1770	*Fashion Display'd*	Philippina Burton	Comic mainpiece	Haymarket
January 12, 1771	*Almida*	Dorothea Celesia	Tragic mainpiece	Drury Lane
May 10, 1771	*The Capricious Lady*	Jael-Henrietta Pye	Comic afterpiece	Drury Lane
March 9, 1772	*A Wife in the Right*	Elizabeth Griffith	Comic mainpiece	Covent Garden
April 12, 1774	*The South Briton*	A Lady	Comic mainpiece	Covent Garden
November 9, 1775	*Old City Manners*	Charlotte Lennox	Comic mainpiece	Drury Lane
March 15, 1776	*The Runaway*	Hannah Cowley	Comic mainpiece	Drury Lane
August 9, 1777	*The Advertisement*	Sarah Cheney Gardner	Comic mainpiece	Haymarket
December 10, 1777	*Percy*	Hannah More	Tragic mainpiece	Covent Garden
April 27, 1778	*The Little French Lawyer*	Ursula Booth	Comic afterpiece	Covent Garden

(*continued*)

TABLE A.1. (*continued*)

Debut	Play	Playwright	Genre/Form	Venue
April 30, 1778	The Lucky Escape	Mary Darby Robinson	Comic opera	Drury Lane
April 10, 1779	Who's the Dupe	Hannah Cowley	Comic afterpiece	Drury Lane
April 28, 1779	The Double Deception	Elizabeth Richardson	Comic mainpiece	Drury Lane
May 6, 1779	The Fatal Falsehood	Hannah More	Tragic mainpiece	Covent Garden
July 31, 1779	Albina	Hannah Cowley	Tragic mainpiece	Haymarket
December 2, 1779	The Times	Elizabeth Griffith	Comic mainpiece	Drury Lane
February 22, 1780	The Belle's Stratagem	Hannah Cowley	Comic mainpiece	Covent Garden
April 4, 1780	The School of Eloquence	Hannah Cowley	Comic interlude	Drury Lane
May 24, 1780	The Miniature Picture	Elizabeth Craven	Comic mainpiece	Drury Lane
August 5, 1780	The Chapter of Accidents	Sophia Lee	Comic mainpiece	Haymarket
January 31, 1781	The Siege of Sinope	Frances Brooke	Tragic mainpiece	Covent Garden
February 24, 1781	The World as It Goes	Hannah Cowley	Comic afterpiece	Covent Garden
March 24, 1781	Second Thoughts Are Best	Hannah Cowley	Comic afterpiece	Covent Garden
July 18, 1781	The Silver Tankard	Elizabeth Craven	Comic opera	Haymarket
February 9, 1782	Which Is the Man?	Hannah Cowley	Comic mainpiece	Haymarket
December 31, 1782	Rosina	Frances Brooke	Comic opera	Covent Garden
February 25, 1783	A Bold Stroke for a Husband	Hannah Cowley	Comic mainpiece	Covent Garden
December 6, 1783	More Ways Than One	Hannah Cowley	Comic mainpiece	Covent Garden

(*continued*)

APPENDIX

TABLE A.1. *(continued)*

Debut	Play	Playwright	Genre/Form	Venue
March 8, 1784	The Double Disguise	Harriet Horncastle Hook	Comic opera	Drury Lane
July 6, 1784	The Mogul Tale	Elizabeth Inchbald	Comic afterpiece	Haymarket
August 4, 1785	I'll Tell You What	Elizabeth Inchbald	Comic mainpiece	Haymarket
October 22, 1785	Appearance Is Against Them	Elizabeth Inchbald	Comic afterpiece	Covent Garden
May 18, 1786	The Peruvian	A Lady	Comic opera	Covent Garden
June 20, 1786	The Widow's Vow	Elizabeth Inchbald	Comic afterpiece	Drury Lane
November 25, 1786	A School for Graybeards	Hannah Cowley	Comic mainpiece	Drury Lane
February 10, 1787	Such Things Are	Elizabeth Inchbald	Comic mainpiece	Covent Garden
May 22, 1787	The Midnight Hour	Elizabeth Inchbald	Comic mainpiece	Covent Garden
November 10, 1787	The New Peerage	Harriet Lee	Comic mainpiece	Drury Lane
December 15, 1787	All on a Summer's Day	Elizabeth Inchbald	Comic mainpiece	Covent Garden
January 31, 1788	The Fate of Sparta	Hannah Cowley	Tragic mainpiece	Drury Lane
April 8, 1788	The Ton	Eglantine Wallace	Comic mainpiece	Covent Garden
April 29, 1788	Animal Magnetism	Elizabeth Inchbald	Comic afterpiece	Covent Garden
May 22, 1788	Marian	Frances Brooke	Comic opera	Covent Garden
August 9, 1788	The Sword of Peace	Mariana Starke	Comic mainpiece	Haymarket
November 28, 1788	The Child of Nature	Elizabeth Inchbald	Comic mainpiece	Covent Garden
May 25, 1789	Half an Hour after Supper	A Lady	Comic afterpiece	Haymarket

(continued)

TABLE A.1. *(continued)*

Debut	Play	Playwright	Genre/Form	Venue
July 15, 1789	The Married Man	Elizabeth Inchbald	Comic mainpiece	Haymarket
March 22, 1790	The Spoiled Child	Attributed to Dorothy Jordan	Comic afterpiece	Drury Lane
May 5, 1790	The Widow of Malabar	Mariana Starke	Tragic mainpiece	Covent Garden
May 11, 1791	The Hue and Cry	Elizabeth Inchbald	Comic afterpiece	Drury Lane
July 9, 1791	Next Door Neighbors	Elizabeth Inchbald	Comic mainpiece	Haymarket
December 3, 1791	A Day in Turkey	Hannah Cowley	Comic mainpiece	Covent Garden
January 18, 1792	Huniades	Hannah Brand	Tragic mainpiece	Drury Lane
February 2, 1792	Agmunda	Hannah Brand	Tragic mainpiece	Drury Lane
April 18, 1792	The Intrigues of a Morning	Eliza Parsons	Comic afterpiece	Covent Garden
June 30, 1792	Young Men and Old Women	Elizabeth Inchbald	Comic afterpiece	Haymarket
August 23, 1792	Cross Partners	Attributed variously to Miss Griffiths and Elizabeth Inchbald	Comic mainpiece	Haymarket
January 29, 1793	Every One Has His Fault	Elizabeth Inchbald	Comic mainpiece	Covent Garden
October 24, 1793	The Ward of the Castle	Miss Burke	Comic opera	Covent Garden
February 25, 1793	Anna	Catherine? Cuthbertson	Comic mainpiece	Drury Lane
May 22, 1794	The Speechless Wife	Mrs. Rainsford	Comic afterpiece	Covent Garden
November 1, 1794	The Wedding Day	Elizabeth Inchbald	Comic mainpiece	Drury Lane
November 29, 1794	Nobody	Mary Darby Robinson	Comic afterpiece	Drury Lane

(continued)

TABLE A.1. *(continued)*

Debut	Play	Playwright	Genre/Form	Venue
December 6, 1794	*The Town before You*	Hannah Cowley	Comic mainpiece	Covent Garden
March 21, 1795	*Edwy and Elgiva*	Frances Burney	Tragic mainpiece	Drury Lane
April 22, 1795	*Mrs. Doggerel in Her Altitudes*	Sarah Cheney Gardner	Comic prelude	Haymarket
April 20, 1796	*Almeyda*	Sophia Lee	Tragic mainpiece	Drury Lane
March 4, 1797	*Wives as They Were, and Maids as They Are*	Elizabeth Inchbald	Comic mainpiece	Covent Garden
April 27, 1798	*Matrimony*	Attributed to Frances Abington	Comic afterpiece	Covent Garden
October 11, 1798	*Lovers' Vows*	Elizabeth Inchbald	Comic mainpiece	Covent Garden
April 19, 1799	*The Princess of Georgia*	Elizabeth Craven	Comic opera	Covent Garden
April 27, 1799	*What Is She?*	Charlotte Smith	Comic mainpiece	Covent Garden
May 3, 1799	*First Faults*	Marie Thérèse du Camp	Comic mainpiece	Drury Lane
November 30, 1799	*The Wise Man of the East*	Elizabeth Inchbald	Comic mainpiece	Covent Garden
April 29, 1800	*De Montfort*	Joanna Baillie	Tragic mainpiece	Drury Lane
October 30, 1800	*Virginia*	Dorothea Plowden	Comic opera	Drury Lane

Source: David D. Mann and Susan Garland, *Women Playwrights in England, Ireland, and Scotland, 1660–1823* (Bloomington: Indiana University Press, 1996), 407–413.

Notes

Introduction

1. Amy Sherman-Palladino, Kate Fodor, and Jen Kirkman, *The Marvelous Mrs. Maisel*, season 2, episode 2, "Mid-way to Mid-town," directed by Amy Sherman-Palladino, Amazon Prime Video, December 5, 2018, 32:50.

2. Sherman-Palladino, Fodor, and Kirkman, 36:30–36:40.

3. Sherman-Palladino, Fodor, and Kirkman, 45:10–45:15.

4. Sherman-Palladino, Fodor, and Kirkman, 48:40–49:30.

5. Susanna Centlivre, *The Platonick Lady* (London: printed for James Knapton, 1707), n.p.

6. Leslie Ritchie, *David Garrick and the Mediation of Celebrity* (Cambridge: Cambridge University Press, 2019), 18–19.

7. Ellen Donkin, *Getting into the Act: Women Playwrights in London, 1776–1829* (London: Routledge, 1995), 1.

8. For a complete list of plays written by women and produced on London's patent stages between 1750 and 1800, the span of this study, see the appendix. Note that there is some margin for error in the total number of plays staged by women during this time period. A small number of plays are attributed to certain playwrights, but not confirmed. Additionally, it's possible that other plays were written and presented under a pseudonym.

9. David D. Mann and Susan Garland Mann, *Women Playwrights in England, Ireland, and Scotland, 1660–1823* (Bloomington: Indiana University Press, 1996), 5; Nancy Cotton, *Women Playwrights in England, c. 1363–1750* (Lewisburg, PA: Bucknell University Press, 1980).

10. See Emily H. Anderson, *Eighteenth-Century Authorship and the Play of Fiction: Novels and the Theater, Haywood to Austen* (New York: Routledge, 2009); Paula Byrne, *Jane Austen and the Theatre* (London: Hambledon and London, 2002); Nora Nachumi, *Acting Like a Lady: British Women Novelists and the Eighteenth-Century Theater* (New York: AMS Press, 2008); and Francesca Saggini, *Backstage in the Novel: Frances Burney and the Theatre Arts* (Charlottesville: University of Virginia Press, 2012).

11. See Lisa Freeman, *Character's Theater: Genre and Identity on the Eighteenth-Century English Stage* (Philadelphia: University of Pennsylvania Press, 2002); Gillian Russell, *Women, Sociability and Theatre in Georgian London* (Cambridge: Cambridge University Press, 2007); Betsy Bolton, *Women, Nationalism, and the Romantic Stage: Theatre and Politics in Britain, 1780–1800* (Cambridge: Cambridge University Press, 2001); Anne K. Mellor, *Mothers of the Nation: Women's Political Writing in England, 1780–1830* (Bloomington: Indiana University Press, 2000); and Daniel O'Quinn, *Staging Governance: Theatrical Imperialism in London, 1770–1800* (Baltimore: Johns Hopkins University Press, 2005).

12. Sarah Apetrei, *Women, Feminism, and Religion in Early Enlightenment England* (Cambridge: Cambridge University Press, 2010), 32.

13. See chapter 3.

14. I am indebted to William Van Lannep, Emmett L. Avery, Arthur H. Scouten, George Winchester Stone Jr., and Charles Beecher Hogan, eds., *The London Stage, 1660–1800: A Calendar of Plays, Entertainments and Afterpieces*, 5 parts in 11 vols. (Carbondale: Southern Illinois University Press, 1960–68). Unless otherwise noted, I have relied on a digitized version of this text. See *Eighteenth Century Drama: Censorship, Society and the Stage* (Marlborough, UK: Adam Matthew, 2016), https://www.eighteenthcenturydrama.amdigital.co.uk/.

15. Aphra Behn, *Sir Patient Fancy*, in *The Works of Aphra Behn*, ed. Janet Todd (Columbus: Ohio State University Press, 1992), 6:5.

16. Aphra Behn, *The Lucky Chance; Or, An Alderman's Bargain*, in Todd, *Works of Aphra Behn*, 7:217.

17. Susan Carlson, *Women and Comedy: Rewriting the British Theatrical Tradition* (Ann Arbor: University of Michigan Press, 1991), 128.

18. Marta Straznicky, "Restoration Women Playwrights and the Limits of Professionalism," *English Literary History* 64, no. 3 (1997): 715.

19. Judith Stanton, "'This New Found Path Attempting': Women Dramatists in England, 1660–1800," in *Curtain Calls: British and American Women in the Theatre*, ed. Mary Anne Schofield and Cecilia Macheski (Athens: Ohio University Press, 1991), 326.

20. Matthew J. Kinservik, *Disciplining Satire: The Censorship of Satiric Comedy on the Eighteenth-Century London Stage* (Lewisburg, PA: Bucknell University Press, 2002), 103–104.

21. See Jane Moody, *Illegitimate Theatre in London, 1770–1840* (Cambridge: Cambridge University Press, 2000).

22. Donkin, *Getting into the Act*, 6.

23. Stanton, "Women Dramatists," 325–336.

24. By the mid-eighteenth century, Black people represented 1 to 3 percent of London's population. It is possible, even likely, that Black women and women of color worked in the theater in various capacities, though not as playwrights. See Gretchen H. Gerzina, ed., *Britain's Black Past* (Liverpool: Liverpool University Press, 2020); and Gretchen H. Gerzina, *Black London: Life before Emancipation* (New Brunswick, NJ: Rutgers University Press, 1995).

25. Berta Joncus presents convincing evidence of Clive's sexual and romantic relationships with other women in *Kitty Clive or, The Fair Songster* (Suffolk, UK: Boydell & Brewer, 2019), 348–354. For more on the experience of same-sex relationships between women in eighteenth-century London, see Rebecca Jennings, *A Lesbian History of Britain: Love and Sex between Women since 1500* (Oxford: Greenwood World Publishing, 2007).

26. Donkin, *Getting into the Act*, 1.

27. See Regina Barecca, *They Used to Call Me Snow White . . . but I Drifted: Women's Strategic Use of Humour in British Literature* (Detroit. MI: Wayne State University Press, 1994), 182.

28. For further discussion of eighteenth-century feminism, see Alice Browne, *The Eighteenth-Century Feminist Mind* (Detroit. MI: Wayne State University Press, 1987); and Katherine M. Rogers, *Feminism in Eighteenth-Century England* (Champagne: University of Illinois Press, 1982).

29. Audrey Bilger, *Laughing Feminism: Subversive Comedy in Frances Burney, Maria Edgeworth, and Jane Austen* (Detroit, MI: Wayne State University Press, 2002), 10.

30. See Misty Anderson, *Female Playwrights and Eighteenth-Century Comedy: Negotiating Marriage on the London Stage* (New York: Palgrave, 2002); and Nancy Copeland, *Staging Gender in Behn and Centlivre: Women's Comedy and the Theatre* (Cornwall, UK: Ashgate, 2004).

31. Jaqueline Pearson, *The Prostituted Muse: Images of Women and Women Dramatists, 1642–1737* (New York: Palgrave Macmillan, 1988), 42.

32. Anderson, *Female Playwrights*, 23.

33. Stanton, "Women Dramatists," 330.

34. Stanton, 330.

35. Gwenn Davis and Beverly A. Joyce, *Drama by Women to 1900: A Bibliography of American and British Writers* (Toronto: University of Toronto Press, 1992), xv.

36. See Robert D. Hume, "Before the Bard: 'Shakespeare' in Early Eighteenth-Century London," *English Literary History* 64, no. 1 (1997): 58.

37. See Diana Solomon, *Prologues and Epilogues of Restoration Theater: Gender and Comedy, Performance and Print* (Newark: University of Delaware Press, 2013).

38. Angela Escott, *The Celebrated Mrs. Cowley: Experiments in Dramatic Genre, 1776–1794* (London: Pickering & Chatto, 2012), 19.

39. Charles Burney to Frances Burney, August 29, 1779, in *The Letters of Dr. Charles Burney*, ed. Alvaro Ribeiro (Oxford: Oxford University Press, 1991), 1:281.

40. Review of *The World as It Goes*, by Hannah Cowley, *Morning Herald* (London), February 26, 1781.

41. Hannah Cowley, *A School for Greybeards; or, The Mourning Bride* (1786), in *The Plays of Hannah Cowley*, ed. Frederick M. Link (New York: Garland, 1979), 2:vii. Subsequent references are from this facsimile edition.

42. See chapters 4 and 5.

43. Donkin, *Getting into the Act*, 60.

44. A. Norman Jeffares, "Sheridan, Richard Brinsley (1751–1816)," *Oxford Dictionary of National Biography*, September 23, 2004, https://doi.org/10.1093/ref:odnb/25367.

45. See Freeman, *Character's Theater*, 193–234.

1. Comic Resurgence

1. Catherine Clive to Jane Pope, December 15, 1774, "Copies of letters to Jane Pope from various people, 1769–1808, in the hand of James Winston" [manuscript], c. 1840, Folger Shakespeare Library, W.b. 73. Quoted in Joncus, *Fair Songster*, 8.

2. For more information on Richard Cumberland's conflicts with theatrical personnel, including David Garrick and Richard Brinsley Sheridan, see Arthur Sherbo, "Cumberland, Richard (1732–1811), Playwright and Novelist," *Oxford Dictionary of National Biography*, September 23, 2004, https://doi.org/10.1093/ref:odnb/6888.

3. All of Clive's plays survive in manuscript at the Huntington Library in the John Larpent Collection: "The Rehearsal; or, Bayes in Petticoats" (1750), LA 86; "Every Woman in Her Humour" (1760), LA 174; "The Sketch of a Fine Lady's Return from a Rout" (1763), LA 220; and "The Faithful Irish Woman" (1765), LA 247. Two additional farces are sometimes attributed to Clive: "The Island of Slaves" (1761), LA 190, and a lost play titled "The London 'Prentice" (1743), but the authorship of these two pieces remains unconfirmed. See Joncus, *Fair Songster*, 378n3.

4. Sallie M. Strange, "Clive, Catherine," in *A Dictionary of British and American Women Writers*, ed. Janet Todd (Lanham, MD: Rowman & Littlefield, 1985), 86; Philip H. Highfill, Kalman A. Burnim, and Edward A. Langhans, eds., "Clive, Catherine," in *A Biographical Dictionary of Actors, Actresses, Musicians, & Other Stage Personnel in London, 1660–1800* (Carbondale: Southern Illinois University Press, 1973), 3:353.

5. There is a small but valuable body of twentieth-century scholarship on Clive's plays, beginning with Patrick J. Crean's dissertation "The Life and Times of Kitty Clive" (University of London, 1933). Crean's research was expanded on by Richard Frushell, who wrote a dissertation and a handful of articles on the topic. See his "An Edition of the Afterpieces of Kitty Clive" (PhD diss., Duquesne University, 1968); "The Textual Relationship and Biographical Significance of Two Petite Pieces by Mrs. Catherine (Kitty) Clive," *Restoration and Eighteenth-Century Theatre Research* 9, no. 1 (1970): 51–58; and "Kitty Clive as Dramatist," *Durham University Journal* 32, no. 2 (1971): 125–132. See also Matthew J. Kinservik, "Garrick's Unpublished Epilogue for Catherine Clive's *The Rehearsal: or, Bays in Petticoats* (1750)," Appendix, *Études Anglaises* 49, no. 3 (1996): 320–326.

6. *Bayes in Petticoats* was performed on March 15, 1750; April 3, 1750; April 26, 1750; April 27, 1750; March 12, 1751; March 19, 1751; May 3, 1751; March 22, 1753; April 3, 1753; May 4, 1753; October 31, 1753; April 19, 1755; March 22, 1762; and May 10, 1762. Harry William Pedicord lists a fourteenth performance on March 27, 1750, but this appears to be an error, as the afterpiece at Drury Lane that evening was Garrick's *Lethe*. See Pedicord, *The Theatrical Public in the Time of Garrick* (Carbondale: Southern Illinois University Press, 1966), 208–209.

7. Fiona Ritchie has argued that Clive, alongside actresses like Hannah Pritchard, played an enormous role in "strengthen[ing] the social standing of theatre performers," especially women. See Ritchie, *Women and Shakespeare in the Eighteenth Century* (New York: Cambridge University Press, 2014), 43.

8. Biographical information on Clive is taken from Joncus's *Fair Songster* and Clive's entry in the *Biographical Dictionary*. See also K. A. Crouch, "Clive [née Raftor], Catherine [Kitty] (1711–1785), Actress," *Oxford Dictionary of National Biography*, September 23, 2004, https://doi.org/10.1093/ref:odnb/5694.

9. William Chetwood, *A General History of the Stage: From Its Origin in Greece Down to the Present Time* (London: printed for W. Owen, 1766), 127.

10. Highfill, Burnim, and Langhans, "Clive," 344.

11. Joncus, *Fair Songster*, 34.

12. Joncus, 36.

13. Joncus, 38.

14. Felicity Nussbaum, *Rival Queens: Actresses, Performance, and the Eighteenth-Century British Theatre* (Philadelphia: University of Pennsylvania Press, 2010), 153.

15. While it has been widely accepted that Catherine and George Clive married in early October 1733—at which time Clive was playing the role of Polly in *The Beggar's Opera*—a recent article by Olive Baldwin and Thelma Wilson in *Theatre Notebook* provides convincing evidence that the couple married years earlier, in 1731. See Baldwin and Wilson, "Kitty Clive: Her Birth and Marriage Dates," *Theatre Notebook*, 74, no. 1 (2020): 4.

16. See Joncus, *Fair Songster*, 153, 348–353.

17. Henry Fielding, epistle to *The Intriguing Chambermaid*, in *The Wesleyan Edition of the Works of Henry Fielding*, ed. Thomas Lockwood (Oxford: Oxford University Press, 2009), 1:582.

18. Nussbaum, *Rival Queens*, 161.

19. Catherine Clive, letter to the editor, *Daily Post* (London), November 19, 1736.

20. *The Beggars' Pantomime* ran for three months and was published in three editions.

21. Review of *The Beggar's Opera*, *London Evening Post*, January 1, 1737.

22. Berta Joncus, "'In Wit Superior, as in Fighting': Kitty Clive and the Conquest of a Rival Queen," *Huntington Library Quarterly* 74, no. 1 (2011): 24.

23. Stuart Sherman, "The Periodical and the Prism: Two Ways of Working at Celebrity in the Careers of Catherine Clive, Eliza Haywood, and Charlotte Charke," in *Making Stars: Biography and Celebrity in Eighteenth-Century Britain*, ed. Nora Nachumi and Kristina Straub (Newark: University of Delaware Press, 2022), 22.

24. See Judith Milhous and Robert D. Hume, "The Drury Lane Actors' Rebellion of 1743," *Theatre Journal* 42, no. 1 (1990): 57–80.

25. Milhous and Hume, 66.

26. Catherine Clive, letter to the editor, *Daily Gazetteer* (London), September 23, 1743.

27. Joncus, *Fair Songster*, 286.

28. Charles Fleetwood, letter to the editor, *Daily Advertiser* (London), October 15, 1743.

29. Catherine Clive, *The Case of Mrs. Clive: Submitted to the Publick* (London: printed for B. Dod, 1744), 18–19.

30. Highfill, Burnim, and Langhans, "Clive," 349.

31. Nussbaum, *Rival Queens*, 166.

32. Tate Wilkinson, *Memoirs of His Own Life* (York: Wilson, Spence, and Mawman), 3:42.

33. Matthew J. Kinservik, "Benefit Play Selection at Drury Lane 1729–1769; the Cases of Mrs Cibber, Mrs Clive, and Mrs Pritchard," *Theatre Notebook* 50, no. 1 (1996): 19.

34. Kinservik, *Disciplining Satire*, 103–104.

35. Donkin, *Getting into the Act*, 6.

36. Kinservik, *Disciplining Satire*, 99.

37. The mysterious Mrs. Hoper earns the title of most prolific woman playwright of the 1740s with her three afterpieces.

38. Kinservik, "Benefit Play Selection," 18. According to the *London Stage*, for Clive's benefit of the previous year, March 13, 1749, she chose *The Suspicious Husband* as the mainpiece and *The Intriguing Chambermaid* as the afterpiece.

39. See the entry for March 15, 1750, in the *London Stage*. *Bayes in Petticoats* was performed for the benefit of Miss Norris (April 3, 1750), Clive's brother, James "Jemmy" Raftor (April 26, 1750, May 3, 1751, May 4, 1753, and April 19, 1755), Charles Leviez (April 27, 1750), Sarah Ward (March 19, 1751), and Mr. Dexter (April 3, 1753). Sometimes these benefit performances were shared with other performers. Joncus lists an additional performance that took place without Clive on May 21, 1753, but this performance appears to have been a production of Buckingham's *The Rehearsal*, not Clive's *Bayes in Petticoats*.

40. Nussbaum, *Rivals Queens*, 178; Frushell, "Dramatist," 126.

41. Catherine Clive, *Every Woman in Her Humour* (1760), The Huntington Library, John Larpent Collection, LA 174, 5–6.

42. Catherine Clive, *The Sketch of a Fine Lady's Return from a Rout* (1763), The Huntington Library, John Larpent Collection, LA 220, 7–8.

43. Catherine Clive, *The Faithful Irish Woman* (1765), The Huntington Library, John Larpent Collection, LA 247, n.p.

44. Felicity Nussbaum, "Straddling: London-Irish Actresses in Performance," in *Ireland, Enlightenment and the English Stage, 1740–1820*, ed. David O'Shaughnessy (Cambridge: Cambridge University Press, 2019), 35.

45. For a discussion of Clive's efforts to frame herself as a gentlewoman, see JoAllen Bradham, "A Good Country Gentlewoman: Catherine Clive's Epistolary Autobiography," *Biography* 19, no. 3 (1996): 259–282.

46. See Robert D. Hume and Harold Love, introduction to *The Rehearsal*, in *Plays, Poems, and Miscellaneous Writings Associated with George Villiers, Second Duke of Buckingham*, ed. Robert D. Hume and Harold Love (Oxford: Oxford University Press, 2007), 1:336–341. While the play was published anonymously, it is certain that Buckingham wrote the text. Others may have contributed as well.

47. George Villiers, Second Duke of Buckingham, *The Rehearsal*, in Hume and Love, *Writings Associated with George Villiers*, 1:401.

48. Hume and Love, introduction to *The Rehearsal*, 363.

49. Frushell, "Edition of the Afterpieces," xxxviii.

50. Charke's rehearsal play, *The Art of Management*, was performed at the York Buildings in 1735 and featured an inept manager, Brainless, who berates a group of actors including Mrs. Tragic, played by Charke.

51. See Lucyle Hook, introduction to *The Female Wits* (1704), by W. M., facsimile ed. (Los Angeles: William Andrews Clark Memorial Library, 1967), xii.

52. W. M., *The Female Wits* (1704), n.p.

53. W. M., n.p.

54. W. M., n.p.

55. W. M., n.p. In the Restoration theater, it was common practice for women in the audience to wear masks as an act of modesty, but masks were also worn by sex workers. For more on the trend of wearing masks at the theater, both on and off the stage, see Will Pritchard, *Outward Appearances: The Female Exterior in Restoration London* (Lewisburg, PA: Bucknell University Press, 2008), 106–111.

56. Claudine van Hensbergen. "The Female Wits: Gender, Satire, and Drama," in *The Oxford Handbook of Eighteenth-Century Satire*, ed. Paddy Bullard (Oxford: Oxford University Press, 2019), 85.

57. Laurie A. Finke, "The Satire of Women Writers in *The Female Wits*," *Restoration: Studies in English Literary Culture* 8, no. 2 (1984): 66.

58. Laura J. Rosenthal, *Playwrights and Plagiarists in Early Modern England: Gender, Authorship, Literary Property* (Ithaca, NY: Cornell University Press, 1996), 173.

59. Nussbaum, *Rival Queens*, 179.

60. Nussbaum, 178.

61. Catherine Clive, *The Rehearsal; or, Bayes in Petticoats*, in *The Clandestine Marriage [by] David Garrick and George Coleman the Elder Together with Two Short Plays*, ed. Noel Chevalier (Peterborough, ON: Broadview Press, 1995), 1.1.19–24. All quotations from *Bayes in Petticoats* are taken from this modern critical edition of the play, which is based on the 1753 published text.

62. Clive, 1.1.35–49.

63. Clive, 1.1.154–170.

64. Clive, 2.1.25–33.

65. Clive, 2.1.46.

66. See Joncus, *Fair Songster*, 387. Though Mrs. Hazard initially describes her musical as an Italian burletta, Joncus explains that the musical interlude is actually a performance of William Boyce's c. 1740 English pastoral *Corydon and Miranda*.

67. Clive, *Bayes in Petticoats*, 2.1.74–75.

68. Joncus, *Fair Songster*, 398.

69. The additional scene is appended to the original manuscript of the play in the Larpent Collection at the Huntington Library (LA 86) and was published in the 1753 edition of the play. *The London Stage* notes that this additional scene was added to the production as of March 12, 1751.

70. Clive, *Bayes in Petticoats*, 2.1.191–194.

71. Clive, 2.1.200–202.

72. Clive, 2.1.258–267.

73. Clive, 2.1.269–270.

74. Donkin, *Getting into the Act*, 20.

75. See *The London Stage*, March 19, 1751.

76. David Garrick, epilogue to *The Rehearsal*, in Kinservik, "Unpublished Epilogue," 322–323. Two manuscript copies of Garrick's epilogue are housed at the Folger Shakespeare Library, but Kinservik's article contains the only publication of the epilogue.

77. Diana Solomon explains that prologues and epilogues that foregrounded the woman playwright, as Garrick's does for Clive's *Bayes in Petticoats*, "offered possibilities for female self-expression yet often reinforced misogyny." See Solomon, *Prologues and Epilogues*, 49.

78. Catherine Clive to David Garrick, February 19, 1768, in Percy Fitzgerald, *The Life of Mrs. Catherine Clive* (London: A. Reader, 1888), 72–73. Fitzgerald retains Clive's original spelling.

79. Donkin, *Getting into the Act*, 42.

80. Nussbaum, *Rival Queens*, 171.

81. Alicia Le Fanu, *Memoirs of the Life and Writings of Mrs. Frances Sheridan* (London: G. and W. B. Whittaker, 1824), 235236.

82. Clive, epilogue to Frances Sheridan's *The Dupe, a Comedy* (London: printed for A. Millar, 1764), 69–70.

83. Sheridan, *Dupe*, 70.

84. Elizabeth Griffith, *The Platonic Wife* (London: printed for W. Johnston in Ludgate Street, 1765), 98.

85. Griffith, 98.

86. Elizabeth Griffith, *The School for Rakes, a Comedy* (London: W. & W. Smith, 1769), 4.

87. Jael-Henrietta Pye, *A Short View of the Principal Seats and Gardens in and about Twickenham* (London: n.p., 1771), 15–16.

88. Catherine Clive to Jane Pope, November 3, 1770, "Copies of letters to Jane Pope," quoted in Clive's entry in the *Biographical Dictionary*.

2. Musical Comedy

1. Roger Fiske, *English Theatre Music in the Eighteenth-Century Theatre Music* (Oxford: Oxford University Press, 1986), 412.

2. Fiske, 456, 468.

3. Donkin, *Getting into the Act*, 43; Jodi L. Wyett, "Frances Brooke on (the) Stage," *Restoration and Eighteenth-Century Theatre Research* 28, no. 2 (2013): 36.

4. Leslie Ritchie, *Women Writing Music in Late Eighteenth-Century England: Social Harmony in Literature and Performance* (London: Routledge, 2016), 160.

5. Betty A. Schellenberg, *The Professionalization of Women Writers in Eighteenth-Century Britain* (Cambridge: Cambridge University Press, 2005), 73.

6. Paula R. Backscheider, "Frances Brooke: Becoming a Playwright," *Women's Writing* 23, no. 3 (2016): 325–338.

7. The Houghton Library has now digitized Brooke and Gifford's correspondence and made it publicly available online. See Frances Brooke letters to Richard Gifford, 1756–72 and undated, MS Eng 1310, Houghton Library, Harvard College Library, https://id.lib.harvard.edu/ead/hou00646/catalog.

8. There is only a brief entry on Brooke in the *Biographical Dictionary*. Thus, unless otherwise noted, all biographical details are drawn from the only existing biography of Brooke, Lorraine McMullen's *An Odd Attempt in a Woman: The Literary Life of Frances Brooke* (Vancouver: University of British Columbia Press, 1983). For a short but thorough biography of Brooke, see Mary Jane Edwards, "Brooke [née Moore], Frances (bap. 1724, d. 1789), Writer and Playwright," *Oxford Dictionary of National Biography*, September 23, 2004. https://doi.org/10.1093/ref:odnb/3540.

9. McMullen, *Odd Attempt*, 2.

10. Backscheider, "Becoming a Playwright," 326.

11. Isobel Hurst, *Victorian Women Writers and the Classics: The Feminine of Homer* (Oxford: Oxford University Press, 2006), 4. A revival of the classical period swept across Europe from the seventeenth through the nineteenth centuries.

12. Frances Brooke, *Virginia* (London: A. Millar, 1756), vii. Brooke does not identify by name the people she says could testify to the veracity of her claim that her manuscript was submitted first. However, she was well connected in London, and possible

readers include Richard Gifford, Mary Cholmondeley (sister of the actress Peg Woffington), and perhaps even Samuel Johnson.

13. With respect to plays by women, Garrick almost exclusively produced comedies, with the exception of Dorothea Celesia's tragedy *Almida*, an adaptation of Voltaire's *Tancrède* (1760), which appeared in 1771 at Drury Lane. He also supported Hannah More with her tragedy *Percy*, but he was retired when it debuted at Covent Garden in 1777.

14. Frances Brooke [Mary Singleton, pseud.], *The Old Maid* (London: A. Miller, 1764), 24.

15. Brooke, 18.

16. See Leigh Woods, "Garrick's King Lear and the English Malady," *Theatre Survey* 27, no. 1–2 (1986): 17–35.

17. Frances Brooke to Richard Gifford, [c. January 1757], MS Eng 1310, 1. Gifford's response to Brooke is dated January 31, 1757, MS Eng 1310, 27.

18. Brooke to Gifford, [c. 1761], MS Eng 1319, 2.

19. *The Letters of David Garrick*, ed. David Little and George Kahrl (Cambridge: Belknap Press, 1963), 2:461.

20. Donkin, *Getting into the Act*, 37.

21. Donkin, 38.

22. On July 6, 1763, Brooke began the three-month journey from England to Canada with her young son, also named John, and her unmarried sister, Sarah. She had published her first novel, *The History of Lady Julia Mandeville* (1763), the same year she moved to Quebec, and she spent her years living in the colony working on another, *The History of Emily Montague* (1769). Set in Quebec, the second novel was published a year after the Brookes returned to England in 1768 and is sometimes called the first Canadian novel. She wrote two more novels: *The Excursion* (1777) and *The History of Charles Mandeville* (1790, published posthumously).

23. *The Early Journals and Letters of Fanny Burney*, vol. 1, ed. Lars E. Troide (Oxford: Oxford University Press, 1990), 273. Hereafter referred to as *EJL*.

24. Brooke to Gifford, November 15, [17??], MS Eng 1310, 12.

25. Brooke to Gifford.

26. The dates of Catley's absence from the patent theaters help date Brooke's efforts to stage *Rosina* as sometime between March 1771 and September 1772.

27. For a meticulously detailed description of the Brookes-Yates partnership, see Ian Woodfield, *Opera and Drama in Eighteenth-Century London: The King's Theatre, Garrick, and the Business of Performance* (Cambridge: Cambridge University Press, 2001).

28. Mary Ann Yates, letter to the editor, *Daily Gazetteer* (London), October 5, 1767.

29. See Peter Thomson, "Yates [née Graham], Mary Ann (1728–1787), Actress and Theatre Manager," *Oxford Dictionary of National Biography*, September 23, 2004, https://doi.org/10.1093/ref:odnb/30196.

30. Woodfield, *King's Theatre*, 119.

31. See Tracy C. Davis, "Female Managers, Lessees and Proprietors of the British Stage (to 1914)," *Nineteenth Century Theatre* 28, no. 2 (2000): 115–144. Davis's list of English women in the theater business up to 1914 reveals only a handful of women working in this field in the eighteenth century, but hundreds in the nineteenth,

confirming that Brooke and Yates's management of the Opera House was indeed pioneering.

32. See Gilli Bush-Bailey, *Treading the Bawds: Actresses and Playwrights on the Late Stuart Stage* (Manchester: Manchester University Press, 2006), 95–96.

33. Thomas C. Crochunis, "Women Theatre Managers," in *The Oxford Handbook of the Georgian Theatre, 1737–1832*, ed. Julia Swindells and David Francis Taylor (Oxford: Oxford University Press, 2014), 568.

34. Russell, *Women, Sociability and Theatre*, 12; Judith Hawley, "Elizabeth and Keppel Craven and the Domestic Drama of Mother-Son Relations," in *Stage Mothers: Women, Work, and the Theater, 1660–1830*, ed. Laura Engel and Elaine M. McGirr (Lewisburg, PA: Bucknell University Press, 2014), 199–215.

35. See Jean Baker, *Sarah Baker and Her Kentish Theatres, 1737–1816: Challenging the Status Quo* (London: Society for Theatre Research, 2019).

36. Garrick to Somerset Draper, [c. December 26,] 1745, *Letters of David Garrick*, 1:74.

37. Ritchie, *Women and Shakespeare*, 49. For more detail on Susannah Cibber's efforts to become a manager, see Helen Brooks, "'Your Sincere Friend and Humble Servant': Evidence of Managerial Aspirations in Susannah Cibber's Letters," *Studies in Theatre and Performance* 28 (2008): 147–159.

38. James T. Kirkman, *Memoirs of the Life of Charles Macklin* (London: Lackington, Allen, 1799), 2:57. Macklin records that actor William Smith left Covent Garden to perform at the Opera House under the new patent. Unfortunately for Smith and all involved, the patent was not granted.

39. Woodfield, *King's Theatre*, 37.

40. Burney, journal, 1774, *EJL*, 1:54–56.

41. Woodfield, *King's Theatre*, 3.

42. Backscheider, "Becoming a Playwright," 327.

43. See Frederick C. Petty, *Italian Opera in London, 1760–1800* (Ann Arbor: UMI Research Press, 1980), 376; and Woodfield, *King's Theatre*, 79.

44. See Woodfield, *King's Theatre*, 77–79.

45. Frances Brooke to Ozias Humphrey, September 8, 1775, MSS Montagu d. 6, f. 239, Bodleian Libraries, Oxford University.

46. Brooke to Humphrey.

47. Woodfield, *King's Theatre*, 219.

48. Brooke, *Old Maid*, 219–220.

49. *Letters of David Garrick*, 3:1041.

50. McMullen, *Odd Attempt*, 160.

51. Frances Brooke to David Garrick, April 17, 1776, quoted in K.J.H. Berland, "Frances Brooke and David Garrick," *Studies in Eighteenth-Century Culture*, 20 (1990): 224.

52. Garrick to Brooke, April 17, 1776, in *Letters of David Garrick*, 3:1006.

53. Wyett, "Frances Brooke on (the) Stage," 32; Katherine Charles, "Staging Sociability in *The Excursion*: Frances Brooke, David Garrick, and the King's Theatre Coterie," *Eighteenth-Century Fiction* 27, no. 2 (2014-15): 259.

54. Frances Brooke, *The Excursion* (1777), ed. Paula R. Backscheider and Hope D. Cotton (Lexington: University Press of Kentucky, 1997), 82.

55. See Edmund Burke to David Garrick, (April 29, 1777), in *The Private Correspondence of David Garrick, with the Most Celebrated Persons of His Time*, ed. James Boaden (London: H. Colburn and Bentley, 1831–32), 331.

56. Garrick to Frances Cadogan, *Letters of David Garrick*, 3:1172.

57. Anderson, *Female Playwrights*, 140.

58. Anderson, 140.

59. David Garrick, review of *The Excursion*, by Frances Brooke, *Monthly Review; Or, Literary Journal* 57 (August 1777): 144.

60. Garrick, 144.

61. Backscheider, "Becoming a Playwright," 328.

62. Backscheider, 328.

63. Quoted in Curtis Price, Judith Milhous, and Robert D. Hume, *The King's Theatre, Haymarket, 1778–1791* (Oxford: Oxford University Press, 1995), 57.

64. Frances Brooke to Thomas Cadell, January 5, [1779], Hyde Collection, Four Oaks Farm, MS file. Quoted in McMullen, *Odd Attempt*, 187.

65. Backscheider, "Becoming a Playwright," 329.

66. Backscheider, 329.

67. Frances Brooke, *The Siege of Sinope* (London: T. Cadell, 1781), 10.

68. Brooke, 11.

69. Review of *The Siege of Sinope*, by Frances Brooke, *Morning Chronicle* (London), February 1, 1781.

70. Review of *The Siege of Sinope*, by Frances Brooke, *Universal Magazine of Knowledge and Pleasure* 68 (February 1781): 86.

71. Review of *The Siege of Sinope*, by Frances Brooke, *Monthly Review; Or, Literary Journal* 64 (1781): 153. Interestingly, this anonymous review was written by George Colman, the previous manager of Covent Garden. Perhaps he was bitter about Brooke's success as manager of the Opera House.

72. Review of *The Siege of Sinope*, by Frances Brooke, *London Magazine* 50 (1781): 63.

73. McMullen, *Odd Attempt*, 194. For more on playwrights' remuneration, see Robert D. Hume, "The Value of Money in Eighteenth-Century England: Incomes, Prices, Buying Power—and Some Problems in Cultural Economics," *Huntington Library Quarterly* 77, no. 4 (2014): 395. After a play's debut, the playwright often chose to sell the publication rights for a fee.

74. Review of *Rosina*, by Frances Brooke, *Lady's Magazine* 14 (1783): 28.

75. Ritchie, *Women Writing Music*, 133. For a record of women's comic operas, see the appendix, 222–225.

76. Terry Gifford, *Pastoral*, 2nd ed. (New York: Routledge, 2020), 2.

77. Gifford, 138.

78. Fiske, *Theatre Music*, 412.

79. Review of *Rosina*, by Frances Brooke, *Public Advertiser* (London), January 1, 1783.

80. "Mrs. Brooke," *British Magazine and Review* (London), February 1783, 101.

81. M. J. Young, *Memoirs of Mrs. Crouch: Including a Retrospect of the Stage, during the Years She Performed* (London: printed for James Asperne, 1806), 1:157.

82. Review of *Rosina*, by Frances Brooke, *Parker's General Advertiser and Morning Intelligencer* (London), January 1, 1783.

NOTES TO PAGES 58–65

83. Frances Brooke, *Rosina: A Comic Opera* (London: T. Cadell, 1783), 5.

84. John Dalton, *Comus* (London: J. Hughs, 1738), 9.

85. Brooke, *Rosina*, v.

86. Brooke, v.

87. Ritchie, *Women Writing Music*, 160.

88. Like many of the newspaper reviews of *Marian*, the review in the *Public Advertiser* makes special note of the lovely "two new scenes . . . painted by Mr. Richards" on May 23, 1788. Such a review contrasts with those of *Rosina*, which did not have new scenery.

89. Frances Brooke, *Marian: A Comic Opera* (London: A. Strahan, 1800), 3, 17.

90. Review of *Marian*, by Frances Brooke, *Gazetteer and New Daily Advertiser* (London), May 23, 1788; review of *Marian*, by Frances Brooke, *London Chronicle* (London), May 23, 1788.

91. Review of *Marian*, by Frances Brooke, *Morning Post* (London), May 23, 1788; review of *Marian*, by Frances Brooke, *Morning Chronicle* (London), May 23, 1788.

92. Review of *Marian*, by Frances Brooke, *World* (London), May 23, 1788.

93. See the entry in *The London Stage* for May 17, 1800.

94. Daniel O'Quinn, *Entertaining Crisis in the Atlantic Imperium, 1770–1790* (Baltimore: Johns Hopkins University Press, 2011), 265.

95. Brooke, *Rosina*, 7.

96. Brooke, 18.

97. Brooke, 18.

98. Linda V. Troost, "Frances Brooke's *Rosina*: Subverting Sentimentalism," in *Paper, Ink, and Achievement: Gabriel Hornstein and the Revival of Eighteenth-Century Scholarship*, edited by Kevin L. Cope and Cedric D. Reverand (Lewisburg, PA: Bucknell University Press, 2021), 108.

99. Brooke, *Marian*, 11.

100. Brooke, 11.

101. Frances Brooke, *Marian of the Grange*, Huntington Library, John Larpent Collection, MS LA 805, 40.

102. Brooke, *Rosina*, 14.

103. Brooke, *Marian*, 24. According to the *Oxford English Dictionary*, in the Scottish and northern dialect, "gear" refers to property. Peggy is telling Sir Henry that he does not own her.

104. Brooke, 13.

105. Brooke, 14.

106. Ritchie, *Women Writing Music*, 164.

107. Backscheider, "Becoming a Playwright," 333.

3. Laughter and Femininity

1. Royall Tyler, *The Contrast* (Philadelphia: Prichard & Hall, 1790), act 4, scene 1.

2. Tyler, act 1, scene 1.

3. Tyler, act 5, scene 2.

4. For further discussion of this relationship, see Willow White, "Comic Collusion: Frances Burney's *The Witlings* and the Mentorship of Arthur Murphy," *Women's Writing* 28, no. 2 (2021): 368–383.

5. See Jesse Foot, *The Life of Arthur Murphy* (London: John Nichols and Son, 1811). Unlike some of his male colleagues, Murphy was supportive of women in the theater industry. His most famous protégée was the actress Ann Elliot, for whom he wrote parts and with whom, for a time, he was romantically involved, but he also had many platonic friendships with theatrical women. For example, he was a close friend of the playwright Frances Brooke and wrote the epilogue to her first staged play, *The Siege of Sinope*, in 1780.

6. Barbara Darby, *Frances Burney, Dramatist: Gender, Performance, and the Late-Eighteenth-Century Stage* (Lexington: University Press of Kentucky, 1997), 23.

7. Margaret Anne Doody, *Frances Burney: The Life in the Works* (New Brunswick, NJ: Rutgers University Press, 1988), 91; Kate Chisholm, *Fanny Burney: Her Life, 1752–1840* (London: Chatto & Windus, 1998), 87.

8. Charles Burney also wrote original songs for Garrick's adaptation of *A Midsummer Night's Dream* in 1763, and his own play, *The Cunning Man*, in 1766. See John Wagstaff, "Burney, Charles (1726–1814), Musician and Author," *Oxford Dictionary of National Biography*, September 23, 2004, https://doi.org/10.1093/ref:odnb/4078.

9. Frances Burney, *Memoirs of Doctor Burney* (London: Edward Moxon, 1832), 1:124.

10. Chisholm, *Fanny Burney*, 216.

11. Frances Burney to Susanna Burney, September 3, 1778, in *The Early Journals and Letters of Frances Burney*, vol. 3, ed. Lars E. Troide and Stewart J. Cooke (Oxford: Oxford University Press, 1994), 133.

12. Frances Burney to Susanna Burney, August 23–[30, 1778], *EJL*, 3:94.

13. Frances Burney to Susanna Burney, January 11, [1779], *EJL*, 3:229.

14. Frances Burney to Susanna Burney, 3:234.

15. Frances Burney to Susanna Burney, 3:235.

16. Donkin, *Getting into the Act*, 140.

17. Saggini, *Backstage in the Novel*, 263n16.

18. Jane Barsanti (?–1795) was a pupil of Dr. Burney who befriended his young daughter. See Frances Burney, journal entry for December 30, 1775, in *The Early Journals and Letters of Frances Burney*, vol. 2, ed. Lars E. Troide (Oxford: Oxford University Press, 1990), 198.

19. Frances Burney, journal for 1777, *EJL*, 2:235–250.

20. Frances Burney to Susanna Burney, February [Streatham, post 16], [1779], *EJL*, 3:243.

21. Frances Burney to Susanna Burney, 3:244.

22. Frances Burney to Susanna Burney, 3:246.

23. Frances Burney to Susanna Burney, February [23?,] 1779, *EJL*, 3:252.

24. Frances Burney to Susanna Burney, February [Streatham, post 16], [1779], *EJL*, 3:246.

25. Frances Burney to Susanna Burney, 3:246.

26. Frances Burney to Susanna Burney, May [21–27, 1779], *EJL*, 3:268.

27. Frances Burney to Susanna Burney, 3:278.

28. Frances Burney to Susanna Burney, May 28, 1779, *EJL*, 3:286–287.

29. Frances Burney to Samuel Crisp, July 30, [1779], *EJL*, 3:342.

30. According to Richard Bevis, the term "laughing comedy" was coined in 1773 in the *Westminster Magazine* by Oliver Goldsmith, though the features of laughing comedy had been debated for decades beforehand. See Richard Bevis, *The Laughing Tradition: Stage Comedy in Garrick's Day* (Athens: University of Georgia Press, 1980), 83.

31. Lisa Freeman, "The Social Life of Eighteenth-Century Comedy," in *The Cambridge Companion to British Theatre, 1730–1830*, ed. Jane Moody and Daniel O'Quinn (Cambridge: Cambridge University Press, 2007), 73.

32. See Misty Anderson, "Genealogies of Comedy," in Swindells and Taylor, *Oxford Handbook of Georgian Theatre*, 352; Freeman, *Character's Theater*, 145–146; and Robert D. Hume, "Goldsmith and Sheridan and the Supposed Revolution in 'Laughing' against 'Sentimental' Comedy," in *Studies in Change and Revolution: Aspects of English Intellectual History, 1640–1800*, ed. Paul J. Korshin (Menston, UK: Scolar Press, 1972), 237–276.

33. Freeman, *Character's Theater*, 146.

34. See Roy E. Aycock, "Arthur Murphy, the *Gray's-Inn Journal*, and the *Craftsman*: Some Publication Mysteries," *Papers of the Bibliographical Society of America* 67, no. 3 (1973): 255–262. Aycock provides a detailed explanation of the complicated publication history of the *Gray's Inn Journal*.

35. Arthur Murphy [Charles Ranger, pseud.], *The Gray's-Inn Journal, 1753–4* (London: W. Faden, 1756), 1:248.

36. Murphy, 2:315.

37. J. Homer Caskey, "Arthur Murphy and the War on Sentimental Comedy," *Journal of English and Germanic Philology* 30, no. 4 (1931): 571; Robert D. Spector, *Arthur Murphy* (Boston: Twayne, 1979), 61.

38. See Saggini, *Backstage in the Novel*, 223–243.

39. Frances Burney, adaptation of scenes from *All in the Wrong*, [c. 1779?], General Collection, Beinecke Rare Book & Manuscript Library, Yale University, MSS. File 459. All subsequent quotations are from this unpaginated manuscript.

40. Arthur Murphy, *All in the Wrong* (London: P. Vaillant, 1761), 46. There is no modern critical edition of this play. Citations are by page number in the original publication.

41. Burney, adaptation of *All in the Wrong*, MSS. File 459.

42. Murphy, *All in the Wrong*, 20.

43. Frances Burney, *The Witlings*, in *The Complete Plays of Frances Burney*, ed. Peter Sabor (London: Pickering & Chatto, 1995), 1:2.22–25. Citations are by act and line number.

44. Burney, 2.494–495.

45. Richard Brinsley Sheridan, *The School for Scandal*, ed. Anne Blake (London: Methuen Drama, 2004), 4.3.100–103. Citations are by act, scene, and line number.

46. Sheridan, 4.3.106–116.

47. Murphy, *All in the Wrong*, 75.

48. Murphy, 78.

49. Burney, *Witlings*, 5.294–296.

50. Burney, 5.458–465.

51. Burney, 5.545.

52. Burney, 5.599.

53. Burney, 5.941–942.

54. Frances Burney, *Evelina, or, The History of a Young Lady's Entrance into the World*, ed. Margaret Anne Doody (New York: Penguin, 1994), 260–261.

55. Amy Louise Erickson, "Esther Sleepe, Fan-Maker, and Her Family," *Eighteenth-Century Life* 42, no. 2 (2018): 15–37.

56. Burney, *Witlings*, 1.

57. Hester Lynch Piozzi, *Thraliana: The Diary of Mrs. Hester Lynch Thrale (Later Mrs. Piozzi), 1776–1809*, ed. Katharine C. Balderston (Oxford: Clarendon Press, 1951), 1:381.

58. Frances Burney to Charles Burney, c. August 13, 1779, *EJL*, 3:347.

59. Samuel Crisp to Frances Burney, December 8, 1778, *EJL*, 3:189–190.

60. Crisp to Burney, 3:187.

61. Crisp to Burney, 3:188.

62. Crisp to Burney, 3:188.

63. Crisp to Burney, 3:189.

64. Crisp to Burney, 3:189.

65. Samuel Crisp to Frances Burney, January 11, [1779], *EJL*, 3:238.

66. James Sambrook, "Crisp, Samuel (1707–1783), Playwright," *Oxford Dictionary of National Biography*, September 23, 2004, https://doi.org/10.1093/ref:odnb/6706.

67. Review of *Virginia*, by Samuel Crisp, *Monthly Review; or, Literary Journal* 10 (1754): 226.

68. Frances Burney to Samuel Crisp, March 11, 1779, *EJL*, 3:255.

69. Samuel Crisp to Sarah Crisp, March 28, 1779, in *Burford Papers; Being Letters of Samuel Crisp to His Sister at Burford; and Other Studies of a Century (1745–1845)*, ed. William Holden Hutton (London: A. Constable, 1905), 29.

70. Samuel Crisp to Frances Burney, January 11, [1779], *EJL*, 3:238.

71. Frances Burney to Charles Burney, c. August 13, 1779, *EJL*, 3:347.

72. Charles Burney to Frances Burney, August 29, 1779, *The Letters of Dr Charles Burney*, ed. Alvaro Ribeiro, S. J. (Oxford: Oxford University Press, 1991), 1:280.

73. Charles Burney's various attacks on Clive are quoted in Joncus, *Fair Songster*, 327–330.

74. Doody, *Frances Burney*, 96; Chisholm, *Fanny Burney*, 88.

75. Frances Burney to Samuel Crisp, January 22, [1780], in *The Early Journals and Letters of Frances Burney*, vol. 4, ed. Betty Rizzo (Oxford: Oxford University Press, 2003), 9.

76. Samuel Crisp to Frances Burney, February 23, 1780, *EJL*, 4:17.

77. Crisp to Burney, August 29, 1779, *EJL*, 3:351–353.

78. Crisp to Burney, 3:351.

79. Frances Burney to Samuel Crisp, January 22, [1780], *EJL*, 4:13.

80. Burney to Crisp, January 22, [1780], *EJL*, 4:13.

81. Frances Burney, journal for June 1788, in *The Court Journals and Letters of Frances Burney*, ed. Lorna J. Clark (Oxford: Oxford University Press, 2014), 3:242.

82. Doody, *Frances Burney*, 173.

83. See Frances Burney to Charles Burney, [February 3, 1800], *The Journals and Letters of Fanny Burney (Madame d'Arblay)*, vol. 4, ed. Joyce Hemlow (Oxford: Oxford University Press, 1973), 392n4. Hereafter referred to as *JL*.

84. Frances Burney to Esther Burney, November 19, 1799, *JL*, 4:361.

85. Tara Ghoshal Wallace, "Fanny Burney and the Theatre," in *A Busy Day* by Frances Burney, ed. Tara Ghoshal Wallace (New Brunswick, NJ: Rutgers University Press, 1984), 197.

86. Frances Burney to Charles Burney, February [10], 1800, *JL*, 4:394–395.

87. Frances Burney to Charles Burney, 4:394–395.

88. Frances Burney to Charles Burney, 4:394–395.

89. Frances Burney, *The Woman-Hater*, in Sabor, *Complete Plays of Frances Burney*, 1:1.11.21. Citations are by act, scene, and line number.

90. Hilary Havens, "'How Is Our Blue Club Cut Up!': Frances Burney's Changing Views of the Bluestockings," *Eighteenth-Century Life* 46, no. 1 (2022): 46–47.

91. Burney, *Woman-Hater*, 1.7.60.

92. Burney, 1.3.21–23.

93. Burney, 1.3.59–60.

94. Burney, 5.14.1–6.

95. Peter Sabor and Geoffrey Sill, introduction to *"The Witlings" and "The Woman-Hater"* (Peterborough, ON: Broadview Press, 2002), 32.

96. Matthew S. Buckley, "The Formation of Melodrama," in Swindells and Taylor, *Oxford Handbook of Georgian Theatre*, 462.

97. Sabor and Sill, introduction to *"The Witlings" and "The Woman-Hater,"* 322. Burney envisioned celebrity siblings Sarah Siddons and John Philip Kemble playing the lead roles, as they had in the failed production of *Edwy and Elgiva*.

98. Frances Burney, Recollections, c. April 12, 1802, in *The Journals and Letters of Fanny Burney (Madame d'Arblay)*, vol. 5, ed. Joyce Hemlow (Oxford: Oxford University Press, 1975), 210. My own translation into English.

99. Frances Burney, *Memoirs of Doctor Burney*, 2:174–175.

100. Hannah Cowley, "On Miss Burney," n.d., MS. British Library, London, Egerton 3700 B.

101. See Emily Allen, "Staging Identity: Frances Burney's Allegory of Genre," *Eighteenth-Century Studies* 31, no. 4 (1998): 433–451; Marcie Frank, "Frances Burney's Theatricality," *English Literary History* 82, no. 2 (2015): 615–635; and Anna Paluchowska-Messing, "'Darts to Wound with Endless Love!': On Hannah Cowley's Response to Frances Burney's *Evelina*," *Studia Anglica Posnaniensia* 54, no.1 (2019): 43–57.

4. The Satirical Seraglio

1. Hannah Gadsby, *Nanette*, directed by Madeline Parry and John Olb, 2018, Netflix, 11:58–11:22.

2. Cowley, *School for Greybeards*, vi–vii.

3. Hannah Gadsby, "Three Ideas. Three Contradictions. Or Not," 2019, TED, 2:32–2:35.

4. This biography was appended to a posthumously published collection of Cowley's plays and poetry. See preface to *The Works of Mrs. Cowley. Dramas and Poems* (London: Wilkie and Robinson, 1813), 1:xvii.

5. Review of *A Day in Turkey*, by Hannah Cowley, *Oracle* (London), December 5, 1791.

6. Review of *A Day in Turkey*, by Hannah Cowley, *Public Advertiser* (London), December 5, 1791.

7. Greg Kucich, "Women's Cosmopolitanism and the Romantic Stage," in *Transnational England: Home and Abroad, 1780–1860*, ed. Monika Class and Terry F. Robinson (Cambridge: Cambridge Scholars, 2009), 24.

8. See Betsy Bolton, "The Balance of Power: Hannah Cowley's *Day in Turkey*," in *Women, Nationalism, and the Romantic Stage: Theatre and Politics in Britain, 1780–1800* (Cambridge: Cambridge University Press, 2001), 173–201.

9. Daniel O'Quinn, "Hannah Cowley's *A Day in Turkey* and the Political Efficacy of Charles James Fox," *European Romantic Review* 14, no. 1 (2003): 19.

10. Anne K. Mellor, "Embodied Cosmopolitanism and the British Romantic Woman Writer," *European Romantic Review* 17, no. 3 (2006): 294; Kucich, "Women's Cosmopolitanism," 28.

11. Anderson, *Female Playwrights*, 141.

12. Mary De la Mahotière, *Hannah Cowley: Tiverton's Playwright and Pioneer Feminist (1743–1809)* (Tiverton, UK: Devon Books, 1997), 19. See also Mary De la Mahotière, "Cowley [née Parkhouse], Hannah (1743–1809), Playwright and Poet," *Oxford Dictionary of National Biography*, September 23, 2004, https://doi.org/10.1093/ref:odnb/6500.

13. Preface to *The Works*, vii.

14. De la Mahotière, *Hannah Cowley*, 11.

15. Donkin, *Getting into the Act*, 23.

16. Hannah Cowley, *The Runaway* (1776), in Link, *Plays of Hannah Cowley*, 1:n.p. Subsequent references are from this facsimile edition.

17. Cowley, n.p.

18. Cowley, n.p.

19. Melinda C. Finberg credits Cowley with being "the first professional female dramatist to draw directly from the works of other professional female playwrights." See Finberg, introduction to *Eighteenth-Century Women Dramatists* (Oxford: Oxford University Press, 2001), xxxix.

20. See Cowley's preface to *Albina, Countess Raimond* (1779), in Link, *Plays of Hannah Cowley*, 1:vii. Subsequent references are from this facsimile edition.

21. Cowley, ii–iii. In her preface to *Albina*, Cowley writes that both Sheridan and Harris were given manuscript copies of the play.

22. De la Mahotière, "Cowley [née Parkhouse], Hannah," n.p.

23. Cowley, *Albina*, v.

24. Cowley, vii.

25. Cowley, vii.

26. Cowley, vii.

27. Donkin, *Getting into the Act*, 53. Donkin argues that an open letter to the *St. James's Chronicle* accusing More of plagiarism "may have been a plant" by Thomas Cowley.

28. Hannah More, letter to the editor, *Morning Post* (London), August 13, 1779.

29. Charles Dibdin, *A Complete History of the English Stage* (London: C. Dibdin, 1795), 5:303.

30. Donkin, *Getting into the Act*, 144.

31. Anne Stott, *Hannah More: The First Victorian* (Oxford: Oxford University Press, 2003), 46.

32. Most recently, on February 22, 2021, Red Bull Theatre, based in New York, produced a professional livestream production of *The Belle's Stratagem*, directed by Gaye Taylor Upchurch.

33. Review of *A School for Greybeards*, by Hannah Cowley, *Morning Chronicle* (London), November 27, 1786.

34. Review of *The Way as It Goes*, by Hannah Cowley, *Morning Herald* (London), February 26, 1781.

35. Cowley, *School for Greybeards*, vi–vii.

36. Kemble's inscription in his copy of the play at the Huntington Library, quoted in Frederick M. Link, introduction to *Plays of Hannah Cowley*, xxxviii.

37. Cowley, *Albina*, v.

38. See Betsy Bolton, introduction to *A Day in Turkey; or, The Russian Slaves*, in *The Routledge Anthology of British Women Playwrights, 1777–1843* (London: Routledge, 2019), 139. Bolton provides more historical detail about the conflict.

39. Hannah Cowley, *A Day in Turkey; or, The Russian Slaves*, in Bolton, *British Women Playwrights, 1777–1843*, 143. There are no line numbers in the original or critical editions of the play, so I have cited by page number. I indicate the act and scene number in the body of the text when possible, but Cowley did not always number her scenes. The text in quotation in Cowley's prologue is by Robert Merry, who, under the name of Della Crusca, had exchanged poetry with Cowley, under the pen name Anna Mathilda.

40. Cowley, 143.

41. Orientalism played an important role in the creation of eighteenth-century English culture, art, novels, and drama. Building on the body of scholarship arising from Edward Said's field-defining *Orientalism* (1978), Suvir Kaul describes Orientalism as a "a capacious, supple and changing discursive system that enables Anglo-European writers to explain and to manage the encounters between themselves and the peoples of lands ranging from Turkey, Egypt, Persia and India to China and Japan." See Kaul, "Styles of Orientalism in the Eighteenth Century," in *Orientalism and Literature*, ed. Geoffrey P. Nash (Cambridge: Cambridge University Press, 2019), 35.

42. For more on Charles II's Ottomanphilia and its influence on the Restoration theater, see Laura J. Rosenthal, *Ways of the World: Theater and Cosmopolitanism in the Restoration and Beyond* (Ithaca, NY: Cornell University Press, 2020), 19–53.

43. See Ros Ballaster, *Fabulous Orients: Fictions of the East in England, 1662–1785* (Oxford: Oxford University Press, 2005); Mita Choudhury, *Interculturalism and Resistance in the London Theater, 1660–1800: Identity, Performance, Empire* (Lewisburg, PA: Bucknell University Press, 2000); Bridget Orr, *Empire on the English Stage, 1660–1714* (Cambridge: Cambridge University Press, 2001); Bridget Orr, "Galland, Georgian Theatre, and the Creation of Popular Orientalism," in *The Arabian Nights in*

Historical Context: Between East and West, ed. Saree Makdisi and Felicity Nussbaum (Oxford: Oxford University Press, 2008), 104–130; O'Quinn, *Staging Governance*, 1–32.

44. Pearson, *Prostituted Muse*, 16. For more on women writers and Orientalism, see Bernadette Andrea, *Women and Islam in Early Modern English Literature* (Cambridge: Cambridge University Press, 2007); and Samara Anne Cahill, *Intelligent Souls? Feminist Orientalism in Eighteenth-Century English Literature* (Lewisburg, PA: Bucknell University Press, 2019).

45. Pearson, *Prostituted Muse*, 16.

46. Elizabeth Inchbald, *The Mogul Tale*, in *The Plays of Elizabeth Inchbald*, ed. Paula R. Backscheider, facsimile edition (New York: Garland, 1980), 2:2. Subsequent references are from this edition.

47. Inchbald, 2:19–20.

48. Daniel O'Quinn, "Theatre and Empire," in Moody and O'Quinn, *British Theatre, 1730–1830*, 233.

49. Paula R. Backscheider, "From the *Emperor of the Moon* to the Sultan's Prison," *Studies in Eighteenth-Century Culture* 43, no. 1 (2014): 16.

50. Escott, *Hannah Cowley*, 168.

51. Cowley, *Turkey*, 152.

52. Cowley, 173.

53. Annibel Jenkins, *I'll Tell You What: The Life of Elizabeth Inchbald* (Lexington: University Press of Kentucky, 2003), 317–319; Frans De Bruyn, "Shakespeare and the French Revolution," in *Shakespeare in the Eighteenth Century*, ed. Fiona Ritchie and Peter Sabor (Cambridge: Cambridge University Press, 2012), 308–309.

54. Review of *A Day in Turkey*, by Hannah Cowley, *Gazetteer and New Daily Advertiser* (London), December 5, 1771.

55. Review of *A Day in Turkey*, by Hannah Cowley, *Oracle* (London), December 5, 1771.

56. Review of *A Day in Turkey*, by Hannah Cowley, *Public Advertiser* (London), December 5, 1771.

57. Cowley, *Turkey*, 142.

58. Cowley, 142.

59. Tanya Caldwell, "'A City Graced with Many a Dome': Hannah Cowley's Domestic Comedies, the Georgic Impulse, and the Female Arts," *Eighteenth-Century Life* 42, no. 1 (2018): 30.

60. Mary Wollstonecraft's *A Vindication of the Rights of Men* had been published in 1790, in response to Edmund Burke's *Reflections on the Revolution in France* (1790). Her *Vindication of the Rights of Woman* was published two years later, in the first three months of 1792, around the same time as *A Day in Turkey*.

61. Cowley, *Turkey*, 174.

62. Link, introduction to *Plays of Hannah Cowley*, xli.

63. Cowley, *Turkey*, 149.

64. Cowley, 149.

65. Both Bolton and O'Quinn draw attention to the semi-autobiographical and metatheatrical qualities of *A Day in Turkey*. See Bolton, "Balance of Power," 191; and O'Quinn, "Political Efficacy," 2.

66. Cowley, *Turkey*, 150. "Mussulman" is an archaic term for someone of the Muslim faith.

67. Cowley, 150.

68. Cowley, 153.

69. Quoted in Bolton, *Turkey*, 189n37.

70. Cowley, *Turkey*, 162.

71. Cowley, 163.

72. Cowley, 171.

73. Cowley, 179.

74. Cowley, 150.

75. Cowley, 170–171.

76. Cowley, 150.

77. Cowley, 171.

78. Cowley, 165.

79. Cowley, 166.

80. Cowley, 166.

81. Cowley, 173.

82. Cowley, 174.

83. Cowley, 180.

84. Cowley, 180.

85. Mellor, *Mothers of the Nation*, 59.

86. Cowley, *Turkey*, 148.

87. Slavery was not abolished in the British colonies until 1833 under the Slavery Abolition Act, which took effect in 1834.

88. Cowley, *Turkey*, 180–181.

89. Hannah Cowley, *The Town Before You* (1795), in Link, *Plays of Hannah Cowley*, 2:x–xi. Subsequent references are from this facsimile edition.

90. De la Mahotière, *Hannah Cowley*, 85.

91. De la Mahotière, 89.

5. Sentimental Comedy and Feminism

1. For a further discussion of this event, see Willow White, "Feminist Sensibilities: The Feud of Elizabeth Inchbald and Mary Wollstonecraft," *Eighteenth-Century Studies* 55, no. 3 (2022): 299–315.

2. Elizabeth Inchbald to William Godwin, April 11, 1797, MS. Abinger, c. 3, fol. 59, Bodleian Libraries.

3. Mary Wollstonecraft to Amelia Alderson, London, April 11, 1797, in *Collected Letters of Mary Wollstonecraft*, ed. Ralph Wardle (Ithaca, NY: Cornell University Press, 1979), 389.

4. William Godwin to Elizabeth Inchbald, September 13, 1797, in *Letters of William Godwin*, ed. Pamela Clemit (Oxford: Oxford University Press, 2011), 1:241.

5. Godwin's diary suggests that a meeting may have taken place between Inchbald and Wollstonecraft on July 15, 1797, three months after their quarrel at the theater. Godwin records: "Call on Inchbald; & Cha. [Charlotte] Smith, w. Wt [Wollstonecraft]."

However, the semicolon separating Inchbald's and Charlotte Smith's names suggests that Godwin actually called on Inchbald alone, as he had on numerous occasions following the theater debacle, and afterward called on Smith with Wollstonecraft. See entry on July 15, 1797, *The Diary of William Godwin*, ed. Victoria Myers, David O'Shaughnessy, and Mark Philp (Oxford: Oxford Digital Library, 2010), http://godwindiary.bodleian.ox.ac.uk.

6. Mary Shelley, "Life of William Godwin," in *Mary Shelley's Literary Lives and Other Writings*, ed. Pamela Clemit (New York: Routledge, 2016), 4:250. Shelley never published the biography of her father that she began writing in 1836, but it survives in fragmentary manuscript form in the Abinger Collection, Bodleian Libraries.

7. C. Kegan Paul, *William Godwin: His Friends and Contemporaries* (London: Henry S. King, 1876), 1:239; S. R. Littlewood, *Elizabeth Inchbald and Her Circle* (London: Daniel O'Connor, 1921), 87.

8. Katherine S. Green, "Mr. Harmony and the Events of January 1793: Elizabeth Inchbald's *Every One Has His Fault*," *Theatre Journal* 56, no. 1 (2004): 50; Ildiko Csengei, "Godwin's Case: Melancholy Mourning in the "Empire of Feeling," in *Sympathy, Sensibility, and the Literature of Feeling in the Eighteenth Century* (London: Palgrave Macmillan, 2012), 172.

9. Inchbald and Godwin discussed plots, characters, and more mundane literary matters. On June 9, 1792, for example, Inchbald asked Godwin to correct the title of one of her new plays, writing, "The title 'Every one his Fault' I am told is not grammar. I am sorry for it. Let me know." See Elizabeth Inchbald to William Godwin, June 9, 1792, National Art Museum, Forster Collection, Letter 48.D.2. While rumors had circulated in the press that Godwin and Inchbald had a romantic relationship—for example, the *True Briton* speculated on February 1, 1797, that "Mrs. Inchbald is said to be on the point of bestowing her hand on Mr. Godwin"—I can find no evidence to validate this claim.

10. August Von Kotzebue (1761–1819) was a famous German dramatist whose plays were regularly translated and adapted for the English stage.

11. Jenkins, *I'll Tell You What*, 463.

12. Anderson, *Female Playwrights*, 199.

13. Biographical details for this chapter are from James Boaden, *Memoirs of Mrs. Inchbald, including her familiar correspondence with the most distinguished persons of her time*, 2 vols. (London: Richard Bentley, New Burlington Street, 1833). Inchbald's surviving pocketbooks have been published in an excellent modern critical edition; see *The Diaries of Elizabeth Inchbald*, ed. Ben P. Robertson, 3 vols. (London: Pickering & Chatto, 2007). I also owe a great debt to the most recent biography of Inchbald, by Annibel Jenkins.

14. For more detail on Digges's company, see Phyllis T. Dircks, "Digges, West (1725?–1786), Actor and Theatre Manager," *Oxford Dictionary of National Biography*, January 3, 2008, https://doi.org/10.1093/ref:odnb/7640.

15. As of 1770, Tate Wilkinson was sole manager of a series of theaters known as the Yorkshire circuit, which included the theatre in Leeds and the York Theatre Royal. See C.M.P. Taylor, "Wilkinson, John Joseph Tate (1769/70–1846), Actor and Theatre Manager," *Oxford Dictionary of National Biography*, September 23, 2004, https://doi.org/10.1093/ref:odnb/38587.

16. Jeffrey Cox, "Cowley's Bold Stroke for Comedy," *European Romantic Review* 17, no. 3 (2006): 362.

17. Both plays were published for the first time by Boaden in his 1833 memoir of Inchbald.

18. Misty G. Anderson, "Women Playwrights," in Moody and O'Quinn, *British Theatre, 1730–1830*, 153; Judith Milhous and Robert D. Hume, "Playwrights' Remuneration in Eighteenth-Century London," *Harvard Library Bulletin* 10, no. 2–3 (1999): 3–90.

19. Jane Wessel, *Owning Performance, Performing Ownership: Literary Property and the Eighteenth-Century British Stage* (Ann Arbor: University of Michigan Press, 2022), 126–133.

20. Wessel, 129.

21. "Article XI. *I'll Tell You What; a Comedy, in Five Acts*; as it is performed at the Theatre-Royal, Hay-Market," *English Review, or, An Abstract of English and Foreign Literature* 8 (November 1786): 378.

22. Jean I. Marsden, *Theatres of Feeling: Affect, Performance, and the Eighteenth-Century Stage* (Cambridge: Cambridge University Press, 2019), 1.

23. Cox, "Cowley's Bold Stroke," 364. Cox explains that melodrama replaced comedy as the genre in greatest demand at the turn of the century.

24. Allardyce Nicoll, *Late Eighteenth-Century Drama 1750–1800*, vol. 3 of *A History of English Drama 1660–1900*, 2nd ed. (Cambridge: Cambridge University Press, 1952), 14; Wendy Nielsen, "A Tragic Farce: Revolutionary Women in Elizabeth Inchbald's *The Massacre* and European Drama," *European Romantic Review* 17, no. 3 (2006): 275–288.

25. Jane Moody, "Suicide and Translation in the Dramaturgy of Elizabeth Inchbald and Anne Plumptre," in *Women in British Romantic Theatre: Drama, Performance, and Society, 1790–1840*, ed. Catherine B. Burroughs (Cambridge: Cambridge University Press, 2000), 279.

26. Daniel O'Quinn, *Corrosive Solace: Theater, Affect, and the Realignment of the Repertoire, 1780–1800* (Philadelphia: University of Pennsylvania Press, 2022), 230.

27. Anderson, *Female Playwrights*, 171.

28. For recent analysis of the English literary radicals, see Nancy E. Johnson, *The English Jacobin Novel on Rights, Property, and the Law: Critiquing the Contract* (Basingstoke, UK: Palgrave Macmillan, 2004); David O'Shaughnessy, *William Godwin and the Theatre* (London: Pickering & Chatto, 2010); and Miriam L. Wallace, *Revolutionary Subjects in the English "Jacobin" Novel, 1790–1805* (Cranbury, NJ: Bucknell University Press, 2009).

29. Gary Kelly, *The English Jacobin Novel, 1780–1805* (New York: Clarendon, 1976), 5.

30. Kelly, *Jacobin*, 7.

31. Inchbald, *Diaries*, 2:314, 317.

32. Elizabeth Inchbald to William Godwin, [1794], quoted in Paul, *William Godwin*, 1:139. *Caleb Williams* was later adapted into a play titled *The Iron Chest* by George Colman the Younger in 1796 and performed with disastrous results (see Jenkins, *I'll Tell You What*, 387–394). Inchbald took no part in the project, but she later criticized Colman's adaptation of the novel.

33. Godwin to Inchbald, [January 30–31, 1794], *Letters of William Godwin*, 2:94.

34. Elizabeth Inchbald, "To the Artist," in *The Artist: A Collection of Essays Relative to Painting, Poetry, Sculpture, Architecture, the Drama, Discoveries of Science, and Various Other Subjects* (London: John Murray et al., 1807), 1:16.

35. Cowley, *School for Greybeards*, vii.

36. Amy Garnai, *Revolutionary Imaginings in the 1790s: Charlotte Smith, Mary Robinson, Elizabeth Inchbald* (New York: Palgrave Macmillan, 2009); Mellor, *Mothers of the Nation*, 39–68; O'Quinn, *Staging Governance*, 125–163.

37. Mellor, *Mothers of the Nation*, 68.

38. Review of *Every One Has His Fault*, by Elizabeth Inchbald, *True Briton* (London), January 30, 1793; Gillian Russell, "Riotous Assemblies: The Army and Navy in the Theatre," in *The Theatres of War: Performance, Politics, and Society 1793–1815* (Oxford: Oxford University Press, 1995), 112.

39. Inchbald's response to the *True Briton* is printed in Boaden, *Memoirs of Mrs. Inchbald*, 1:311.

40. Anderson, *Female Playwrights*, 183.

41. Boaden, *Memoirs of Mrs. Inchbald*, 1:330.

42. Littlewood, *Circle*, 87.

43. Jenkins, *I'll Tell You What*, 518.

44. Kelly, *Jacobin*, 113.

45. A second novel by Wollstonecraft, *Maria: or, The Wrongs of Woman*, was published posthumously in 1798.

46. Mary Wollstonecraft, *A Vindication of the Rights of Woman*, in *A Vindication of the Rights of Man; A Vindication of the Rights of Woman; An Historical and Moral View of the French Revolution*, ed. Janet Todd (Oxford: University Press, 1999), 113. Henceforth referred to as *Rights of Woman*.

47. Janet Todd, *Mary Wollstonecraft: A Revolutionary Life* (New York: Columbia University Press, 2000), 185.

48. Inchbald, *Every One Has His Fault* (1793), in Backscheider, *Plays of Elizabeth Inchbald*, facsimile edition, 2:i. Subsequent references are from this edition.

49. Green, "Mr. Harmony," 52.

50. See Cowley, *Turkey*, 142.

51. Wollstonecraft to Godwin, London, August 2, 1796, in *Collected Letters*, 333. See also Wollstonecraft to Godwin, London, August 24, 1796, in *Collected Letters*, 340.

52. Wollstonecraft to Godwin, London, September 4, 1796, in *Collected Letters*, 346. In this letter, Wollstonecraft appears to suggest that she and Godwin believe that Inchbald has romantic feelings for him.

53. Wollstonecraft wrote to Amelia Alderson on April 11, 1797, that the Twisses had ended their friendship with her after they learned of the marriage, and Godwin later named Siddons as doing the same in his memoir of Wollstonecraft published in 1798.

54. Todd, *Mary Wollstonecraft*, 417.

55. Ben Robertson, *Elizabeth Inchbald's Reputation* (London: Pickering & Chatto, 2013), 11; Anna Lott, introduction to *A Simple Story*, by Elizabeth Inchbald (Toronto: Broadview, 2007), 20.

56. William Godwin, *An Enquiry Concerning Political Justice* (London: G.G.J. and J. Robinson, 1793), 2:850.

57. Harriet Guest, *Unbounded Attachment: Sentiment and Politics in the Age of the French Revolution* (Oxford: Oxford University Press, 2013), 99.

58. Godwin to Inchbald, September 10, 1797, *Letters of William Godwin*, 1:238.

59. Inchbald to Godwin, September 10, 1797, *Letters of William Godwin*, 1:238n1.

60. Inchbald to Godwin, September 14, 1797, *Letters of William Godwin*, 1:243n4.

61. Inchbald to Godwin, September 10, 1797, 1:238n1.

62. See Mary Wollstonecraft, "Contributions to the *Analytical Review*," in *The Works of Mary Wollstonecraft*, ed. Janet Todd and Marilyn Butler (London: Pickering & Chatto, 1989), 7:13–487. All subsequent references to Wollstonecraft's essays for the *Analytical Review* are from this edition.

63. Review of *A Simple Story*, by Elizabeth Inchbald, *Gentleman's Magazine and Historical Chronicle* 61 (1791): 225.

64. Review of *A Simple Story*, by Elizabeth Inchbald, *Lady's Magazine* 21 (1791): 59–61.

65. Wollstonecraft, *Analytical Review* 10 (1791): 101.

66. Wollstonecraft, 101.

67. Wollstonecraft, 102.

68. Wollstonecraft, *Rights of Woman*, 272.

69. Wollstonecraft, 271.

70. For further discussion of Wollstonecraft's complex treatment of sentiment and sensibility, see Syndy McMillen Conger, *Mary Wollstonecraft and the Language of Sensibility* (Rutherford, NJ: Fairleigh Dickinson University Press, 1994); Harriet Guest, "Remembering Mary Wollstonecraft," in *Unbounded Attachment: Sentiment and Politics in the Age of the French Revolution* (Oxford: Oxford University Press, 2013), 88–122; and Mitzi Myers, "Sensibility and the 'Walk of Reason': Mary Wollstonecraft's Literary Reviews as Cultural Critique," in *Sensibility in Transformation: Creative Resistance to Sentiment from the Augustans to the Romantics*, ed. Syndy McMillen Conger (Rutherford, NJ: Fairleigh Dickinson University Press, 1990), 120–144.

71. Wollstonecraft, *Rights of Woman*, 74.

72. Anna Laetitia Barbauld, introduction to "A Simple Story," in *The British Novelists*, 50 vols (London: F. C. and J. Rivington, 1810), 28:iv.

73. Boaden, *Memoirs of Mrs. Inchbald*, 2:353.

74. Boaden, 2:353.

75. Wollstonecraft, *Analytical Review* 23 (1796): 511.

76. Wollstonecraft, 511.

77. Wollstonecraft, 511.

78. For a detailed analysis of Inchbald's revisions to various editions of *Nature and Art*, see Janice Marie Cauwels, "Authorial 'Caprice' vs. Editorial 'Calculation': The Text of Elizabeth Inchbald's *Nature and Art*," *Papers of the Bibliographical Society of America* 72, no. 2 (1978): 169–185.

79. Wollstonecraft, *Analytical Review* 23 (1796): 511.

80. See Ralph M. Wardle, "Mary Wollstonecraft, Analytical Reviewer," *PMLA* 62, no. 4 (1947): 1000–1009. Wardle was the first to attribute all reviews signed "M," "W," and "T" to Wollstonecraft. For more recent analysis of Wollstonecraft's work for the *Analytical Review*, see Anne Chandler, "The 'Seeds of Order and Taste': Wollstonecraft,

the *Analytical Review*, and Critical Idiom," *European Romantic Review* 16, no. 1 (2005): 1–21; Fiore Sireci, "'Writers Who Have Rendered Women Objects of Pity': Mary Wollstonecraft's Literary Criticism in the *Analytical Review* and *A Vindication of the Rights of Woman*," *Journal of the History of Ideas* 79, no. 2 (2018): 243–265; and Mary A. Waters, "'The First of a New Genus—': Mary Wollstonecraft, Mary Hays, and *The Analytical Review*," in *British Women Writers and the Profession of Literary Criticism, 1789–1832* (New York: Palgrave Macmillan, 2004), 86–120.

81. Todd, *Mary Wollstonecraft*, 382.

82. Lott, introduction to *A Simple Story*, 21.

83. Wollstonecraft, *Analytical Review* 8 (1790), 223; Wollstonecraft, *Analytical Review* 1 (1788), 333.

84. Elizabeth Inchbald, "Remarks for *John Bull*," in *The British Theatre; or, a Collection of Plays, Which Are Acted at the Theatres Royal, Drury Lane, Covent Garden, and Haymarket* (London: Longman, Hurst, Rees, and Orme, 1808), 24:4. Here, Inchbald is commenting on a play by George Colman the Younger.

85. *London Chronicle*, October 11–13, 1798.

86. John Loftis, "Political and Social Thought in the Drama," in *The London Theatre World, 1660–1800*, ed. Robert D. Hume. (Carbondale: Southern Illinois University Press, 1980), 282.

87. Review of *The Stranger*, by Richard Brinsley Sheridan, *Anti-Jacobin Review* (London), September 4, 1799. Despite facing criticism, *The Stranger* was a success, in large part due to performances by celebrity siblings Sarah Siddons and John Philip Kemble. The two did not perform in *Lovers' Vows* as they were acting at Drury Lane when the play was first acted at Covent Garden.

88. Moody, "Suicide and Translation," 262.

89. See Loftis, "Political and Social," 283.

90. Elizabeth Inchbald, *Lovers' Vows* (1798), in Backscheider, *Plays of Elizabeth Inchbald*, facsimile edition, 2:i. Subsequent citations are from this edition. When possible, act and scene numbers are referred to in the main body of the text.

91. Christoph Bode. "Unfit for an English Stage? Inchbald's *Lovers' Vows* and Kotzebue's *Das Kind der Liebe*," *European Romantic Review* 16, no. 3 (2005): 303.

92. See Bode, "Unfit," 303–304.

93. See Byrne, *Jane Austen*, 149–177. Byrne offers a detailed analysis of the *Lovers' Vows* scene in *Mansfield Park*.

94. Inchbald, *Lovers' Vows*, iii.

95. Inchbald, 21–22.

96. Inchbald, 41–42.

97. Anne Plumptre, preface to *The Natural Son*, by August Von Kotzebue (London: R. Phillips, 1798), v. For a discussion of Plumptre's and Inchbald's different approaches to translating *Lovers' Vows*, see Moody, "Suicide and Translation," 264–272.

98. Byrne, *Jane Austen*, 158.

99. Inchbald, *Lovers' Vows*, 10.

100. Inchbald, 13.

101. Inchbald, 84.

102. Inchbald, 88.

103. See *The British Theatre; or, A Collection of Plays, Which Are Acted at the Theatres Royal, Drury Lane, Covent Garden, and Haymarket. Printed Under the Authority of the Managers from the Prompt Books. With Biographical and Critical Remarks*, by Mrs. Inchbald, 25 vols. (London: Longman, Hurst, Rees and Orme, 1808). *The British Theatre* was initially published serially between 1806 and 1808, and later released as a twenty-five-volume collected edition in 1808 with each play paginated separately. All subsequent references to Inchbald's prefaces are from the 1808 edition and are cited by volume and page number when available. Five of Inchbald's own works were included in the collection: *Every One Has His Fault* (1793), *Lovers' Vows* (1798), *Such Things Are* (1787), *To Marry, or Not to Marry* (1793), and *Wives as They Were and Maids as They Are* (1797).

104. Elizabeth Inchbald, remarks in *The British Theatre*, 23:7.

105. Inchbald, 23:n.p.

106. Mary Wells, *Memoirs of the life of Mrs. Sumbel, late Wells: Of the Theatres-Royal, Drury-Lane, Covent-Garden, and Haymarket* (London: C. Chapple, 1811), 2:203.

107. Boaden, *Memoirs of Mrs. Inchbald*, 1:332–333.

108. For further discussion of Inchbald's theatrical criticism see Marvin Carlson, "Elizabeth Inchbald: A Woman Critic in Her Theatrical Culture," in *Women in British Romantic Theatre: Drama, Performance, and Society, 1790–1840*, ed. Catherine B. Burroughs (Cambridge: Cambridge University Press, 2000), 207–222; Lisa Freeman, "On the Art of Dramatic Probability: Elizabeth Inchbald's Remarks for *The British Theatre*," *Theatre Survey* 62, no. 2 (2021): 163–181; Katharine M. Rogers, "Britain's First Woman Drama Critic: Elizabeth Inchbald," in *Curtain Calls: British and American Women and the Theater, 1660–1820*, ed. Mary Anne Schofield and Cecilia Macheski (Athens: Ohio University Press, 1991), 277–290; and Mary A. Waters, "Renouncing the Forms: The Case of Elizabeth Inchbald," in *Profession of Literary Criticism*, 57–81.

109. Freeman, "Art of Dramatic Probability," 164–165.

110. Inchbald, remarks in *The British Theatre*, 11:3–6, 24:3.

111. Jenkins, *I'll Tell You What*, 484.

112. Inchbald, remarks in *The British Theatre*, 21:v.

113. Inchbald, 21:4.

114. Printed in William McKee, *Elizabeth Inchbald, Novelist* (Washington, DC: Catholic University of America, 1954), appendix 1, 151.

115. Some of Edgeworth's letters to Inchbald's are printed in Boaden, *Memoirs of Mrs. Inchbald*, 2:192–199. Other letters are housed today in the Archive of Maria Edgeworth and the Edgeworth Family, Oxford, Bodleian Libraries MSS. Eng. lett. c. 696–747.

116. Jacky Bratton, *The Making of the West End Stage: Marriage, Management and the Mapping of Gender in London, 1830–1870* (Cambridge: Cambridge University Press, 2011), 7.

117. Moody, *Illegitimate Theatre*, 45–46.

118. See Katherine Newey, *Women's Theatre Writing in Victorian Britain* (New York: Palgrave Macmillan, 2005), 1–9.

119. Jeffrey Cox and Michael Gamer, introduction to *The Broadview Anthology of Romantic Drama* (Peterborough, ON: Broadview Press, 2003), xiii.

Conclusion

1. Phoebe Waller-Bridge, *Fleabag*, season 2, episode 2, directed by Harry Bradbeer, BBC Three, March 5, 2019, 15:20–15:30.

2. Waller-Bridge, *Fleabag*, season 2, episode 2, 15:30.

3. Phoebe Waller-Bridge, *Fleabag*, season 2, episode 4, directed by Harry Bradbeer, BBC Three, March 11, 2019, 3:20–3:25.

4. Phoebe Waller-Bridge, *Saturday Night Live*, season 45, episode 2, NBC, October 5, 2019, 9:15–9:28.

5. "Black Women and the Pay Gap," American Association of University Women, 2019, https://www.aauw.org/resources/article/black-women-and-the-pay-gap/.

6. Issa Rae, *Insecure*, season 2, episode 1, "Hella Great," directed by Melina Matsoukas, HBO, July 23, 2017, 20:45–20:54.

7. Issa Rae, *Insecure*, season 2, episode 1, 21:10–21:15.

8. Abbi Jacobson and Ilana Glazer, *Broad City*, season 3, episode 10, "Jews on a Plane," directed by John Lee, Comedy Central, April 20, 2016, 8:05.

9. Jacobson and Glazer, *Broad City*, season 3, episode 10, 8:10–8:31.

10. Jacobson and Glazer, *Broad City*, season 3, episode 10, 8:47–8:52.

11. Ali Wong, *Baby Cobra*, directed by Jay Karas, Netflix, 2016, 22:00–20:55.

12. Leslie Bennetts, "Joan Rivers's Remarkable Rise to (and Devastating Fall from) Comedy's Highest Rank," *Vanity Fair*, November 3, 2016, https://www.vanityfair.com/hollywood/2016/11/joan-rivers-last-girl-before-freeway-excerpt.

13. Ali Wong, *Hard Knock Wife*," directed by Jay Karas, Netflix, 2018, 3:15–3:35.

14. Tig Notaro, *Tig Notaro Live*, Spotify, 2013, 0:45–0:50.

15. Notaro, *Tig Notaro Live*, 1:13–1:35.

16. See Sarah Silverman, *The Sarah Silverman Podcast*, episode 97, "Mom, Religion, Drag," Spotify, August 4, 2022, 40:30–40:40.

17. Quoted in Michelle Ruiz, "In *Oh God, a Show about Abortion*, Alison Leiby Shares Her Unvarnished Truth," *Vogue*, May 13, 2022, https://www.vogue.com/article/oh-god-a-show-about-abortion-alison-leiby-interview.

18. See Laura Collins-Hughs, "*The Appointment* Review: A Chorus Line at the Abortion Clinic," *New York Times*, January 24, 2023, https://www.nytimes.com/2023/01/24/theater/the-appointment-review.html.

Bibliography

Archives Consulted

Beinecke Rare Book and Manuscript Library, Yale University, New Haven, CT.
    "Frances Burney, Adaptation of scenes from *All in the Wrong*" (c. 1779). General Collection. GEN MSS File 459.

Bodleian Library Special Collections, Oxford University, Oxford, England. Abinger Papers.
    Archive of Maria Edgeworth and the Edgeworth Family. MSS. Eng. lett. c. 696–747.
    Frances Brooke to Ozias Humphrey (September 8, 1775). MSS. Montagu d. 6, ff. 239–240.

British Library, London.
    Cowley, Hannah. "On Miss Burney" (n.d.). Manuscript Collections. Egerton MS 3700 B.
    Evelyn Papers.
    Garrick Collection of English Plays.
    Letters from Edgeworth family. Manuscript Collections. Egerton MS 2158.
    Papers of Charles Burney. Barrett Collection. Egerton MS 3700 B.

Chawton House Library, Alton, England Women's Writing in English Collection.

Christ Church Library, Oxford University, Oxford, England F. B. Brady Collection.

Folger Shakespeare Library, Washington, DC.
    "Copies of letters to Jane Pope from various people, 1769–1808, in the hand of James Winston" (c. 1840). W.b. 73.

Houghton Library, Harvard University, Cambridge, MA.
    Frances Brooke Letters to Richard Gifford. MS Eng 1310.

Huntington Library, San Marino, CA.
    Brooke, Frances. "Marian of the Grange" (1788). MS John Larpent Collection, LA 805.
    Clive, Catherine. "Every Woman in Her Humour" (1760). MS John Larpent Collection, LA 174.
    Clive, Catherine. "The Faithful Irish Woman" (1765). MS John Larpent Collection, LA 247.
    Clive, Catherine. "The Rehearsal; or, Bayes in Petticoats" (1750). MS John Larpent Collection, LA 86.
    Clive, Catherine. "The Sketch of a Fine Lady's Return from a Rout" (1763). MS John Larpent Collection, LA 220.

McGill Rare Books and Special Collections, McGill University, Montreal, QC. Enlightenment Collections.

National Art Library, London.
    Elizabeth Inchbald to William Godwin (June 9, 1792). Forster Collection, Letter 48. D.2.

BIBLIOGRAPHY

Primary Sources

American Association of University Women. "Black Women and the Pay Gap." 2019. https://www.aauw.org/resources/article/black-women-and-the-pay-gap/.

"Article XI. *I'll Tell You What; a Comedy, in Five Acts*; as it is performed at the Theatre-Royal, Hay-Market." *English Review, or, An Abstract of English and Foreign Literature* 8 (November 1786): 374–380.

Barbauld, Anna Laetitia. Introduction to *A Simple Story* by Elizabeth Inchbald. In *The British Novelists*, 50 vols. London: F. C. and J. Rivington, 1810, vol. 28.

Behn, Aphra. *The Lucky Chance; Or, An Alderman's Bargain*. In *The Works of Aphra Behn*, edited by Janet Todd, 7:210–285. Columbus: Ohio State University Press, 1992.

———. *Sir Patient Fancy*. In *The Works of Aphra Behn*, edited by Janet Todd, 6:1–82. Columbus: Ohio State University Press, 1992.

Boaden, James. *Memoirs of Mrs. Inchbald, including her familiar correspondence with the most distinguished persons of her time*. 2 vols. London: Richard Bentley, New Burlington Street, 1833.

Brooke, Frances. *The Excursion*. Edited by Paula R. Backscheider and Hope D. Cotton. Lexington: University Press of Kentucky, 1997.

———. *Marian: A Comic Opera*. London: A. Strahan, 1800.

——— [Mary Singleton, pseud.]. *The Old Maid*. London: A. Miller, 1764.

———. *Rosina: A Comic Opera*. London: T. Cadell, 1783.

———. *The Siege of Sinope*. London: T. Cadell, 1781.

———. *Virginia*. London: A. Millar, 1754.

Burney, Charles. *The Letters of Dr. Charles Burney*. Vol. 1, *1751–1784*. Edited by Alvaro Ribeiro. Oxford: Oxford University Press, 1991.

Burney, Frances. *The Court Journals and Letters of Frances Burney*. Edited by Lorna J. Clark. Vol. 3. Oxford: Oxford University Press, 2014.

———. *The Early Journals and Letters of Fanny Burney*. Vol. 1. Edited by Lars E. Troide. Oxford: Oxford University Press, 1990.

———. *The Early Journals and Letters of Fanny Burney*. Vol. 3. Edited by Lars E. Troide and Stewart J. Cooke. Oxford: Oxford University Press, 1994.

———. *The Early Journals and Letters of Fanny Burney*. Vol. 4. Edited by Betty Rizzo. Oxford: Oxford University Press, 2003.

———. *Evelina, or, The History of a Young Lady's Entrance into the World*. Edited by Margaret Anne Doody. New York: Penguin, 1994.

———. *The Journals and Letters of Fanny Burney (Madame d'Arblay)*. Edited by Joyce Hemlow. vol. 4. Oxford: Oxford University Press, 1973.

———. *The Journals and Letters of Fanny Burney (Madame d'Arblay)*. Edited by Joyce Hemlow. vol. 5. Oxford: Oxford University Press, 1975.

———. *Memoirs of Doctor Burney*. 3 vols. London: Edward Moxon, 1832.

———. *The Witlings*. In *The Complete Plays of Frances Burney*, edited by Peter Sabor, 1:7–101. London: Pickering & Chatto, 1995.

———. *The Woman-Hater*. In *The Complete Plays of Frances Burney*, edited by Peter Sabor, 1:195–285. London: Pickering & Chatto, 1995.

Centlivre, Susanna. *The Platonick Lady*. London: printed for James Knapton, 1707.

Chetwood, William. *A General History of the Stage: From Its Origin in Greece Down to the Present Time*. London: printed for W. Owen, 1766.

Clive, Catherine. *The Case of Mrs. Clive: Submitted to the Publick*. London: printed for B. Dod, 1744.

———. "The Rehearsal; or, Bayes in Petticoats (1753)." In *"The Clandestine Marriage" by David Garrick & George Coleman the Elder Together with Two Short Plays*, edited by Noel Chevalier, 187–213. Peterborough, ON: Broadview Press, 1995.

Congreve, William. "Concerning Humour in Comedy." In *The Works of William Congreve*, edited by D. F. McKenzie, 3:63–72. Oxford: Oxford University Press, 2011.

Cowley, Hannah. *Albina, Countess Raimond* (1779). In *The Plays of Hannah Cowley*, edited by Frederick M. Link, 1:i–84. New York: Garland, 1979.

———. *A Day in Turkey; or, The Russian Slaves*. In *The Routledge Anthology of British Women Playwrights, 1777–1843*, edited by Betsy Bolton, 138–181. London: Routledge, 2019.

———. *The Runaway* (1776). In *The Plays of Hannah Cowley*, edited by Frederick M. Link, 1:1–72. New York: Garland, 1979.

———. *A School for Greybeards; Or, The Mourning Bride* (1786). In *The Plays of Hannah Cowley*, edited by Frederick M. Link, 2:iii–74. New York: Garland, 1979.

———. *The Town Before You* (1795). In *The Plays of Hannah Cowley*, edited by Frederick M. Link, 2:v–103. New York: Garland, 1979.

———. *The Works of Mrs. Cowley*, v–xxi. London: Wilkie and Robinson, 1813.

Crisp, Samuel. *Burford Papers; Being Letters of Samuel Crisp to His Sister at Burford; and Other Studies of a Century (1745–1845)*. Edited by William Holden Hutton. London: A. Constable, 1905.

Dalton, John. *Comus*. London: J. Hughs, 1738.

Dibdin, Charles. *A Complete History of the English Stage*. 5 vols. London: C. Dibdin, 1795.

Fielding, Henry. *The Intriguing Chambermaid*. In *The Wesleyan Edition of the Works of Henry Fielding, Plays*, vol. 2, 1731–1734, edited by Thomas Lockwood, 561–617. Oxford: Oxford University Press, 2009.

Foot, Jesse. *The Life of Arthur Murphy*. London: John Nichols and Son, 1811.

Gadsby, Hannah. *Nanette*. Netflix, 2018.

———. "Three Ideas. Three Contradictions. Or Not." TED Talks, April 2019. https://www.youtube.com/watch?v=87qLWFZManA.

Garrick, David. *The Letters of David Garrick*. Edited by David Little and George Kahrl. 3 vols. Cambridge, MA: Belknap Press, 1963.

———. *The Private Correspondence of David Garrick with the most Celebrated Persons of his Time*. Edited by James Boaden. London: Colburn and Bentley, 1831.

Godwin, William. *The Diary of William Godwin*. Edited by Victoria Myers, David O'Shaughnessy, and Mark Philp. Oxford: Oxford Digital Library, 2010.

———. *An Enquiry Concerning Political Justice*. 2 vols. London: G.G.J. and J. Robinson, 1793.

———. *The Letters of William Godwin*. Edited by Pamela Clemit. 2 vols. Oxford: Oxford University Press, 2011.

Griffith, Elizabeth. *The Platonic Wife, a Comedy*. London: W. Johnston, 1765.

———. *The School for Rakes, a Comedy*. London: W. & W. Smith, 1769.
Hurst, Isobel. *Victorian Women Writers and the Classics: The Feminine of Homer*. Oxford: Oxford University Press, 2006.
Inchbald, Elizabeth. *The Diaries of Elizabeth Inchbald*. Edited by Ben P. Robertson. 3 vols. London: Pickering & Chatto, 2007.
———. *Every One Has His Fault* (1793). In *The Plays of Elizabeth Inchbald*, edited by Paula R. Backscheider, facsimile edition, 2:1–116. New York: Garland, 1980.
———. *Lovers' Vows* (1798). In *The Plays of Elizabeth Inchbald*, edited by Paula Backscheider, facsimile edition, 2:1–90. New York: Garland, 1980.
———. *The Mogul Tale*. In *The Plays of Elizabeth Inchbald*, edited by Paula R. Backscheider, facsimile edition, 2:1–20. New York: Garland, 1980.
———. "Remarks for *John Bull*." In *The British Theatre; or, a Collection of Plays, Which Are Acted at the Theatres Royal, Drury Lane, Covent Garden, and Haymarket*, 21:3–5. London: Longman, Hurst, Rees, and Orme, 1808.
———. "Remarks for *Lovers' Vows*." In *The British Theatre; or, A Collection of Plays, Which Are Acted at the Theatres Royal, Drury Lane, Covent Garden, and Haymarket*, 23:7–9. London: Longman, Hurst, Rees, and Orme, 1808.
———. "To The Artist." In *The Artist: A Collection of Essays Relative to Painting, Poetry, Sculpture, Architecture, the Drama, Discoveries of Science, and Various Other Subjects*, 1:9-19. London: John Murray et al., 1807.
Jacobson, Abbi, and Ilana Glazer. *Broad City*. Season 3, episode 10, "Jews on a Plane." Directed by John Lee. Comedy Central, April 20, 2016.
Kirkman, James T. *Memoirs of the Life of Charles Macklin*. 3 vols. London: Lackington, Allen, 1799.
Le Fanu, Alicia. *Memoirs of the Life and Writings of Mrs. Frances Sheridan*. London: G. and W. B. Whittaker, 1824.
Murphy, Arthur. *All in the Wrong*. London: P. Vaillant, 1761.
——— [Charles Ranger, pseud.]. *The Gray's-Inn Journal*. London: W. Faden, 1753–54.
Notaro, Tig. *Tig Notaro Live*. Spotify, 2013.
Plumptre, Anne. Preface to *The Natural Son*, by August von Kotzebue, i–vii. London: R. Phillips, 1798.
Pye, Jael-Henrietta. *A Short View of the Principal Seats and Gardens in and About Twickenham*. London: n.p., 1771.
Rae, Issa. *Insecure*. Season 2, episode 1, "Hella Great." Directed by Melina Matsoukas. HBO, July 23, 2017.
Shelley, Mary. "Life of William Godwin." In *Mary Shelley's "Literary Lives" and Other Writings*, vol. 4, edited by Pamela Clemit, 3–116. New York: Routledge, 2016.
Sheridan, Frances. *The Dupe, a Comedy*. London: printed for A. Millar, 1764.
Sheridan, Richard Brinsley. *The School for Scandal*. Edited by Anne Blake. London: Methuen Drama, 2004.
Sherman-Palladino, Amy, Kate Fodor, and Jen Kirkman. *The Marvelous Mrs. Maisel*. Season 2, episode 2, "Mid-way to Mid-town." Directed by Amy Sherman-Palladino. Amazon Prime Video, December 5, 2018.
Silverman, Sarah. *The Sarah Silverman Podcast*. Episode 97, "Mom, Religion, Drag." Spotify, August 4, 2022.

Thrale, Hester. *Thraliana: The Diary of Mrs. Hester Lynch Thrale (Later Mrs. Piozzi), 1776–1809*. Edited by Katherine C. Balderston. 2 vols. Oxford: Clarendon Press, 1951.

Tyler, Royall. *The Contrast*. Philadelphia: Prichard & Hall, 1790.

Villiers, George, Second Duke of Buckingham. *The Rehearsal*. In *Plays, Poems, and Miscellaneous Writings associated with George Villiers, Second Duke of Buckingham*, edited by Robert D. Hume and Harold Love, 1:396–453. Oxford: Oxford University Press, 2007.

Waller-Bridge, Phoebe. *Fleabag*. Season 2, episode 2. Directed by Harry Bradbeer. BBC Three, March 5, 2019.

———. *Fleabag*. Season 2, episode 4. Directed by Harry Bradbeer. BBC Three, March 11, 2019.

———. *Saturday Night Live*. Season 45, episode 2. NBC, October 5, 2019.

Wells, Mary. *Memoirs of the life of Mrs. Sumbel, late Wells: of the Theatres-Royal, Drury-Lane, Covent-Garden, and Haymarket*. 2 vols. London: C. Chapple, 1811.

Wilkinson, Tate. *Memoirs of His Own Life*. 3 vols. York: Wilson, Spence, and Mawman, 1790.

W. M. *The Female Wits* (1704). Facsimile ed., with an introduction by Lucyle Hook. Los Angeles: William Andrews Clark Memorial Library, 1967.

Wollstonecraft, Mary. *Collected Letters of Mary Wollstonecraft*. Edited by Ralph Wardle. Ithaca, NY: Cornell University Press, 1979.

———. "Contributions to the *Analytical Review*." In *The Works of Mary Wollstonecraft*, edited by Janet Todd and Marilyn Butler, 7:14–487. London: Pickering & Chatto, 1989

———. *A Vindication of the Rights of Woman*. In *A Vindication of the Rights of Man; A Vindication of the Rights of Woman; An Historical and Moral View of the French Revolution*, edited by Janet Todd, 63–284. Oxford: Oxford University Press, 1999.

Wong, Ali. *Baby Cobra*. Directed by Jay Karas. Netflix, 2016.

———. *Hard Knock Wife*. Directed by Jay Karas. Netflix, 2018.

Young, M. J. *Memoirs of Mrs. Crouch: Including a Retrospect of the Stage, During the Years She Performed*. 2 vols. London: printed for James Asperne, 1806.

Secondary Sources

Allen, Emily. "Staging Identity: Frances Burney's Allegory of Genre." *Eighteenth-Century Studies* 31, no. 4 (1998): 433–435.

Anderson, Emily H. *Eighteenth-Century Authorship and the Play of Fiction: Novels and the Theater, Haywood to Austen*. New York: Routledge, 2009.

Anderson, Misty G. *Female Playwrights and Eighteenth-Century Comedy: Negotiating Marriage on the London Stage*. New York: Palgrave, 2002.

———. "Genealogies of Comedy." In *The Oxford Handbook of the Georgian Theatre, 1737–1832*, edited by Julia Swindells and David Francis Taylor, 347–367. Oxford: Oxford University Press, 2014.

———. "Women Playwrights." In *The Cambridge Companion to British Theatre, 1730–1830*, edited by Jane Moody and Daniel O'Quinn, 145–158. Cambridge: Cambridge University Press, 2007.

Andrea, Bernadette. *Women and Islam in Early Modern English Literature*. Cambridge: Cambridge University Press, 2007.

Apetrei, Sarah. *Women, Feminism, and Religion in Early Enlightenment England*. Cambridge: Cambridge University Press, 2010.

Aycock, Roy E. "Arthur Murphy, the *Gray's-Inn Journal*, and the *Craftsman*: Some Publication Mysteries." *Papers of the Bibliographical Society of America* 67, no. 3 (1973): 255–262.

Backscheider, Paula R. "Frances Brooke: Becoming a Playwright." *Women's Writing* 23, no. 3 (2016): 325–338.

———. "From *The Emperor of the Moon* to the Sultan's Prison." *Studies in Eighteenth-Century Culture* 43, no. 1 (2014): 1–26.

Backscheider, Paula R., and Hope D. Cotton. Introduction to *The Excursion*, by Frances Brooke, x–xlvi. Lexington: University Press of Kentucky, 2015.

Baker, Jean. *Sarah Baker and Her Kentish Theatres, 1737–1816: Challenging the Status Quo*. London: Society for Theatre Research, 2019.

Ballaster, Ros. *Fabulous Orients: Fictions of the East in England, 1662–1785*. Oxford: Oxford University Press, 2005.

Barecca, Regina. *They Used to Call Me Snow White . . . but I Drifted: Women's Strategic Use of Humor in British Literature*. Detroit, MI: Wayne State University Press, 1994.

Bennetts, Leslie. "Joan Rivers's Remarkable Rise to (and Devastating Fall from) Comedy's Highest Rank." *Vanity Fair*, November 3, 2016. https://www.vanityfair.com/hollywood/2016/11/joan-rivers-last-girl-before-freeway-excerpt.

Berland, K.J.H. "Frances Brooke and David Garrick." *Studies in Eighteenth-Century Culture* 20 (1990): 217–230.

Bevis, Richard. *The Laughing Tradition: Stage Comedy in Garrick's Day*. Athens: University of Georgia Press, 1980.

Bilger, Audrey. *Laughing Feminism: Subversive Comedy in Frances Burney, Maria Edgeworth, and Jane Austen*. Detroit, MI: Wayne State University Press, 2002.

Bode, Christoph. "Unfit for an English Stage? Inchbald's *Lovers' Vows* and Kotzebue's *Das Kind der Liebe*." *European Romantic Review* 16, no. 3 (2005): 297–309.

Bolton, Betsy. "The Balance of Power: Hannah Cowley's *Day in Turkey*." In *Women, Nationalism, and the Romantic Stage: Theatre and Politics in Britain, 1780–1800*, 173–201. Cambridge: Cambridge University Press, 2001.

———. Introduction to *A Day in Turkey*, by Hannah Cowley. In *The Routledge Anthology of British Women Playwrights, 1777–1843*, edited by Thomas C. Crochunis and Michael E. Sinatra, 138–142. London: Routledge, 2019.

———. *Women, Nationalism, and the Romantic Stage: Theatre and Politics in Britain, 1780–1800*. Cambridge: Cambridge University Press, 2001.

Bradham, JoAllen. "A Good Country Gentlewoman: Catherine Clive's Epistolary Autobiography." *Biography* 19, no. 3 (1996): 259–282.

Bratton, Jacky. *The Making of the West End Stage: Marriage, Management and the Mapping of Gender in London, 1830–1870*. Cambridge: Cambridge University Press, 2011.

Brooks, Helen. "'Your Sincere Friend and Humble Servant': Evidence of Managerial Aspirations in Susannah Cibber's Letters." *Studies in Theatre and Performance* 28 (2008): 147–159.

Browne, Alice. *The Eighteenth-Century Feminist Mind*. Detroit, MI: Wayne State University Press, 1987.

Buckley, Matthew S. "The Formation of Melodrama." In *The Oxford Handbook of the Georgian Theatre, 1737–1832*, edited by Julia Swindells and David Francis Taylor, 457–475. Oxford: Oxford University Press, 2014.

Bush-Bailey, Gilli. *Treading the Bawds: Actresses and Playwrights on the Late Stuart Stage*. Manchester: Manchester University Press, 2006.

Byrne, Paula. *Jane Austen and the Theatre*. London: Hambledon and London, 2002.

Cahill, Samara Anne. *Intelligent Souls? Feminist Orientalism in Eighteenth-Century English Literature*. Lewisburg, PA: Bucknell University Press, 2019.

Caldwell, Tanya. "'A City Graced with Many a Dome': Hannah Cowley's Domestic Comedies, the Georgic Impulse, and the Female Arts." *Eighteenth-Century Life* 42, no. 1 (2018): 28–57.

Carlson, Marvin. "Elizabeth Inchbald: A Woman Critic in Her Theatrical Culture." In *Women in British Romantic Theatre: Drama, Performance, and Society, 1790–1840*, edited by Catherine B. Burroughs, 207–222. Cambridge: Cambridge University Press, 2000.

Carlson, Susan. *Women and Comedy: Rewriting the British Theatrical Tradition*. Ann Arbor: University of Michigan Press, 1991.

Caskey, J. Homer. "Arthur Murphy and the War on Sentimental Comedy." *Journal of English and Germanic Philology* 30, no. 4 (1931): 563–577.

Cauwels, Janice Marie. "Authorial 'Caprice' vs. Editorial 'Calculation': The Text of Elizabeth Inchbald's *Nature and Art*." *Bibliographical Society of America* 72, no. 2 (1978): 169–185.

Chandler, Anne. "The 'Seeds of Order and Taste': Wollstonecraft, the *Analytical Review*, and Critical Idiom." *European Romantic Review* 16, no. 1 (2005): 1–21.

Charles, Katherine. "Staging Sociability in *The Excursion*: Frances Brooke, David Garrick, and the King's Theatre Coterie." *Eighteenth-Century Fiction* 27, no. 2 (2014–15): 257–284.

Chisholm, Kate. *Fanny Burney: Her Life, 1752–1840*. London: Chatto & Windus, 1998.

Choudhury, Mita. *Interculturalism and Resistance in the London Theater, 1660–1800: Identity, Performance, Empire*. Lewisburg, PA: Bucknell University Press, 2000.

Collins-Hughs, Laura. "*The Appointment* Review: A Chorus Line at the Abortion Clinic." *New York Times*, January 24, 2023, https://www.nytimes.com/2023/01/24/theater/the-appointment-review.html.

Copeland, Nancy. *Staging Gender in Behn and Centlivre: Women's Comedy and the Theatre*. Cornwall, UK: Ashgate, 2004.

Cotton, Nancy. *Women Playwrights in England, c. 1363–1750*. Lewisburg, PA: Bucknell University Press, 1980.

Cox, Jeffrey. "Cowley's Bold Stroke for Comedy." *European Romantic Review* 17, no. 3 (2006): 361–375.

Cox, Jeffrey, and Michael Gamer. Introduction to *The Broadview Anthology of Romantic Drama*, vii–xxiv. Peterborough, ON: Broadview Press, 2003.

Crean, Patrick J. "The Life and Times of Kitty Clive." Doctoral diss., University of London, 1933.

Crochunis, Thomas C. "Women Theatre Managers." In *The Oxford Handbook of the Georgian Theatre, 1737–1832*, edited by Julia Swindells and David Francis Taylor, 568–584. Oxford: Oxford University Press, 2014.

Crouch, K. A. "Clive [née Raftor], Catherine [Kitty] (1711–1785), Actress." *Oxford Dictionary of National Biography*. September 23, 2004. https://doi.org/10.1093/ref:odnb/5694.

Csengei, Ildiko. "Godwin's Case: Melancholy Mourning in the "Empire of Feeling." In *Sympathy, Sensibility and the Literature of Feeling in the Eighteenth Century*, 169–194. London: Palgrave Macmillan, 2012.

Darby, Barbara. *Frances Burney, Dramatist: Gender, Performance, and the Late-Eighteenth-Century Stage*. Lexington: University Press of Kentucky, 1997.

Davis, Gwenn, and Beverly A. Joyce. *Drama by Women to 1900: A Bibliography of American and British Writers*. Toronto: University of Toronto Press, 1992.

Davis, Tracy C. "Female Managers, Lessees and Proprietors of the British Stage (to 1914)." *Nineteenth Century Theatre* 28, no. 2 (2000): 115–144.

De Bruyn, Frans. "Shakespeare and the French Revolution." In *Shakespeare in the Eighteenth Century*, edited by Fiona Ritchie and Peter Sabor, 297–313. Cambridge: Cambridge University Press, 2012.

De la Mahotière, Mary. "Cowley [née Parkhouse], Hannah (1743–1809), Playwright and Poet." *Oxford Dictionary of National Biography*. September 23, 2004. https://doi.org/10.1093/ref:odnb/6500.

———. *Hannah Cowley: Tiverton's Playwright and Pioneer Feminist (1743–1809)*. Tiverton. UK: Devon Books, 1997.

Dircks, Phyllis T. "Digges, West (1725?–1786), Actor and Theatre Manager." *Oxford Dictionary of National Biography*. January 3, 2008. https://doi.org/10.1093/ref:odnb/7640.

Donkin, Ellen. *Getting into the Act: Women Playwrights in London, 1776–1829*. London: Routledge, 1995.

Doody, Margaret Anne. *Frances Burney: The Life in the Works*. New Brunswick, NJ: Rutgers University Press, 1988.

Edwards, Mary Jane. "Brooke [née Moore], Frances (bap. 1724, d. 1789), Writer and Playwright." *Oxford Dictionary of National Biography*. September 23, 2004. https://doi.org/10.1093/ref:odnb/3540.

Erickson, Amy Louise "Esther Sleepe, Fan-Maker, and Her Family." *Eighteenth-Century Life* 42, no. 2 (2018): 15–37.

Escott, Angela. *The Celebrated Mrs Cowley: Experiments in Dramatic Genre, 1776–1794*. London: Pickering & Chatto, 2012.

Finberg, Melinda C. Introduction to *Eighteenth-Century Women Dramatists*, ix–xlviii. Oxford: Oxford University Press, 2001.

Finke, Laurie A. "The Satire of Women Writers in *The Female Wits*." *Restoration: Studies in English Literary Culture* 8, no. 2 (1984): 64–71.

Fiske, Roger. *English Theatre Music in the Eighteenth Century*. Oxford: Oxford University Press, 1986.

Fitzgerald, Percy. *The Life of Mrs. Catherine Clive: With an Account of Her Adventures on and off the Stage, a Round of Her Characters, Together with Her Correspondence*. London: A. Reader, 1888.

Frank, Marcie. "Frances Burney's Theatricality." *English Literary History* 82, no. 2 (2015): 615–635.

Freeman, Lisa. *Character's Theater: Genre and Identity on the Eighteenth-Century English Stage*. Philadelphia: University of Pennsylvania Press, 2002.

———. "On the Art of Dramatic Probability: Elizabeth Inchbald's Remarks for *The British Theatre*." *Theatre Survey* 62, no. 2 (2021): 163–181.

———. "The Social Life of Eighteenth-Century Comedy." In *The Cambridge Companion to British Theatre, 1730–1830*, edited by Jane Moody and Daniel O'Quinn, 73–86. Cambridge: Cambridge University Press, 2007.

Frushell, Richard. "An Edition of the Afterpieces of Kitty Clive." PhD diss., Duquesne University, 1968.

———. "Kitty Clive as Dramatist." *Durham University Journal* 32, no. 2 (1971): 125–132.

———. "The Textual Relationship and Biographical Significance of Two Petite Pieces by Mrs. Catherine (Kitty) Clive." *Restoration and Eighteenth-Century Theatre Research* 9, no. 1 (1970): 51–58.

Garnai, Amy. *Revolutionary Imaginings in the 1790s Charlotte Smith, Mary Robinson, Elizabeth Inchbald*. New York: Palgrave Macmillan, 2009.

Gerzina, Gretchen H. *Black London: Life before Emancipation*. New Brunswick, NJ: Rutgers University Press, 1995.

———, ed. *Britain's Black Past*. Liverpool: Liverpool University Press, 2020.

Gifford, Terry. *Pastoral*. 2nd ed. New York: Routledge, 2020.

Green, Katherine S. "Mr. Harmony and the Events of January 1793: Elizabeth Inchbald's *Every One Has His Fault*." *Theatre Journal* 56, no. 1 (2004): 47–62.

Guest, Harriet. *Unbounded Attachment: Sentiment and Politics in the Age of the French Revolution*. Oxford: Oxford University Press, 2013.

Havens, Hilary. "'How Is Our Blue Club Cut Up!': Frances Burney's Changing Views of the Bluestockings." *Eighteenth-Century Life* 46, no. 1 (2022): 37–55.

Hawley, Judith. "Elizabeth and Keppel Craven and the Domestic Drama of Mother-Son Relations." In *Stage Mothers: Women, Work, and the Theater, 1660–1830*, edited by Laura Engel and Elaine M. McGirr, 199–215. Lewisburg, PA: Bucknell University Press, 2014.

Highfill, Philip H., Jr., Kalman A. Burnim, and Edward A. Langhans. *A Biographical Dictionary of Actors, Actresses, Musicians, Dancers, Managers & Other Stage Personnel in London, 1660–1800*. 16 vols. Carbondale: Southern Illinois University Press, 1973–93.

Hook, Lucyle. Introduction to *The Female Wits* (1704), by W. M., i–xvi. Facsimile ed. Los Angeles: William Andrews Clark Memorial Library, 1967.

Hume, Robert D. "Before the Bard: 'Shakespeare' in Early Eighteenth-Century London." *English Literary History* 64, no. 1 (1997): 41–75.

———. "Goldsmith and Sheridan and the Supposed Revolution in 'Laughing' against 'Sentimental' Comedy." In *Studies in Change and Revolution: Aspects of English Intellectual History, 1640–1800*, edited by Paul J. Korshin, 313–320. Menston, UK: Scolar Press, 1972.

———. "The Value of Money in Eighteenth-Century England: Incomes, Prices, Buying Power—and Some Problems in Cultural Economics." *Huntington Library Quarterly* 77, no. 4 (2014): 373–416.

Hume, Robert D., and Harold Love. Introduction to *The Rehearsal*. In *Plays, Poems, and Miscellaneous Writings Associated with George Villiers, Second Duke of Buckingham*, edited by Robert D. Hume and Harold Love, 1:333–395. Oxford: Oxford University Press, 2007.

Jeffares, A. Norman. "Sheridan, Richard Brinsley (1751–1816)." *Oxford Dictionary of National Biography*. September 23, 2004. https://doi.org/10.1093/ref:odnb/25367.

Jenkins, Annabel. *I'll Tell You What: The Life of Elizabeth Inchbald*. Lexington: University Press of Kentucky, 2003.

Jennings, Rebecca. *A Lesbian History of Britain, Love and Sex between Women since 1500*. Oxford: Greenwood World Publishing, 2007.

Johnson, Nancy E. *The English Jacobin Novel on Rights, Property, and the Law: Critiquing the Contract*. Basingstoke, UK: Palgrave Macmillan, 2004.

Joncus, Berta. "'In Wit Superior, as in Fighting': Kitty Clive and the Conquest of a Rival Queen." *Huntington Library Quarterly* 74, no. 1 (2011): 23–42.

———. *Kitty Clive, or the Fair Songster (1728–1765)*. Suffolk, UK: Boydell & Brewer, 2019.

Kaul, Suvir. "Styles of Orientalism in the Eighteenth Century." In *Orientalism and Literature*, edited by Geoffrey P. Nash, 35–49. Cambridge: Cambridge University Press, 2019.

Kelly, Gary. *The English Jacobin Novel, 1780–1805*. New York: Clarendon, 1976.

Kinservik, Matthew J. "Benefit Play Selection at Drury Lane 1729–1769: The Cases of Mrs Cibber, Mrs Clive, and Mrs Pritchard." *Theatre Notebook* 50, no. 1 (1996): 15–28.

———. *Disciplining Satire: The Censorship of Satiric Comedy on the Eighteenth-Century London Stage*. Lewisburg, PA: Bucknell University Press, 2002.

———. "Garrick's Unpublished Epilogue for Catherine Clive's *The Rehearsal: or, Bays in Petticoats* (1750)." *Études Anglaises* 49, no. 3 (1996): 320–326.

Kucich, Greg. "Women's Cosmopolitanism and the Romantic Stage." In *Transnational England: Home and Abroad, 1780–1860*, edited by Monika Class and Terry F. Robinson, 22–40. Cambridge: Cambridge Scholars, 2009.

Link, Frederick M. Introduction to *The Plays of Hannah Cowley*, facsimile edition, 1:v–xlv. New York: Garland, 1979.

Littlewood, S. R. *Elizabeth Inchbald and Her Circle*. London: Daniel O'Connor, 1921.

Loftis, John. "Political and Social Thought in the Drama." In *The London Theatre World, 1660–1800*, edited by Robert D. Hume, 253–285. Carbondale: Southern Illinois University Press, 1980.

Lott, Anna. Introduction to *A Simple Story*, by Elizabeth Inchbald, 13–46. Toronto: Broadview Press, 2007.

Mann, David D., and Susan Garland Mann. *Women Playwrights in England, Ireland, and Scotland, 1660–1823*. Bloomington: Indiana University Press, 1996.

Marsden, Jean I. *Theatres of Feeling: Affect, Performance, and the Eighteenth-Century Stage*. Cambridge: Cambridge University Press, 2019.

McKee, William. *Elizabeth Inchbald, Novelist*. Washington, DC: Catholic University of America, 1954.

McMillen Conger, Syndy. *Mary Wollstonecraft and the Language of Sensibility*. Rutherford, NJ: Fairleigh Dickinson University Press.

McMullen, Lorraine. *An Odd Attempt in a Woman: The Literary Life of Frances Brooke.* Vancouver: University of British Columbia Press, 1983.

Mellor, Anne K. "Embodied Cosmopolitanism and the British Romantic Woman Writer." *European Romantic Review* 17, no. 3 (2006): 289–300.

———. *Mothers of the Nation: Women's Political Writing in England, 1780–1830.* Bloomington: Indiana University Press, 2000.

Milhous, Judith, and Robert D. Hume. "The Drury Lane Actors' Rebellion of 1743." *Theatre Journal* 42, no. 1 (1990): 57–80.

———. "Playwrights' Remuneration in Eighteenth-Century London." *Harvard Library Bulletin* 10, no. 2–3 (1999): 3–90.

Moody, Jane. *Illegitimate Theatre in London, 1770–1840.* Cambridge: Cambridge University Press, 2000.

———. "Suicide and Translation in the Dramaturgy of Elizabeth Inchbald and Anne Plumptre." In *Women in British Romantic Theatre: Drama, Performance, and Society, 1790–1840*, edited by Catherine B. Burroughs, 257–284. Cambridge: Cambridge University Press, 2000.

Myers, Mitzi. "Sensibility and the 'Walk of Reason': Mary Wollstonecraft's Literary Reviews as Cultural Critique." In *Sensibility in Transformation: Creative Resistance to Sentiment from the Augustans to the Romantics*, edited by Syndy McMillen Conger, 120–144. Rutherford, NJ: Fairleigh Dickinson University Press, 1990.

Nachumi, Nora. *Acting Like a Lady: British Women Novelists and the Eighteenth-Century Theater.* New York: AMS Press, 2008.

Newey, Katherine. *Women's Theatre Writing in Victorian Britain.* New York: Palgrave Macmillan, 2005.

Nicoll, Allardyce. *Late Eighteenth-Century Drama, 1750–1800.* Vol. 3 of *A History of English Drama 1660–1900.* Cambridge: Cambridge University Press, 1952.

Nielsen, Wendy. "A Tragic Farce: Revolutionary Women in Elizabeth Inchbald's *The Massacre* and European Drama." *European Romantic Review* 17, no. 3 (2006): 275–288.

Nussbaum, Felicity. *Rival Queens: Actresses, Performance, and the Eighteenth-Century British Theatre.* Philadelphia: University of Pennsylvania Press, 2010.

———. "Straddling: London-Irish Actresses in Performance." In *Ireland, Enlightenment and the English Stage, 1740–1820*, edited by David O'Shaughnessy, 31–56. Cambridge: Cambridge University Press, 2019.

O'Quinn, Daniel. *Corrosive Solace: Theater, Affect, and the Realignment of the Repertoire, 1780–1800.* Philadelphia: University of Pennsylvania Press, 2022.

———. *Entertaining Crisis in the Atlantic Imperium, 1770–1790.* Baltimore: Johns Hopkins University Press, 2011.

———. "Hannah Cowley's *A Day in Turkey* and the Political Efficacy of Charles James Fox." *European Romantic Review* 14, no. 1 (2003): 17–30.

———. *Staging Governance: Theatrical Imperialism in London, 1770–1800.* Baltimore: Johns Hopkins University Press, 2005.

———. "Theatre and Empire." In *The Cambridge Companion to British Theatre, 1730–1830*, edited by Jane Moody and Daniel O'Quinn, 233–246. Cambridge: Cambridge University Press, 2007.

Orr, Bridget. *Empire on the English Stage 1660–1714*. Cambridge: Cambridge University Press, 2001.

———. "Galland, Georgian Theatre, and the Creation of Popular Orientalism." In *The Arabian Nights in Historical Context: Between East and West*, edited by Saree Makdisi and Felicity Nussbaum, 104–130. Oxford: Oxford University Press, 2008.

O'Shaughnessy, David. *William Godwin and the Theatre*. London: Pickering & Chatto, 2010.

Paluchowska-Messing, Anna. "'Darts to Wound with Endless Love!': On Hannah Cowley's Response to Frances Burney's *Evelina*." *Studia Anglica Posnaniensia* 54, no. 1 (2019): 43–57.

Paul, C. Kegan. *William Godwin: His Friends and Contemporaries*. 2 vols. Boston: Roberts Brothers, 1876.

Pearson, Jaqueline. *The Prostituted Muse: Images of Women and Women Dramatists, 1642–1737*. New York: Palgrave Macmillan, 1988.

Pedicord, Harry William. *The Theatrical Public in the Time of Garrick*. Carbondale: Southern Illinois University Press, 1966.

Petty, Frederick C. *Italian Opera in London, 1760–1800*. Ann Arbor: UMI Research Press, 1980.

Price, Curtis, Judith Milhous, and Robert D. Hume. *The King's Theatre, Haymarket, 1778–1791*. Vol. 1 of *Italian Opera in Late Eighteenth-Century London*. Oxford: Oxford University Press, 1995.

Pritchard, Will. *Outward Appearances: The Female Exterior in Restoration London*. Lewisburg, PA: Bucknell University Press, 2008.

Ritchie, Fiona. *Women and Shakespeare in the Eighteenth Century*. New York: Cambridge University Press, 2014.

Ritchie, Leslie. *David Garrick and the Mediation of Celebrity*. Cambridge: Cambridge University Press, 2019.

———. *Women Writing Music in Late Eighteenth-Century England: Social Harmony in Literature and Performance*. London: Routledge, 2016.

Robertson, Ben. *Elizabeth Inchbald's Reputation*. London: Pickering & Chatto, 2013.

Rogers, Katharine M. "Britain's First Woman Drama Critic: Elizabeth Inchbald." In *Curtain Calls: British and American Women and the Theater, 1660–1820*, edited by Mary Anne Schofield and Cecilia Macheski, 277–290. Athens: Ohio University Press, 1991.

———. *Feminism in Eighteenth-Century England*. Champagne: University of Illinois Press, 1982.

Rosenthal, Laura J. *Playwrights and Plagiarists in Early Modern England: Gender, Authorship, Literary Property*. Ithaca, NY: Cornell University Press, 1996.

———. *Ways of the World: Theater and Cosmopolitanism in the Restoration and Beyond*. Ithaca, NY: Cornell University Press, 2020.

Ruiz, Michelle. "In *Oh My God, a Show about Abortion*, Alison Leiby Shares Her Unvarnished Truth." *Vogue*, May 13, 2022. https://www.vogue.com/article/oh-god-a-show-about-abortion-alison-leiby-interview.

Russell, Gillian. "Riotous Assemblies: The Army and Navy in the Theatre." In *The Theatres of War: Performance, Politics, and Society 1793–1815*, 95–121. Oxford: Oxford University Press, 1995.

———. *Women, Sociability and Theatre in Georgian London*. Cambridge: Cambridge University Press, 2007.

Sabor, Peter, and Geoffrey Sill. Introduction to *"The Witlings" and "The Woman-Hater,"* by Frances Burney, 9–35. Peterborough, ON: Broadview Press, 2002.

Saggini, Francesca. *Backstage in the Novel: Frances Burney and the Theater Arts*. Translated by Laura Kopp. Charlottesville: University of Virginia Press, 2012.

Sambrook, James. "Crisp, Samuel (1707–1783), Playwright." *Oxford Dictionary of National Biography*. September 23, 2004. https://doi.org/10.1093/ref:odnb/6706.

Schellenberg, Betty A. *The Professionalization of Women Writers in Eighteenth-Century Britain*. Cambridge: Cambridge University Press, 2005.

Sherbo, Arthur. "Cumberland, Richard (1732–1811), Playwright and Novelist." *Oxford Dictionary of National Biography*. September 23, 2004. https://doi.org/10.1093/ref:odnb/6888.

Sherman, Stuart. "The Periodical and the Prism: Two Ways of Working at Celebrity in the Careers of Catherine Clive, Eliza Haywood, and Charlotte Charke." In *Making Stars: Biography and Celebrity in Eighteenth-Century Britain*, edited by Nora Nachumi and Kristina Straub, 17–42. Newark: University of Delaware Press, 2022.

Sireci, Fiore. "'Writers Who Have Rendered Women Objects of Pity': Mary Wollstonecraft's Literary Criticism in the *Analytical Review* and a *Vindication of the Rights of Woman*." *Journal of the History of Ideas* 79, no. 2 (2018): 243–265.

Solomon, Diana. *Prologues and Epilogues of Restoration Theater: Gender and Comedy, Performance and Print*. Newark: University of Delaware Press, 2013.

Spector, Robert D. *Arthur Murphy*. Boston: Twayne, 1979.

Stanton, Judith. "'This New-Found Path Attempting': Women Dramatists in England." In *Curtain Calls: British and American Women and the Theater, 1660–1820*, edited by Mary Anne Schofield and Cecilia Macheski, 325–356. Athens: Ohio University Press, 1991.

Stott, Anne. *Hannah More: The First Victorian*. Oxford: Oxford University Press, 2003.

Strange, Sallie M. "Clive, Catherine." In *A Dictionary of British and American Women Writers*, edited by Janet Todd, 86. Lanham, MD: Rowman & Littlefield, 1985.

Straznicky, Marta. "Restoration Women Playwrights and the Limits of Professionalism." *English Literary History* 64, no. 3 (1997): 703–726.

Taylor, C.M.P. "Wilkinson, John Joseph Tate (1769/70–1846), Actor and Theatre Manager." *Oxford Dictionary of National Biography*. September 23, 2004. https://doi.org/10.1093/ref:odnb/38587.

Thomson, Peter. "Yates [née Graham], Mary Ann (1728–1787), Actress and Theatre Manager." *Oxford Dictionary of National Biography*. September 23, 2004. https://doi.org/10.1093/ref:odnb/30196.

Todd, Janet. *Mary Wollstonecraft: A Revolutionary Life*. New York: Columbia University Press, 2000.

Troost, Linda V. "Frances Brooke's *Rosina*: Subverting Sentimentalism." In *Paper, Ink, and Achievement: Gabriel Hornstein and the Revival of Eighteenth-Century Scholarship*, edited by Kevin L. Cope and Cedric D. Reverand, 101–114. Lewisburg, PA: Bucknell University Press, 2021.

Van Hensbergen, Claudine. "The Female Wits: Gender, Satire, and Drama." In *The Oxford Handbook of Eighteenth-Century Satire*, edited by Paddy Bullard, 74–91. Oxford: Oxford University Press, 2019.

Van Lannep, William, Emmett L. Avery, Arthur H. Scouten, George Winchester Stone Jr., and Charles Beecher Hogan, eds. *The London Stage, 1660–1800: A Calendar of Plays, Entertainments and Afterpieces*. 5 parts in 11 vols. Carbondale: Southern Illinois University Press, 1960–68.

Wagstaff, John. "Burney, Charles (1726–1814), Musician and Author." *Oxford Dictionary of National Biography*. September 23, 2004. https://doi.org/10.1093/ref:odnb/4078.

Wallace, Miriam L. *Revolutionary Subjects in the English "Jacobin" Novel, 1790–1805*. Lewisburg, PA: Bucknell University Press, 2009.

Wallace, Tara Ghoshal. "Fanny Burney and the Theatre." In *A Busy Day*, by Frances Burney, edited by Tara Ghoshal Wallace, 197–198. New Brunswick, NJ: Rutgers University Press, 1984.

Wardle, Ralph. "Mary Wollstonecraft, Analytical Reviewer." *PMLA* 62, no. 4 (1947): 1000–1009.

Waters, Mary A. "'The First of a New Genus—': Mary Wollstonecraft, Mary Hays, and the *Analytical Review*." In *British Women Writers and the Profession of Literary Criticism, 1789–1832*, 86–120. New York: Palgrave Macmillan, 2004.

———. "Renouncing the Forms: The Case of Elizabeth Inchbald." In *British Women Writers and the Profession of Literary Criticism, 1789–1832*, 57–81. New York: Palgrave Macmillan, 2004.

Wessel, Jane. *Owning Performance, Performing Ownership: Literary Property and the Eighteenth-Century British Stage*. Ann Arbor: University of Michigan Press, 2022.

White, Willow. "Comic Collusion: Frances Burney's *The Witlings* and the Mentorship of Arthur Murphy." *Women's Writing* 28, no. 2 (2021): 368–383.

———. "Feminist Sensibilities: The Feud of Elizabeth Inchbald and Mary Wollstonecraft." *Eighteenth-Century Studies* 55, no. 3 (2022): 299–315.

Woodfield, Ian. *Opera and Drama in Eighteenth-Century London: The King's Theatre, Garrick, and the Business of Performance*. Cambridge: Cambridge University Press, 2001.

Woods, Leigh. "Garrick's King Lear and the English Malady." *Theatre Survey* 27, no. 1–2 (1986): 17–35.

Wyett, Jodi L. "Frances Brooke on (the) Stage." *Restoration and Eighteenth-Century Theatre Research* 28, no. 2 (2013): 25–43.

Index

abortion, 141, 145
activism, 17, 143
afterpieces, 3, 7, 11, 14, 18–19, 25–28, 35, 38–44, 55–59, 94, 119, 143
American Revolution, 60
Anderson, Emily H., 3
Anderson, Misty, 4, 52, 115
antisemitism, 2
Apetrei, Sarah, 4
Appointment, The, 145
aristocracy. *See* class
Aristophanes: *Frogs, The*, 28
Arne, Thomas: *Comus*, 56, 58
Astley's Royal Amphitheatre, 138
Austen, Jane: *Mansfield Park*, 132

Backscheider, Paula R., 41, 49, 52–54, 64
Baillie, Joanna, 128, 137–138
Baker, Sarah, 47
Ball, Lucille, 2
Barbauld, Anna Laetitia, 115, 128
Barecca, Regina, 9
Barry, Elizabeth, 47
Barry, Spranger, 44
Barsanti, Jane, 69
Beard, John, 13
Beaumont, Francis (*Knight of the Burning Pestle, The*), 29
Becket, Thomas, 45
Behn, Aphra, 5–14, 94, 97–100, 104; *Abdelazer, or, the Moor's Revenge*, 100; *Emperor of the Moon, The*, 101; *Lucky Chance, The*, 5, 12, 94, 97
Bilger, Audrey, 9
Birmingham patent, 52
Bluestockings, 82, 85
Boaden, James (*Memoirs of Mrs. Inchbald*), 122, 173n13, 174n17
Bode, Christoph, 131
Bolton, Betsy, 3, 106, 170n39, 171n65
Bolton, Duke of, 20
Booth, Ursula, 8

Boothby, Frances (*Marcelia; or, The Treacherous Friend*), 5
Boyce, William (*Corydon and Miranda*), 32–33, 159n66
Bracegirdle, Ann, 47
British Theatre series, 136–137
Brooke, Frances, 3, 9–15, 38–64, 80, 92–95, 140, 143, 160n8, 160n12, 161n22, 161n26, 161n31, 165n5; *Clandestine Marriage, The*, 46; and David Garrick, 15, 39, 41–52, 58–64; *Excursion, The*, 51–53, 161n22; *History of Emily Montague, The*, 45, 161n22; *History of Lady Julia Mandeville, The*, 45, 161n22; *Marian*, 15, 39–41, 44, 55–64, 143; *Old Maid, The*, 43–45, 52; in Quebec, 45, 161n22; 45; *Rosina*, 15, 55–64, 143, 161n26, 164n88; *Shepherd's Wedding, The*, 44–45; *Siege of Sinope, The*, 39, 53–58; *Virginia*, 15, 39–43, 52–54, 60, 80, 95, 160n12
Brooke, John, 42, 48
Brosnahan, Rachel. See *Marvelous Mrs. Maisel, The*
Burke, Edmond, 52, 123, 171n60
Burnett, Carol, 2
Burney, Dr. Charles, 15, 66–67, 78–87, 97, 165n18
Burney, Frances, 3–16, 45, 48–49, 64–88, 97, 11, 119, 139, 143; *All in the Wrong*, 15, 66, 69, 71–78, 87; and Arthur Murphy, 15, 67–87; *Busy Day, A*, 84; *Evelina*, 15, 65, 67, 69, 78–80, 84, 88; *Love and Fashion*, 15; *Witlings, The*, 4, 15, 65–67, 70, 72, 74–88, 97, 111; *Woman-Hater, The*, 84–87
Byrne, Paula, 3, 133

Cadell, Thomas, 53, 55
Cadogan, Frances, 52
Caldwell, Tanya, 103
Carey, Henry, 29

195

INDEX

Carlisle House, 47
Carlson, Susan, 6
Catholic, 9, 117, 126
Catley, Ann, 46, 161n26
Celesia, Dorothy, 8, 13
censorship, 7, 15, 78–84, 92, 97, 121, 131
Centlivre, Susanna, 7, 9, 12, 14, 25, 64, 94, 137; *Basset Table, The*, 7; *Bold Stroke for a Wife*, A, 7; *Busy Body, The*, 7, 64; *Stolen Heiress, The*, 94
Chamberlain, Lord, 7, 12, 23–25, 33, 46, 62, 104, 121
Charke, Charlotte, 7, 26, 29, 47, 158n50; *Art of Management, The*, 29
Charles, Katherine, 51
Charles II, 5, 100
Chetwood, William, 20
Chisholm, Kate, 66, 82
Christianity, 101, 109, 132
Cibber, Colley, 21, 26, 29; *Rival Queens with the Humors of Alexander the Great*, 29
Cibber, Susannah, 22, 26, 35, 43, 47; *Oracle, The*, 26, 35, 91
Cibber, Theophilus, 22, 48
class, 2, 8–9, 41, 55, 59–63, 65, 74, 77–78, 83, 100, 108, 120–122, 132; aristocracy, 41, 61–63, 74, 102, 61; and laughter, 65, 77
Clive, Catherine, 3, 7, 18–38, 43, 47, 50, 61, 81, 118, 138, 140–143; *Case of Mrs. Clive, Submitted to the Publick, The*, 24; *Every Woman in Her Humour*, 18, 26, 28, 35, 18, 27, 35, 156n3; *Faithful Irish Woman, The*, 18, 27–28, 34–35; *Rehearsal; or, Bayes in Petticoats, The*, 7, 28–35, 38, 61; and the role of Polly, 19–25, 157n15; *Sketch of a Fine Lady's Return from a Rout, The*, 18, 27, 35, 148
Clive, George, 21, 157n15
Colman, George the Elder, 13, 45–47, 72, 95, 117, 119, 137; *Clandestine Marriage, The*, 46
Colman, George the Younger, 13, 137, 174n32; *Heir at Law*, 137
colonialism, 91, 101, 120
comedy: angry, 89; contemporary, 16–17, 139–146; farce, 11, 18–22, 29, 44, 67, 69, 71, 82–83, 91, 100, 118, 156n3; laughing, 14–16, 66, 70–74, 78–88, 166n30; male domination in the industry, 1, 3–4, 14, 18, 93; and masculinity, 67, 101, 143; and morality, 12, 71, 77, 79, 82–84, 96–97, 121, 125, 128–135; musical, 3, 13–15, 39–64, 91, 145; Oriental, 99–112, 170n41; parody, 28–33; pastoral, 11, 32, 41–44, 55, 59–61; politics, 4, 7, 9–10, 25, 91–92, 99, 102–104, 121–123, 131, 142; renaissance of women's, 3, 19, 142; Restoration style, 70–71, 75, 97, 101; satire, 14, 16, 29–30, 37, 43, 52, 66, 71, 74, 82–83, 89–112, 143; sentimental, 14, 16, 70–72, 79, 86, 113–138, 143; stage, 2–3, 11–14, 17, 67, 80, 89, 111, 119, 142, 145. *See also* opera
Congreve, William, 71, 110–111
Cooper, Elizabeth, 7
Corneille, Pierre (*La Mort de Pompeé*), 5
Cornelys, Teresa, 47
Cotton, Nancy, 3
Covent Garden, 7, 13, 16, 21, 24–29, 39–47, 50–53, 58, 60, 84, 94, 97–98, 102, 117, 119, 122–123, 130, 162n38, 163n71, 177n87
Cowley, Hannah, 3, 8–16, 63–64, 87–112, 119, 121, 124, 137, 140, 143; adaptation of Behn's *The Lucky Chance*, 22; adaptation of Centlivre's *The Stolen Heiress*, 94; *Albina*, 13, 94–98, 111; *Belle's Stratagem, The*, 64, 91, 97; *Day in Turkey; or, The Russian Slaves, A*, 10, 63, 91, 170n39; *Fate of Sparta, The*, 98; and Hannah More, 94–97; *Runaway, The*, 16, 92–94; *School for Greybeards, A*, 12, 89, 97–98, 103, 111; *Town Before You, The*, 110–111; *Way as it Goes*, 98; *World as it Goes, The*, 12
Craven, Elizabeth, 8, 47
Crevier, Jean-Baptiste Louis, 42
Crisp, Samuel, 15, 41–43, 66, 78–85, 87, 95, 97; *Pitches, The*, 82–83; *Virginia*, 42, 80
Cross, Richard, 26
Crouch, Anna, 56
Csengei, Ildiko, 114
Cumberland, Richard, 18, 137; *The Choleric Man*, 18

Dalton, John, 56, 58; *Comus*, 56
Davenant, William (*Siege of Rhodes, The*), 100
Davis, Gwenn, 11

desire, 62, 77, 10, 106, 109, 132–134, 140, 145
Dibdin, Charles (*Complete History of the British Stage*), 96–97
Digges, West, 117
Diller, Phyllis, 2
discrimination, 9, 12, 30, 89, 143
Divorce, 7, 97
Donkin, Ellen, 4, 34, 40, 45, 69, 93, 97
Doody, Margaret Anne, 66, 82
Drury Lane, 7, 9, 13, 15–30, 34, 37, 42–53, 67–72, 80, 86, 92–95, 113, 156n6, 161n13
Dryden, John, 28–29, 98; *Conquest of Granada, The*, 28
du Camp, Marie Thérèse, 138
Durfey, Thomas (*Two Queens of Brentford; or, Bayes no Poetaster, The*), 29

Edgeworth, Maria, 137, 178n115
education, 10, 12, 33, 41–42, 92, 114, 123, 127, 136
epilogues, 11, 34–38, 110, 139

farce. *See* comedy: farce
Favart, Charles Simon (*Moissonneurs, Les*), 59
Female Wits, 6–7, 12, 29–30
feminism, 3–4, 9, 109–111, 113–138
Fenton, Lavinia, 21–22
Ferrouh Effendim, Ismail, 60
Fielding, Henry, 7, 20–21, 29, 80; *Author's Farce, The*, 29; *Covent Garden Tragedy, The*, 21, 29; *Intriguing Chambermaid, The*, 21–22; *Miser, The*, 21; *Old Debauchees, The*, 21
finance, 6, 22–23, 25–26, 35–37, 41–42, 45, 49–50, 55–56, 61–62, 92, 119. *See also* salary
Fink, Laurie, 30
Fiske, Roger, 39
Fleabag (Waller-Bridge), 139–140
Fleetwood, Charles, 23–24
Foot, Jesse (*The Life of Arthur Murphy*), 66
Foote, Samuel, 13, 46, 72
Freeman, Lisa, 3, 71, 136
French Revolution, 91, 102, 104, 120
Frushell, Richard, 26, 29, 156n5

Gadsby, Hannah, 16, 89, 91, 145; *Nanette*, 89, 145

Gardner, Sarah Cheyney, 8
Garnai, Amy, 122
Garrick, David, 13–15, 19, 23–25, 29, 33–48, 50–53, 58, 61, 64, 67, 70–72, 80, 92–95; *Florizel and Perdita*, 61; and Frances Brooke, 15, 39, 41–52, 58–64; *Peep behind the Curtain; or, The New Rehearsal, A*, 29, 36
gatekeeping, 3, 7, 12–13, 26, 35
Gay, John, 21, 29; *Beggar's Opera, The*, 21, 25, 157n15; *Rehearsal at Gotham, The*, 29
genre sérieux, 120
Germaine de Staël, Anne Louise, 137
Gifford, Richard, 41, 44
Gifford, Terry, 55
Glazer, Ilana, 17, 141–142; *Broad City*, 141–142
Godwin, William, 11, 102, 113–114, 120–126, 130, 172n5, 173n6, 173n9; *Caleb Williams*, 12, 174n32; *Enquiry Concerning Political Justice, An*, 121; *Political Justice*, 121, 125
Goldsmith, Oliver, 71–72, 166n30
Goodman Fields Theatre, 23
Green, Katherine S., 114, 123
Griffith, Elizabeth, 8, 34–35; *Platonic Wife, The*, 34–35, 37; *School for Rakes, The*, 34, 38
Guest, Harriet, 125

harem. *See* seraglio
Harris, Thomas, 13, 53, 64, 84, 94, 117, 119
Haymarket Theatre, 7, 13, 26, 46, 50, 95, 117–119
Haywood, Eliza, 7, 9
Holcroft, Thomas, 120–122, 125
homosexuality, 21
Hoper, Mrs., 26
Hume, Robert D., 23, 71, 119
Humphrey, Ozias, 49

Imlay, Gilbert, 113, 124
Imperialism, 60, 92
Inchbald, Elizabeth, 3, 8–16, 63–64, 86, 100, 102, 104, 112–138, 140, 143, 172n5, 173n9, 173n13, 174n32; *Animal Magnetism*, 64; *Case of Conscience, The*, 119; *Child of Nature, The*, 64, 133; *Every One Has His Fault*, 104, 120,

INDEX

Inchbald, Elizabeth (cont.)
122–123, 129; *I'll Tell You What*, 33, 119; *Lovers' Vows*, 16, 86, 114, 116, 130–136; *Massacre, The,* 11, 102, 119; *Midnight Hour, The,* 64; *Mogul Tale, The,* 63, 100, 118; *Nature and Art,* 114, 121, 128, 129; *Simple Story, A,* 114, 121, 126–129; *Such Things Are,* 64, 120; *To Marry or Not to Marry,* 136; *Wise Man of the East,* 120
interludes, 11, 32, 108

Jacobson, Abbi, 17, 141–142; *Broad City,* 141–142
Jenkins, Annibel, 114, 122
Joncus, Berta, 21–25, 32, 154n25, 159n66
Jonson, Ben: *Every Man in His Humour,* 26; *Poetaster,* 29
Joyce, Beverly A., 11
Judaism, 1, 9, 141

Kelly, Gary, 120–122
King's Theatre. *See* Opera House, The
Kinservik, Matthew J., 25–26, 35
Kotzebue, August von, 16, 114, 130–133, 173n10; *Child of Love,* 131; *Das Kind der Liebe,* 16, 114, 130–133
Kucich, Greg, 92

Lampe, John, 29
Laughter: and femininity, 65–88; and morality, 79. *See also* comedy: laughing
Le Fanu, Alicia, 36
Leiby, Alison, 145
Lennox, Charlotte, 8, 13, 129
libretto, 40, 56–60
Link, Frederick, 104
Linley, Elizabeth Ann, 13
Littlewood, S. R., 114, 122
London Opera House, 15, 47, 64
Lott, Anna, 125
Lovattini, Giovanni, 49
Lyceum Theatre, 138

Mabley, Jackie "Moms," 2
Macklin, Charles, 23
Macnamara, Morgan (*Sheep Sheering, The*), 61
Manley, Delarivier, 6, 29–30, 100; *Almyna, or, The Arabian Vow,* 100

Mann, David D., 3
Mann, Susan G., 3
marriage, 4, 10–11, 62–63, 94, 97, 108, 120, 125, 128–129, 133–134
Marvelous Mrs. Maisel, The, 1–2
Masculinity. *See* comedy: masculinity
Mazzinghi, Joseph, 104
McMullen, Lorraine, 42, 51
Mellor, Anne K., 4, 92, 109, 122
melodrama, 16, 104, 120, 128–129, 138, 174n23
Metcalfe, Catherine, 8
Milhous, Judith, 23, 119
Mingotti, Regina, 50
misogyny, 14, 19, 29, 33, 35, 52, 140
Moncrief, John (*Appius*), 42–43
Montagu, Elizabeth, 82
Montagu, Mary Wortley (*Turkish Embassy Letters*), 100
Moody, Jane, 120, 131
Moore, Thomas, 41–42
morality. *See* comedy: morality
More, Hannah, 8, 13, 52, 54, 94–97, 114; *Fatal Falsehood, The,* 94, 96; and Hannah Cowley, 94–97; *Percy,* 13, 54, 94–95, 97, 161n13
Murphy, Arthur, 15, 65–66, 69–87, 165n5; *All in the Wrong,* 15, 66, 69, 71–72, 74–78, 87; *Apprentice, The,* 71; *Citizen, The,* 69; and Frances Burney, 15, 69–87; *Know Your Own Mind,* 69, 71, 73, 87; *Upholsterer, The,* 69, 84; *Way to Keep Him, The,* 69, 71, 87
musicals. *See* comedy: musical

Nachumi, Nora, 3
Nares, Robert, 123
Newey, Katherine, 138
Nicoll, Allardyce, 120
Nielsen, Wendy, 120
Norwich Company, 117
Notaro, Tig, 17, 144–145; *One Mississipi,* 144
novels, 3, 16, 45, 80, 114, 121–122, 126–130
Nussbaum, Felicity, 21

opera: comic, 15, 38–41, 45, 49–50, 59, 64, 91, 143; English, 47, 59; French, 59; Italian, 47

198

INDEX

Opera House, The, 39, 46–54, 58, 162n31, 162n38, 163n71
oppression, 1–2, 4, 9, 17
O'Quinn, Daniel, 60, 92, 101, 106, 120, 122
Orientalism, 99–104, 170n41. *See also* comedy
Ottoman Empire, 98–100
Otway, Thomas (*Venice Preserv'd*), 54

Parkhouse, Philip, 92
parody. *See* comedy: parody
pastoral. *See* comedy: pastoral
patriarchy, 2, 4, 9–10, 14–17, 41, 54, 62, 89, 94, 101, 105, 114–121, 126–127, 140–145. *See also* oppression
Pearson, Jaqueline, 10, 100
Periodicals, reviews in: *Analytical Review*, 126–127, 129; *Artist, The*, 137; *British Magazine and Review*, 56; *British Theatre, The*, 135–137, 178n103; Daily *Gazetteer*, 23, 60, 92, 96, 103; *Gentleman's Magazine*, 126; *Gray's-Inn Journal*, 71; *Lady's Magazine*, 55, 57, 126; *London Chronicle*, 60, 130; *Monthly Review*, 80–81; *Morning Chronicle*, 55, 60, 97; *Morning Herald*, 98; *Morning Post*, 60, 96; *New Daily Advertiser*, 60, 103; *Public Advertiser*, 56, 91, 103; *True Briton*, 122, 173n9
Philips, Katherine, 5
Pilkington, Letitia, 26
Pix, Mary, 6, 29–30, 100; *Ibrahim, the Thirteenth Emperor of the Turks*, 100
plagiarism, 30, 43, 95–96, 169n27
Plumptre, Anne, 133
politics: feminist, 64, 114; gender, 30, 89, 92, 98; radical, 4, 104, 120–126. *See also* comedy: politics
Polly Row, 19–25
Pope, Jane, 8, 18, 38; *Young Couple, The*, 38
Poullain de Saint-Foix, Germain Francois (*L'Oracle*), 26
pregnancy, 124, 128, 130, 143–145
Pritchard, Hannah, 23, 156n7
prologues, 11, 30, 35, 44, 93, 99, 104, 123, 129, 139, 159n77
Pye, Jael-Henrietta, 9, 38

racism, 2, 100, 140–141
Radcliffe, Anne (*Patronage*), 137
radicalism. *See* politics: radical
Rae, Issa, 17, 140–141; *Awkward Black Girl*, 140; *Insecure*, 140–141
reform movement, 116, 120–123
Rehearsal play, 28–33, 36, 158n50
Restoration, 10, 19, 30. *See also* comedy: Restoration style
Revolutionary War, 60
Riccoboni, Marie Jeanne: *History of Miss Jenny Salisbury, The*, 44–45; *Lettres de milady Juliette Catesby à milady Henriette Campley, son amie*, 44–45
Rich, John, 13, 24, 35, 42
Richardson, Elizabeth, 8
Ritchie, Fiona, 48, 156n7
Ritchie, Leslie, 41, 55
Robertson, Ben, 125
Robinson, George, 120
Robinson, Mary, 121
Roe v. Wade, 145
Rosenthal, Laura J., 30
Royal Circus, 110–111, 138
Russel, Gillian, 3
Russian-Turkish War, 91, 99, 104

Sacchini, Antonio (*Mithridates*), 54
Sadler's Wells, 110–111, 138
Saggini, Francesca, 3, 69
salary, 23–24, 47. *See also* finance
Sans Pareil Theatre, 138
satire. *See* comedy: satire
scenery, 43, 55, 58, 60
Schellenberg, Betty, 41
Schumer, Amy, 144
Scott, Jane M., 138
screen scene, 75–77
sensibility, 16, 71
seraglio, 16, 105, 89–112
sexism, 2–3, 16, 28, 41, 44, 64, 89–92, 96, 119, 137, 140–141
sex work, 78, 128–129, 136, 158n55
Shakespeare, 75, 82, 102, 117, 137; *Coriolanus*, 102; *Hamlet*, 25; *King Lear*, 43, 117; *Measure for Measure*, 61; *Midsummer Night's Dream, A*, 28–29; *Winter's Tale, The*, 44, 61
Shelley, Mary, 114, 173n6

199

INDEX

Sheridan, Frances, 1, 7, 13, 19, 34–38, 44, 119; *Discovery, The*, 1, 34–35, 38; *Dupe, The*, 34–37

Sheridan, Richard Brinsley, 13, 16, 19, 53, 63, 67–69, 72, 94–95, 119, 131; *Critic; or, A Tragedy Rehearsed, The*, 29; *School for Scandal, The*, 72, 75–77, 94; *Stranger, The*, 131, 177n87; *Trip to Scarborough, A*, 94

Sherman, Stuart, 23

Sherman-Palladino, Amy. See *Marvelous Mrs. Maisel, The*

Shield, William, 56–60

Siddons, Sarah, 97, 124–125, 168n97

Silverman, Sarah, 145

Singleton, Mary. See Brooke, Frances

slavery, 63, 91–92, 101–110, 120–122, 172n87

Smith, Charlotte, 8, 121, 129, 172n5

spoken drama, 46–50, 53, 138

Stage Licensing Act, The, 7, 19, 25

Stanton, Judith, 10

Starke, Mariana, 8

Steevens, Roger, 42

Steevens, Sarah, 42

Streatham, 65–70, 72, 78–83, 87. See also Thrale, Hester

Sturm und Drang, 120

Tate, Nahum, 43

Taylor, Thomas (*Vindication of the Rights of Brutes, A*), 123

Thomson, James (*Seasons, The*), 59

Thrale, Hester, 65, 67, 69–70, 78, 79, 81. See also Streatham

Todd, Janet, 124–125, 129

tragedy, 11–12, 15, 39, 42–43, 47, 51–54, 80, 94–98, 119, 138, 144–145

Treaty of Paris, 60

Trotter, Catherine, 6, 29–30

Twiss, Frances, 124–125, 175n53

Tyler, Royall (*Contrast, The*), 65

United Company, 47

unities, 33, 42, 59

van Hensbergen, Claudine, 30

Villiers, George Duke of Buckingham (*Rehearsal, The*), 28–31, 33, 36, 61, 158n39

violence: domestic, 7; patriarchal, 15; sexual, 62–64, 89, 145

Waller-Bridge, Phoebe (*Fleabag*), 16, 139–140

Walpole, Horace, 38

Webster, John (*Appius and Virginia*), 42

Wells, Mary, 136

Wells Theatre, 110–111

Wilberforce, William, 110

Wilkinson, Tate, 25, 173n15

Wollstonecraft, Mary, 4, 16, 111; and Elizabeth Inchbald, 16, 103–104, 113–116, 123–130, 136, 172n5; *Maria: or, The Wrongs of Women*, 128; *Mary: A Fiction*, 123, 128; *Thoughts on the Education of Daughters*, 122; *Vindication of the Rights of Men*, 123, 171n60; *Vindication of the Rights of Woman, A*, 4, 113, 123–124, 127, 171n60; *Wrongs of Woman, The*, 129

Wong, Ali, 16; *Baby Cobra*, 143; *Hard Knock Wife*, 144

Woodfield, Ian, 48–49

Woodward, Henry (*The Beggar's Pantomime; or, the Contending Columbines*), 22

Wycherley, William (*Country Wife, The*), 71, 75

Wyett, Jody L., 41, 51

Yates, Mary Ann, 46–55, 161n31

Yates, Richard, 48–50

About the Author

Willow White is a feminist literary historian and assistant professor of English Literature and Indigenous Studies at the University of Alberta. Her research focuses on English and Indigenous women writers of the long eighteenth century. She coedited *A Narrative of the Life of Mrs. Mary Jemison* and her work has appeared in such journals as *Women's Writing* and *Eighteenth-Century Studies*.